PRAISE FOR *MANAGING BY DEFINING MOMENTS*

"Managing generational cohorts by their shared defining moments is a novel and creative approach to management. Read this book and learn how to identify these moments in order to create values and motivation in the workplace."

— Ken Blanchard, co-author of *The One Minute Manager*

"If you're a manager and want to get inside the heads of your employees, you've got to read this book. *Managing by Defining Moments* has brought refreshing new insight to understanding the diversity of the workforce. This book will enable any company to harness the power of its employees by understanding the values that motivate different generational cohorts."

— Wayne Marks, Senior Vice President, The Forum Corporation

"A fresh and exciting way to think about how to motivate your people. A provocative read."

— Bob Nelson, PhD, President of San Diego-based Nelson Motivation Inc. and author of *1001 Ways to Reward Employees* and *Please Don't Just Do What I Tell You! Do What Needs to Be Done*

"A very thought-provoking work, with new insights on how leaders can improve the productivity of their workforce."

— Ed Gambrell, Dow Business President

"Why is fun a key motivational ingredient in the workplace today? Older employees don't expect it but want it. Today's youth craves it. What gives? This book answers this question and many more age-related motivational issues as well. It surely will change and improve your management style forever."

— Harry Paul, co-author of *FISH! A Remarkable Way to Boost Morale and Improve Results*

"Fascinating reading. *Managing by Defining Moments* soundly explains common dilemmas we experience in the workplace. It gives you new tools for solving some of the age-old problems."

— Jan Becker, Senior Vice President of Human Resources, Autodesk

PRAISE FOR *DEFINING MARKETS, DEFINING MOMENTS*

"Dr. Schewe's latest book should be on the must reading list for all direct marketers. In our catalogue and e commerce businesses we have discovered that many of the old rules of target marketing no longer apply. We have been using generational cohort marketing for our catalogue positioning with great success. This is not a book of theory. It offers actionable opportunities in every chapter."

— Bob Allen, President/CEO, The Vermont Country Store

"Back when I was working for Nestle, I was introduced to Geoff Meredith's generational cohort theory and experienced its successful application to chocolate beverages, a category that was in dire need of excitement and innovation. I witnessed a narrowly defined 2-D consumer target transform into a 3-D consumer landscape that helped us identify several highly profitable new business opportunities. Like all great strides in Marketing theory, this new approach was an obvious epiphany . . . one that makes sense immediately despite the realization that no one has done this before."

— Lisa Steere, Executive Vice President of Marketing, Gloria Jean's Coffees

"There's nothing academic about cohort marketing. It's global. It's practical. And it adds richness, texture, and definition to one's target market."

— Jeff Manning, Executive Director, California Milk Processor Board (Godfather of the "Got Milk?" advertising campaign)

"Cohort analysis really works. We have used it as a primary tool to help us understand motivations and differences in consumption patterns in 14 countries around the world. This book describes the concept in a way that brings it to life and is fun reading."

— David Garrett, Director, Consumer Insight and Opportunity Planning, Coca-Cola North America

Managing by Defining Moments

By Geoffrey E. Meredith
Charles D. Schewe, PhD
and Alexander Hiam

With Janice Karlovich

Hungry Minds™

Best-Selling Books · Digital Downloads · e-Books · Answer Networks
e-Newsletters · Branded Web Sites · e-Learning

New York, NY · Cleveland, OH · Indianapolis, IN

Managing by Defining Moments

Published by
Hungry Minds, Inc.
909 Third Avenue
New York, NY 10022
www.hungryminds.com

Library of Congress Control Number: 2002100167

ISBN: 0-7645-5412-3

Printed in the United States of America

10 9 8 7 6 5 4 3 2 1

Distributed in the United States by Hungry Minds, Inc.

For general information on Hungry Minds' products and services please contact our Customer Care Department within the U.S. at 800-762-2974, outside the U.S. at 317-572-3993 or fax 317-572-4002.

For sales inquiries and reseller information, including discounts, premium and bulk quantity sales, and foreign-language translations, please contact our Customer Care Department at 800-434-3422, fax 317-572-4002, or write to Hungry Minds, Inc., Attn: Customer Care Department, 10475 Crosspoint Boulevard, Indianapolis, IN 46256.

DEDICATION

This book is dedicated to all those who perished in the terrorist attacks of September 11, 2001. Not only was this a great tragedy for them and their loved ones, it was also a defining moment in our history — one that will alter the ways in which business is conducted and life is lived for those left behind.

ACKNOWLEDGMENTS

We have benefited from the support of so many people who helped us put this book in your hands. We would like to thank them for all they have done.

Much of the research was unearthed by Amy Wales, a very bright and conscientious graduate student at the University of Massachusetts. We thank her for her tenacity. Stephanie Noble, now an Assistant Professor at the University of Mississippi, also conducted secondary and primary research with findings that were folded into the book. She, too, is an excellent researcher and a great contributor.

We also praise and appreciate the dedication of Ben Nussbaum, our developmental editor at Hungry Minds. Not only is he responsible for dotting the i's and crossing the t's, his vision helped make this book a great deal more enjoyable to read. His probing questions also challenged us and dramatically improved the conceptual underpinnings of this book. We don't know how he is able to accommodate all that parallel processing and multi-tasking, but are glad he can.

From the start we had great support from many at Hungry Minds. We would like to thank Kathy Nebenhaus for believing in our concept for the book, Melisa Duffy for her marketing skills par excellence, and Kate Fischer for her contributions to creating marketplace awareness of this book. Celia Rocks and Dottie DeHart (of Rocks-DeHart Public Relations) with Megan Johnson are fabulous publicists who have reached new heights in getting the word out about this and our earlier books. We truly appreciate all they do for us . . . and if you really like this book, what they do for you too!

Our agent, Bob Linsenman, also deserves a round of applause for hammering out the details and for encouraging us when we needed it most.

Writing a book is not a trivial endeavor, as we suspect you know. It takes a great deal of time . . . time away from family. So we would like to salute our spouses for putting up with us, and for giving us encouragement while we squirreled away to put this book together. These generous souls are Anne Schewe, Val Meredith, Heather White, and Ken Foster. We fully expect that these wonderful friends will share in the rewards of this book along with us. Finally, we must thank Sean Foster, born in March, 2001, for finally learning to sleep through the night at age seven months. His mom could not have worked and reworked this manuscript to the degree that she did without cooperation from him. We wish him only the best of defining moments as he grows into adulthood.

TABLE OF CONTENTS

6 UNDERSTANDING YOUR LEADING-EDGE BABY BOOMER EMPLOYEES   81

ABOUT THE AUTHORS

Geoffrey E. Meredith is President and founder of Lifestage Matrix Marketing, the strategic planning and marketing consulting company that pioneered cohort and lifestage segmentation techniques, especially as they apply to the global aging phenomenon. Clients include the Coca-Cola Company, Nestle, Levi's, Kodak, SCI, and Kellogg's. Prior to starting Lifestage Matrix Marketing in 1992, he spent over 20 years in advertising and marketing, holding Senior Vice President and General Manager positions at Ogilvy & Mather, Ketchum Communications, Age Wave, Inc., and Hal Riney & Partners. He has extensive experience with clients in financial services (The Prudential, Bank of America), packaged goods (Procter & Gamble, Pillsbury, 7-Up, Clorox, Campbell Soup), healthcare (Aetna, Blue Cross and Blue Shield), consumer electronics (Pacific Bell, Fujitsu America, Convergent Technologies), cable television (Viacom, Goodlife Television Network), and retail (McDonald's, Marine World, Princess Tours). Geoff is currently acting as Executive Vice President and Chief Marketing Officer of connectME.tv, a broadband video telephony and Internet access company. A noted writer and keynote speaker, he has lectured in the Stanford, University of San Francisco, and St. Mary's MBA programs. He has a BA from Princeton University in Art and Archeology and an MBA from Stanford.

You can reach Geoff at:
Geoffrey E. Meredith
Lifestage Matrix Marketing
3517 Eagle Point Road
Lafayette, California 94549-2329
925.283.4806 [Voice]
925.283.4276 [Fax]
Lifestage@aol.com [email]

Charles D. Schewe is Professor of Marketing at the Eugene M. Isenberg School of Management at the University of Massachusetts at Amherst and a principal in Lifestage Matrix Marketing. Dr. Schewe has researched and written extensively about the marketing implications of the aging process. For three years, Dr. Schewe was executive consultant for Age Wave, the Emeryville, California, strategic planning and consulting company that focused on the aging of America. His client engagements included Kmart, Grand Metropolitan, Prudential Bache, Nabisco, Sara Lee, Procter & Gamble, and Lucky Stores. He has also advised IBM, Spalding Sports Worldwide, and Kraft General Foods. It was at Age Wave that he met Geoff, and shortly thereafter they joined in Lifestage Matrix Marketing. The author of over 50 articles in academic journals and more than 10 books, including the bestselling *Portable MBA in Marketing,* Dr. Schewe has been the keynote speaker for a wide range of U.S. and global audiences. His talks are wildly received. He received his PhD from the Kellogg Graduate School of Management at Northwestern University, and his MBA and BA from the University of Michigan. He was a Fulbright Scholar and frequent visiting professor to Lund University in Sweden, as well as other universities in Europe and South America.

You can reach Charles at:

Charles D. Schewe, PhD
Lifestage Matrix Marketing
23 Ash Lane
Amherst, Massachusetts 01002
413.256.0914 [Voice]
413.253.3338 [Fax]
Schewe@mktg.umass.edu [email]

Alexander Hiam is an Executive Consultant with Lifestage Matrix Marketing and the principal and founder of a training company that provides courses and publishes course materials for the corporate training industry. In his capacity at Lifestage Matrix Marketing, he has worked on numerous cohort-related projects for clients such as Coca-Cola, Eastman Kodak, Vermont Country Store, and Kellogg's. His own training firm specializes in management training in areas such as leadership, supervision, conflict management, sales and service, creativity, and employee motivation. Clients include the U.S. Senate, Ford Motor Company, General Motors, the U.S. Army, 3M, the U.S. Postal Service, AT&T, the National Association of Independent Trust companies, and many other organizations. Alex's training programs and materials in the areas of leadership, motivation, and creativity are integrated into this book's treatment of the subjects.

Alex has taught at several business schools, including the Eugene M. Isenberg School of Management at the University of Massachusetts at Amherst. He is the author of numerous books on management issues, including *The Vest-Pocket CEO* (Prentice Hall), *Closing the Quality*

Gap: Lessons from America's Leading Companies (Prentice Hall and The Conference Board), *The Manager's Pocket Guide to Creativity* (HRD Press), *The 24 Hour MBA* (Adams), and *Motivating & Rewarding Employees: New and Better Ways to Inspire Your People* (Adams).

Alex received his AB in anthropology from Harvard and his MBA in marketing and strategic planning from the Haas School of Business at the University of California at Berkeley.

Alex's business is based in Amherst, Massachusetts. His website is www.alexhiam.com.

Janice Karlovich is a freelance writer and a proud member of the Generation X Cohort. She has a BS in journalism from the University of Illinois at Urbana-Champaign, and has written for such publications as the *Chicago Tribune, The New York Times,* and *The Fort Wayne, Indiana, Journal Gazette.* She also does marketing communications writing for several Fortune 500 companies and other clients from her home-based office. Janice lives in Michigan with her husband, son, and two border collies.

PROLOGUE

An ancient Arabian proverb states, "Men resemble the times more than they resemble their fathers." It captures the underlying theme of this book. By today's standards, this statement would clearly be considered sexist. But when this saying was first voiced, the value of gender equality was not only not a relevant social consideration, the concept of sexism was not even acknowledged.

The point is that what we value depends as much on the shared experiences that we have with our peers as on what we learn or inherit from our family. Now, we don't dispute the importance of the family — or of schools and churches, for that matter — in determining what we all value in life. But our extensive work and research has uncovered a fresh angle on how we gain many of our core values. And we want to share that with you in this book.

From academic research and countless consulting engagements, we have come to learn that many values are fashioned from what we call *defining moments,* those significant emotional events that we experience when we are roughly between the ages of 17 and 23 — our coming-of-age years. As we are becoming responsible, economically active adults, our societal antennae are extended. When faced with an event such as a war, a severe economic change, or a terrorist attack during these impressionable years, we're impacted in a way that creates values that stay with us, relatively unchanged, throughout our lives.

We all know or have known people who experienced the Great Depression as they were coming of age. They are in their 80s now. You certainly can sense their concern for their own financial security, even today! This is a value shared by most Americans in their 80s. And we all know Baby Boomers in their late 40s and 50s. These people came of age during the social revolution of the 1960s . . . and they are fixated on remaining youthful in every facet of their lives. Their coming-of-age years defined them, and they do not want to let go of those memories. In essence, the members of each of these groups have a common bond with each other, shaped by common experiences during that late adolescent/early adulthood period. These bonds are the basis on which generational cohorts are made, and are what makes these groups different from each other.

Earlier, we wrote *Defining Markets, Defining Moments: America's 7 Generational Cohorts, Their Shared Experiences, and Why Businesses Should Care.* In it, we described seven age groups that encompass those in their 80s today to those coming of age right now. We believe that the members of these groups are similar to each other in terms of values. In our earlier book, we focused on how these values can be used as platforms for marketing, for developing products and promotional campaigns. Generational cohort values are clearly motivational foundations for buying and consumption behavior. But they are also clearly valuable clues for how to stir employee productivity. This book explores the theory of generational cohorts and applies this powerful body of knowledge to the field of management.

Motivation is now a key issue in the field of management. Employees are even hired based in good part on their perceived motivation, and rewards are doled out based on what will motivate employees. Organizations want to retain good employees, and the way to keep them (and to make sure they stay good employees) is to appeal to and increase their motivation. Because different generational cohorts possess different values and motivations, understanding these values and motivations is a powerful avenue for managerial excellence. This book details these age-related values and motives.

In addition, we offer you concrete ideas about how to use your newfound knowledge to improve the way you manage these different generational cohorts. In particular, we believe that one management style will not be very effective in a workplace that includes several generational cohorts — and that there are four management paths that can and should be employed. This approach is so very new that many of these ideas are just that, ideas. We know they are theoretically sound, and we are certain they're useful. But in many cases, we leave their operational interpretation and execution to you. We are sure they will offer some very fresh approaches and sharpen your managerial thinking. And we know you will find these ideas fascinating and exciting.

We want you to have fun reading this book. After all, fun is as important on the job as it is in the rest of your life, isn't it? Well, maybe yes, maybe no! Read on and see the importance of fun, among other things, in today's workplace.

CHAPTER 1

TROUBLE BREWING

On a recent afternoon at the Coors Brewery in Golden, Colorado, a giant vat began to sputter and fail. The equipment clearly needed immediate repair. But many of the younger employees looked at their watches, realized it was only a short while until quitting time, and flat out refused to put in the extra time needed to do the repairs. They'd done all that was required to collect their paychecks. Why go to any extra trouble for the sake of the company? They would get to it first thing tomorrow.

Fortunately, a group of older employees heard about the problem, stepped forward, and worked long into the night to fix the broken equipment and keep the plant running.

What happened? Why wouldn't the majority of the employees take responsibility or demonstrate appropriate concern and initiative? And perhaps more to the point, what should management's response have been? Is rewarding the volunteers and punishing those who did not help appropriate? Should the people who refused to fix the problem still be eligible for raises and promotions? Should they be fired? And how might the brewery's managers ensure that the entire shift will show more commitment and cooperation the next time a crisis occurs?

All difficult questions, to be sure — ones you may have grappled with yourself. Before taking action, before making any plans or disciplining anyone, managers in this kind of situation need to first recognize that they have just witnessed what we call a *generational cohort effect.* A generational cohort is a group of people about the same age who share the same coming-of-age experiences and core values.

A review of those Coors workers who volunteered reveals that they were older workers who belong to a generational cohort whose members value their jobs and naturally feel a strong obligation in times of crisis. Those workers who left were from a younger cohort whose members typically prize their personal time more highly and feel less sense of duty. But they weren't teenagers. They were mature adults holding responsible long-term jobs, working side by side with members of an older cohort in apparent harmony until this crisis demonstrated their different underlying attitudes toward work.

The brewery's managers have every right to wish that their employees would all care enough to step forward and resolve an urgent problem, even if doing so is inconvenient. Yet managers can't reasonably expect to get that desired behavior from each cohort *unless they use a different strategy with each.* The way the brewery currently designs, supervises, and rewards its employees is effective with members of the older cohort — who didn't walk away from the problem. There are good ways to motivate and manage other employees also, but they are *different* ways, as you'll see in this book. (We propose a solution for Coors in Chapter 3.)

LOYALTY ON THE DECLINE

Today, workers don't feel the same level of loyalty to their jobs and their employers that their parents did. They gripe around water coolers and in chat rooms, sounding for all the world like less-humorous versions of Dilbert. In survey after survey, employees say they don't like their bosses or employers, and that they would take a better job in a heartbeat if they could find one.

Add to that the growing problem of employee dishonesty. Estimates put typical costs of employee pilferage and expense-account padding at 6% to 10% of revenues. A new survey by KPMG International, one of the world's largest accounting and consulting firms, finds that 76% of employees have seen illegal activities in their workplaces in the past year. And at large corporations where most employees are online, it's estimated that an average of over two hours per day per employee are spent on the Internet, on personal e-mail, or even playing games or accessing porn. A small percentage of workers are even downloading files to sell to competitors or are planning vandalistic hacking attacks.

THE CHANGING NATURE OF WORK

The type of situation described at Coors is a common problem for many American managers. Many times their expectations don't match those of their employees, and the end result is frustration and stress on both sides. A recent Gallup survey found that more than half of all employees are demotivated and aren't engaged with their work. Turnover has reached record levels in many industries in recent years, and even when the economy softens, the better employees are hard to hold on to.

The new challenges facing managers have a lot to do with the changing work environment. Today, we do more with fewer people. We work with less hierarchy, wider spans of control, and flatter organizations. Thus, more initiative and cooperation are needed from employees. At the same time, the nature of our work is less structured and requires us to be more improvisational, flexible, and solution oriented, because our organizations must grow and change rapidly just to stay alive. This makes for a high-contact work environment in which we have to work well with lots of different people instead of just doing our own little jobs and then passing our work off to someone else.

The workplace has changed so dramatically that most companies are in a permanent state of chaos trying to figure out what to do. The average mid-size to large company embraces at least one major new management theory or program each year. We've done total quality management, management by walking around, matrix management, organizational development, flat organizations, systems thinking, quality improvement teams, process reengineering, change management, just-in-time inventories, outsourcing, supplier integration, employee recognition, suggestion systems, and who knows what else.

And many companies have flirted with even more radical notions, such as self-directed teams, open-book management, and employee ownership plans — all of which seem to run counter to the very essence of the typical business organization, with its top-down control and separation of owners from workers. Yet, in spite of the apparent contradictions, many companies persist in trying to make such ideas work. They have to. They can't think of anything else to do, and they continue to face frustrations and obstacles in their efforts to manage and motivate their people.

There's nothing wrong with many of the new management ideas. But they haven't added up to a silver bullet. In fact, they don't even create a clear idea of what the modern workplace should be like or how it should be managed. If anything, managers seem less in control and more frustrated today than they did 30 years ago, when the idea of wholesale training of managers in MBA programs was just getting started. Time after time, the new idea falls short, the new solution fails, and the chase has to start again.

A Tough Business Environment for Managers

These days, many managers complain that business is tougher than it used to be. First we had the "new economy," with its fast rate of technological change. Then we plunged into a recession and are struggling to come out the other side. And if these relatively recent economic challenges weren't enough, there has been a long-term trend toward faster cycles of technology and product change, along with a high rate of entrepreneurship and increased competition from thousands of new companies entering the economy each year. Add the increasingly global nature of competition, and you have a far larger and less stable playing field for the fast-paced game of business.

It's important to recognize that business does get tougher in tangible ways over time. We say this not to discourage anyone, but rather to encourage everyone to be open-minded about the need for new and improved approaches to management. New challenges can certainly be overcome — and may even provide significant business opportunities. But new challenges probably will not be overcome using the same old methods.

As things get tougher, we can still remember that the fundamentals of success involve motivating employees to perform well and providing customers with the goods and services that satisfy them.

THE NEW DIVERSIFICATION

In this book, you're going to see that there is no one right way to run a business anymore. Instead, there's such a wide diversity of basic work values among employees that most businesses need to present multiple faces and provide parallel work paths in order to get the most out of their people. The economy is changing fundamentally, and these changes are driven by changes in the makeup of the population itself.

In an earlier book, *Defining Markets, Defining Moments,* we wrote about the marketing side of this new economic equation. In *Managing by Defining Moments,* we join forces with Alex Hiam, a management consultant and author, to focus on what goes on inside a company and how to get the management side of the equation right, both today and in the coming years.

One of the most important findings from our work on generational cohorts and management is that most workplaces now have a surprisingly diverse mix of different employees — but not in the way you think. Race, gender, and religion may seem like the key drivers of diversity in businesses today, but in our research we find that the core attitudes and values that are formed during a person's coming-of-age years are often more important determinants of workplace behavior.

In today's workplaces, multiple generational cohorts with very different values and attitudes often work side by side. They coexist in uneasy truces that hide a great deal of underlying tension and misunderstandings. To manage everyone well and overcome common business ailments, such as high turnover and low motivation, managers need to understand and work with these subtle but powerful divisions.

Each cohort needs a culture it can identify with and work within comfortably and naturally. Having one single culture that everyone must make his or her home in is no longer effective. Having just one corporate culture ensures that *no one* feels completely at home in the workplace. No wonder managers can't seem to make any of the new management theories work!

THE VALUE OF COHORT ANALYSIS

In the search for new and better ways of creating productive, motivated workforces, some managers are turning to the insights of sociology to gain a better understanding of their employees. Since the 1920s, sociologists have understood that significant political, social, or economic events can shape core values and attitudes of entire groups of people — groups of people called cohorts. While cohort analysis is well known in sociology, this book is the first time this theoretical construct is being applied to management.

Our approach focuses on the idea that to develop a more effective work environment, managers must learn to identify, profile, and tap into the latent feelings and values that were formed when their employees were coming of age, roughly when they were between the ages of 17 and 23. This was a time when they were falling in love for the first time, becoming economic beings, developing their own value systems, exploring new ideas — in essence, becoming adults. It is a very powerful time, and the lessons learned during it last a lifetime. We believe that if managers understand the impact of these shared experiences, they can better understand how to manage these cohort groups in the workplace. In this book, we explore some new ways of looking at and working with employees, new ways that can help maximize performance in challenging business environments.

In North America today, there are a number of different generational cohorts, all of which play a major role in the workplace. Each has its own values and perceptions, and the members of each cohort find it far easier to understand and work with fellow cohort members than to cross cohort divides. Yet bridging these gaps and forging effective teams out of diverse groups of employees is vitally important.

You may be surprised to find out that differences between generational cohorts are at the root of many of the most prominent and important workforce issues in the headlines and boardrooms of our era. In the coming chapters, we demonstrate that a better understanding of each cohort can resolve many problems and create powerful new opportunities for you and your business today.

While many managers would like to develop a kinder, gentler management style, one that taps into people's unique personalities and strengths, the fact is that most don't know how to do it. They fall back on old-style command-and-control methods that have sat on the shelf collecting dust for years. These managers may value independence themselves, yet many end up micromanaging their employees' every move.

Research has shown that the single most important factor in individual performance is an employee's relationship with his or her immediate supervisor. The best, most efficient way to achieve peak performance from your employees is not to focus on their weaknesses, but to promote diversity of thought and revel in employees' strengths. Managing by cohort — or defining moment — is one effective way to do this.

THE LONG SHADOWS OF DEFINING MOMENTS

We use the term *generational cohort* to refer to groups of people who came of age at roughly the same time. Each generational cohort is deeply influenced by the significant events that were happening during its key coming-of-age years. External events such as economic changes, wars, political ideologies, technological innovations, and social upheavals act to redefine social values, attitudes, and preferences. And these cohort effects stay with the members of that cohort and influence their behavior throughout the rest of their lives.

For example, Americans now in their late 70s and early 80s lived through the Great Depression. Individuals who are now in their 40s and 50s witnessed the assassination of JFK, saw other political assassinations, shared the experience of the Vietnam War, and lived through the energy crisis. These events, which we call *defining moments,* shape values, attitudes, beliefs, and behaviors to such an extent that these shared experiences distinguish one cohort from another.

Cohort-formed values, attitudes, and preferences do not change as a function of age or lifestyle. Individuals who came of age during the Great Depression tend to be compulsive savers and risk-averse throughout their lives because they experienced great economic hardship in their early adulthood. Similarly, individuals who came of age during the freewheeling '60s still value self-expression, individuality, and youth.

Think about the values and culture of America (and much of Europe, too) during the 1960s. Now ask yourself: Would people who internalized those values in their youth fit comfortably in a strict, top-down corporate hierarchy? Would they want to follow orders without knowing why or having a chance to voice their views? Would they want to sit in a workstation in a long row of workstations that all look just alike?

Of course not! Anyone whose consciousness was branded by the self-expressive '60s retains a kernel of that self-expressive free spirit even today. They may wear pinstriped suits when need be, but they much prefer their jeans and T-shirts. When they start and run their own companies, they create very different corporate cultures than the ones their parents created and left to them. But when they go to work for others, these square pegs still must squeeze into round holes. This is an ongoing struggle that is leaving shavings all over the carpet in many companies today.

Seven American Cohorts

By the end of this book, you will be intimately acquainted with each of the cohorts that currently exist in the U.S. For now, we simply want to introduce you to the cohorts and give you a feel as to how each is unique. We have identified the following seven generational cohorts:

+ **Depression Cohort:** Born from 1912 to 1921, ages 81 to 90 in 2002. This group's coming-of-age years were marked by economic strife and elevated unemployment rates. The members of this cohort had to take menial jobs to survive. Financial security — what they most lacked when coming of age — rules their thinking. They are no longer in the workforce, but they have a clear impact on many of today's management practices.

+ **World War II Cohort:** Born from 1922 to 1927, ages 75 to 80 in 2002. Sacrifice for the common good was widely accepted among members of the World War II Cohort, as evidenced by women working in factories for the war effort and men going off to fight. This cohort was focused on defeating a common enemy during their coming-of-age years, and the members of this cohort are more team oriented and patriotic than those of other generational cohorts. They represent a very small portion of today's workforce, but they, too, have impacted today's managers.

✦ **Postwar Cohort:** Born from 1928 to 1945, ages 57 to 74 in 2002. These individuals experienced a time of remarkable economic growth and social tranquility, a time of family togetherness, school dress codes, and houses in the suburbs, although they also experienced McCarthyism and the Korean conflict. This cohort participated in the rise of the middle class, sought a sense of security and stability, and expected prosperous times to continue indefinitely. Many CEOs and upper-level managers are members of this cohort.

✦ **Leading-Edge Baby Boomer Cohort:** Born from 1946 to 1954, ages 48 to 56 in 2002. This group remembers the assassinations of John and Robert Kennedy and Martin Luther King, Jr. The loss of JFK had the largest influence on this cohort's values. They became adults during the Vietnam War, and watched as the first man walked on the moon. Leading-Edge Boomers championed causes (Greenpeace, civil rights, women's rights), yet were simultaneously hedonistic and self-indulgent (pot, free love, sensuality). They are now beginning their ascent into upper-middle and upper management.

✦ **Trailing-Edge Baby Boomer Cohort:** Born from 1955 to 1965, ages 37 to 47 in 2002. This group witnessed the fall of Vietnam, Watergate, and Nixon's resignation. The oil embargo, the raging inflation rate, and the more than 30% decline in the S&P Index led these individuals to be less optimistic about their financial future than the Leading-Edge Boomers. Many middle managers, mid-level and senior employees, and entrepreneurs are from this cohort, as are members of the rank and file.

✦ **Generation X Cohort:** Born from 1965 to 1976, ages 26 to 36 in 2002. Many members of this cohort were latchkey children or have parents who divorced. They have delayed marriage and children, and they don't take those commitments lightly. More than other groups, this cohort accepts cultural diversity and puts personal life ahead of work life. They're free agents, not team players. And yet, they are being forced to participate in a fundamental workplace shift from individual to team-based tasks and organizations . . . a serious mistake, as we shall see.

Despite a rocky start into adulthood, this group shows a spirit of entrepreneurship unmatched by any other cohort. Take a look at many Internet startups, and you'll find successful Gen-Xers who did it their way. Members of this group mainly fill rank-and-file positions, although some are beginning to move into management positions.

✦ **N Generation Cohort:** Born from 1977, ages 25 and under in 2002. We call the youngest cohort the N Generation or N Gen, because the advent of the Internet is a defining event for them and because they will be the engine of growth over the next two decades. While still a work in progress, their core value structure is different than that of Gen X. They are more idealistic and social-cause oriented, without the cynical, what's-in-it-for-me, free-agent mindset of many Xers. This group mainly fills entry-level positions today, but N-Gens are destined to step up to more important roles relatively rapidly because they outnumber their older Gen-X associates.

As you can see from the list above, age is a determining factor in cohort analysis, but by no means are we suggesting that you hire or make management decisions based on age. As Ford Motor Company recently learned when it implemented a forced ranking system, making management decisions based on age can have dire consequences. In Ford's case, it resulted in a slew of age-discrimination lawsuits filed by older white-collar employees who claimed they were unfairly penalized by the system, which called for 10% of workers to receive a C grade, a grade that could lead to termination. A large number of older employees received Cs after their managers were forced to rank them against younger colleagues. Ford is now in settlement discussions with the employees' attorneys.

What we're advocating in *Managing by Defining Moments* is not to use employees' ages against them, but to use age as a clue to get to know your employees better, to manage them in ways they find most effective, to diversify teams, and to ensure you get the very best performance from the people that work for you. In tough economic times, older, higher-paid employees are often the first to go, but we believe this is short-sighted. The experience and institutional knowledge this group brings to the table is irreplaceable, and intangible in economic terms. Cohort analysis can help you to integrate these older employees with younger employees and create a workplace where people feel energized and motivated and are able to achieve peak performance.

FROM REACTIVE TO PROACTIVE

There have been many changes in the workplace in recent years. Does that mean we are already adapting to the newer cohorts? Yes and no.

Some of the newer workplace practices are, in fact, geared to workers from the younger cohorts, but these are relatively superficial changes and rarely get at the heart of the problem. Casual Fridays are the norm . . . and casual everyday is often found as well. In fact, casual has become so much the norm that several West coast companies have recently instituted Dress-Up Fridays, so that employees can show off their finery and be ready for a fancy night on the town! Twenty-something techies are given the option of when they show up for work, and many can even drift into the office at 9:30 in the morning only to hit the fitness center. At the height of the Internet boom, Gen-Xers and N-Gens were coddled by being given signing bonuses, being allowed to have their pets, even birds, on the job, and being allowed to design their workspaces to fit their individuality.

Even as standardized and buttoned-down a company as Microsoft found that it had to accommodate its younger workers' need for individuality. When the company designed the Xbox, Microsoft's video-game system, it had to hire gaming code–writers from the outside. Facing a rebellion, the company moved the group from the cookie-cutter buildings on the Redmond, Washington campus to their own funky, three-building complex, and allowed the 50 key game designers to organize and decorate their own workspaces. With few exceptions, the gamers were Gen-Xers.

As the Microsoft example shows, the current work environment is certainly different than what it used to be, and the preferences of younger cohorts are clearly responsible for these changes. Yet most of the changes to date have been quite superficial, for the simple reason

9-11 as a Defining Moment

On September 11, 2001, much of the world watched news reports of a series of massive and devastating terrorist attacks on the United States. In addition to being a terrible tragedy, 9-11 was also a defining moment for many Americans, particularly young adults who were old enough to appreciate the events fully, but young enough not to have been tempered by other major events.

We go into greater detail about this cohort in later chapters, especially Chapter 9, but you probably already know something about it from the occasional media coverage of Generation Y, as the emerging cohort is sometimes called. As we noted earlier, we call the newest cohort N Gen, because its members are the first cohort to grow up with the Internet, and also because it is expected to be the engine of growth in the coming years because of its large size.

Young adults in North America grew up in a world of economic prosperity, at least for the average person. No major national tragedies had shattered their protective bubble. The overall economy grew, and those who wished to participate in the high-tech economy could

that most managers are unaware of the fundamental cohort-based values underlying their employees' preferences. No level of investment in surface issues is going to prevent problems of commitment, turnover, communications, and the other management issues that are on the business pages today. Utilizing cohort effects to shift from reactive to proactive engagement is a significant strategic step, and one that we will help you take in this book.

have a crack at almost instant wealth, at least on paper. September 11, plus the onset of recession and the bioterrorist attacks that came on the heels of the terrorist attacks, changed everything.

For N-Gens, who had relatively little life experience, the sudden puncturing of their sense of security has no doubt had a lasting effect. You don't need to be a sociologist to anticipate that compared to Generation X — the next youngest cohort — this group will tend to be:

✦ More patriotic
✦ More fearful and vigilant of danger

Sociology tell us that these values are likely to be imprinted at a very deep level and will endure throughout N-Gens' lives.

Add to this picture the likelihood that N-Gens are probably going to be more group and team oriented — they will remember vividly the ways in which their communities pulled together in response to the terrorist attacks during their coming-of-age years. A workplace is, among other things, a *community*, and we can anticipate that N-Gen employees may feel strong emotional ties to their co-workers.

CHAPTER 2

MANY WORKERS, ONE WORKPLACE

The senior executives of software consulting firm NovaSoft Information Technology generated a lot of news coverage when they offered maxed-out sales incentives to employees. The bait for achieving high sales goals? A C-class Mercedes-Benz sports car, a Rolex watch, and $20,000 in cold, hard cash.

With incentives like that, who wouldn't work night and day to outsell the competition?

Well, in some media reports, 20-something employees were quoted as saying they were tired of working 12-hour days to win prizes and were planning to relax a bit and take more time off in the future. Material rewards are beginning to lose their appeal.

The sorts of employee incentives offered by NovaSoft are especially appropriate for people who came of age during the affluent postwar period of the 1950s. The prosperity the nation experienced during their coming-of-age years gave many of them a lifelong taste for status-oriented luxuries. Working hard to earn luxury goods that say "I made it!" is okay with this cohort. Leading-Edge and Trailing-Edge Boomers also tend to appreciate these kinds of status objects. They make them feel good.

Not surprisingly, Postwars and Boomers are typically the ones who come up with incentive programs. But what about those young sales-people who the programs are targeting?

Their response is likely to be along the lines of "whatever." They typically are not impressed by fancy cars and other status objects, and would prefer to have their evenings and weekends free. According to a Gen-X senior account executive, "It's against my religion to work weekends." To them, quality of life is paramount, and they are cynical about a lot of things, including the incentive programs of senior managers. We have here a clash of two cultures, cultures that the managers and their employees brought to the workplace without even realizing it or meaning to. Their formative experiences gave them differing views of work and incompatible attitudes about performance and incentives.

Senior managers naturally try to design incentives that *would work for them.* That's fine, as long as they're managing people from their own cohort, people who share the same underlying attitudes and work values. It leads to trouble when they are managing employees from other cohorts. Better to put together a team (a loose, informal, maybe even virtual team) of Gen-X employees and ask it to design the sales incentive program. The Gen-Xers would come up with very different rewards than what the senior managers created — maybe time off instead of status products.

Oh, and why should it be a loose, virtual team and not a formal committee? Because, while Postwar managers like to be assigned to formal teams and groups, Gen-Xers are more independent and react to teams like they are bits to chafe against.

The moral? Managing people who are different from you is impossible unless you first take the time to get to know them well.

Fortunately, that's an interesting thing to do as we look more deeply at the cohorts in today's workplace. The quest for understanding our diverse human economy leads to fascinating insights, not only into our employees, but also into ourselves. Our quest begins with a more detailed look at the power of defining moments.

DEFINING MOMENTS DEFINE VALUES

We all experience a wide range of events during our coming-of-age years. Not all are defining moments, however. Only those events — either short-term or long-term — that are strong enough to have a lasting social consequence become defining moments. The death of President John F. Kennedy and the AIDS crisis were two such events because they had lasting effects. The deaths of John Lennon and Princess Diana, two events that shocked the world, were not defining moments because they had no lasting significant social consequences.

Our work shows that defining moments create the ties that bind generational cohorts together. This is because defining moments help to define cohort values. The Vietnam War and the social turmoil of the late '60s and early '70s, for example, prompted the oldest Baby Boomers to value personal and social expression and individualism. This was quite a departure from societal norms at the time — their parents had just the opposite values. These kinds of defining moments help to create a patch-work of core values that stay with the members of a particular cohort, virtually unchanged, throughout their lives. Predictable patterns of behavior are the result.

UNCHANGING VALUES ARE WHAT CREATE COHORTS

Values are the bedrock on which Generational Cohort Analysis is built. Research shows that people's values are largely determined during their coming-of-age years, between the ages of 17 and 23. Shared defining moments play a huge role in shaping the values of a generational cohort. Not surprisingly, generational cohort values affect everything from personal relationships to career choices to financial decisions and more. Either directly or indirectly, all of these things affect the work environment as well.

Values can be broken down into two broad categories:

+ **Core values:** Molded by external events, and they do not change during a person's lifetime. In most cases, these core values define a specific cohort, and they provide cues for

behavior. If the external events during your coming-of-age
years were such that you learned to value security, for example,
you always tend to seek out security.

✦ **Changeable values:** Not held as long-term and often are ancil-
lary to core values. For example, say that one of your core
values is self-fulfillment. Acquiring material possessions may
enhance your self-fulfillment in your younger years, but this
may change as you grow older. As you age, you may well
choose other means of self-fulfillment, such as building a
strong relationship with your grandchildren. The means change
over time, but the core value of self-fulfillment remains constant.

In some cases, people's value structure is most influenced by what
they lacked during their coming-of-age years. For example, a sense of
belonging is often quite important to those who felt less nurtured when
they were coming of age. Security is often important for those who felt
unsettled or threatened during their early adult years. In other cases,
values are more influenced by surplus or by emulation. In these cases,
people tend to hold values similar to what their role models, such as
their parents or teachers, had.

Our research shows that generational cohort values are more closely
related to core values than to changeable values. They provide ongoing
cues for employee behavior. And because these values do not change
over one's life, they provide a solid platform on which to build effective
relationships in the workplace.

As you can see from Table 2.1, each cohort holds unique values that
differentiate it from other cohorts.

TABLE 2.1: GENERATIONAL COHORTS

Cohort	Population in 2000	Defining Moments	Values and Concerns
Depression	13 million (6%)	The Great Depression	✦ Sense of purpose ✦ Safety and security ✦ Social connectedness and companionship ✦ Comfort and convenience ✦ Waste not, want not

Cohort	Population in 2000	Defining Moments	Values and Concerns
World War II	17 million (8%)	World War II	✦ Patriotic ✦ Respect for authority ✦ Romance ✦ Self-reliance
Postwar	47 million (21%)	End of World War II Prosperity Moving to the suburbs Cold War Korean War McCarthyism Emergence of rock 'n' roll Civil rights movements	✦ The American Dream ✦ Conformity ✦ Stability ✦ Family ✦ Self-fulfillment
Leading-Edge Boomers	31 million (14%)	Assassination of JFK, RFK, and Martin Luther King, Jr. Vietnam War First man on the moon	✦ Personal and social expression ✦ Protected individualism ✦ Youth ✦ Health and wellness
Trailing-Edge Boomers	49 million (22%)	Fall of Vietnam Watergate Nixon resigns Energy crisis	✦ Lonely individualism ✦ Cynicism/distrust of government ✦ Family commitments
Generation X	42 million (19%)	Reaganomics Stock market crash of 1987 Challenger explosion Fall of Berlin Wall Gulf War AIDS crisis	✦ Free agency/independence ✦ Friendships important ✦ Cynical about future ✦ Savvy ✦ Pursuit of quality of life ✦ Acceptance of violence and sex

TABLE 2.1: (CONT.)

Cohort	Population in 2000	Defining Moments	Values and Concerns
Generation N	26 million (12%)	The Internet Good economic times School shootings Clinton's impeachment 9-11 terrorist attacks	◆ Hopeful about future ◆ Heightened fears ◆ Change is good ◆ Tolerance/diversity ◆ Team players ◆ Greater belief in institutions

THE COHORT EFFECT CREATES FLASHPOINTS IN THE WORKPLACE

The varied values of each cohort produce a constellation of workplace issues and problems. Values are durable and difficult (if not impossible) to change, so they tend to assert themselves in the workplace just as they do elsewhere. Being aware of various value-based conflicts, or *flashpoints,* as we often call them, is an important first step in dealing with them more productively. Employees and managers who appreciate these value differences are able to recognize value-driven behaviors for what they are and not overreact to them. And companies can prevent damage by providing education, conflict-resolution processes, and organizational designs that accommodate value differences and lessen value-based flashpoints.

Managers frequently supervise younger employees from newer cohorts. As a result, many value clashes occur that leave both the employee and manager feeling confused, angry, or frustrated. These value-based differences can have serious effects on employee perform-ance, damaging workplace relations and dampening job motivation. They can also lead to difficult incidents involving accusations of sexual harassment, discrimination, and wrongful discharge. Many employee lawsuits are at least partially due to differences between the employee's and the manager's cohort-driven values.

Table 2.2 lists some of the most damaging cohort flashpoints in the workplace today. These flashpoints are covered in detail in Chapter 10.

TABLE 2.2: BEWARE! COHORT FLASHPOINTS

Cohort Value	Flashpoint
N-Gen expectation for immediate success	A tight labor market and good economic times have given N-Gens an unrealistically high expectation of work, which often frustrates older managers who had to pay their dues along the way.
Gen-X values of informality, cynicism, and street smarts	These attitudes may offend older supervisors, leading to accusations of poor attitude and insubordination. The employee feels these charges are unjustified. Gen-Xers' communications with their managers are usually quite poor.
Gen-X need for emotional and financial security, also desire for independence	Managers often misread the independence value as indicating that the Gen-X employee resents direction and does not want attention. The Gen-X employee does not know how to elicit the desired emotional support and reassurance/security from supervisors.
Trailing-Edge Baby Boomers' desire to shape their own experiences	Because Trailing-Edge Boomers seek a greater level of control over their lives, younger workers often label them micromanagers or control freaks.
Trailing-Edge Baby Boomers' tendency toward lonely individualism, combined with a desire to have access to information	Older managers often fail to recognize that these Boomers resent being excluded from information flows and need to be given a chance to express their opinions. Many Trailing-Edge Boomers actually quit their jobs over this issue.
Trailing-Edge Boomers' leaning toward sexual promiscuity	This cohort's core values are more open to sexuality and explicit sexual language and behavior than many other cohorts. Without sensitivity training and proper coaching in sexual harassment issues, these Boomers can generate many harassment claims and problems when they become managers. Trailing-Edge Boomers may not realize that Gen-X employees value sexual caution more than they do.

TABLE 2.2: (CONT.)

Cohort Value	Flashpoint
Leading-Edge Boomers' desire for self-expression and treatment of work as self-fulfillment	Whether an employee or a manager, the Leading-Edge Boomer has a need to stamp each project with his or her personal touch. This can be a positive source of motivation, but more often it causes conflict over what is to be done, how to do it, and where to give the credit. Leading-Edge Boomers' employees may feel they are not getting the individual recognition they deserve and frequently complain their boss is taking all the credit.
Leading-Edge Boomers' individualism, skepticism, and questioning nature	Leads to conflicts with senior executives and boards when these Boomers gain management responsibility and use it to make radical changes without building sufficient support from older cohorts. The radical in the corner office often gets turned out — one reason why executive turnover rates are dangerously high today.
The Postwar Cohort's emphasis on stability, formality, structure, and institutions	These employees are slow to change and find it difficult to cooperate with younger, less respectful coworkers. At the executive level, the Postwar Cohort frequently fails to recognize the need for change until it is too late. Postwar CEOs and board members have been known to block needed changes and ride their organizations into the ground. Members of younger cohorts have to learn how to talk to this cohort about change, and must learn how to overcome Postwars' instinctive resistance.

Without the language of cohort values to explain problems such as the ones presented in Table 2.2, employees and managers are often mystified as to what went wrong and are unable to resolve the problem and move on. People fail to cooperate or communicate well, employees lose commitment and drag their heels or resign, managers complain about performance and agitate for dismissal, and employees file EEOC claims or accuse managers and employers of sexual harassment or wrongful dismissal. And worst of all, poor decisions are made, poor strategies are pursued, and bottom-line results are hurt, all as a result of a lack of appreciation of cohort-based values and the flashpoints where they clash.

OTHER FACTORS ALSO AFFECT A COHORT'S PROFILE

In addition to cohort values, other key factors play an important role in determining a generational cohort's preferred work style:

✦ **Current and next lifestage:** Husband, mother, grandmother, empty-nester. These are all examples of lifestages, or the roles we take on and act out during the course of our lives. Values impact how a person adjusts to a certain lifestage (whether to accept the stereotypical image of grandparenting or to redefine it, for example). Lifestages, in turn, help to define attitudes, outlooks, and daily activities.

Lifestages affect the work environment, too. As Leading-Edge Baby Boomers get older, for example, their priorities shift away from work toward family and inner fulfillment. This shift is having a huge impact at work.

It's critical to know what is going on in your employees' lives. Current and next lifestages can offer many clues for the astute manager. If a large percentage of your employees are in the parenting lifestage, for example, flex time is likely to be a good fit. Flex time also indulges the independence of Boomers and younger cohorts, and sends a very clear message of trust.

✦ **Physiographic profile:** As we age, certain physical changes are inevitable. Vision and hearing become more limited, arthritis and muscle pain become more common, and strength gradually is reduced. These effects of aging create many obvious opportunities for marketing, but they also create opportunities for management. For example, if you employ older workers, make company memos easy to read by using larger fonts and invest in ergonomically correct office furniture and equipment. For older workers who aren't in it just for the paycheck, a comfortable work environment is critical.

23

✦ **Emotions and affinities:** These are the desires and wants that emerge at various ages and that change over time. Socializing is a top priority for most 20 year olds, while career development and children's education play a larger role to many workers who are in their 30s. Taking into account an employee's emotions and affinities can sometimes mean the difference between a happy employee and a disgruntled one. For example, Boomers prefer a casual work environment, and would much rather wear jeans and golf shirts than suits and ties. If you have a Boomer-heavy workforce (or even one with a lot of Gen-Xers and N-Gens), relaxing the dress code can boost morale and improve employee effectiveness with no out-of-pocket costs to you.

These factors combine with a cohort's core values to give a vivid profile of a particular generational cohort. This profile, in turn, provides clues about the type of work environment a particular cohort prefers. In Chapter 3, we talk in greater detail about how to use cohort analysis. In Chapters 4 through 9, we profile each of the generational cohorts that currently dominate the workplace. In Chapters 10 through 14, we show you how to apply your new understanding of the different cohorts.

CHAPTER 3

USING COHORT ANALYSIS

Imagine a work environment in which you were expected to take a creative approach to routine tasks, find ways to turn work into play, create a unique character for yourself to amuse customers, share your personal feelings and experiences, and embrace the philosophy of your workplace in all aspects of your life.

Sound pretty good?

Now, imagine that this job also required you to catch big, smelly, raw fish that were thrown at you by your co-workers! Still sound appealing?

It's possible that you're the type of person who would love this sort of environment. But, obviously, the job isn't for everyone. It all depends on your personal work style.

This work environment actually exists, by the way. It's Pike Place Fish, a fish market in Seattle that has become world-famous for the crazy antics and incredibly high morale of its employees. The market has a highly committed workforce and far lower turnover than the industry average. A bestselling book, called *Fish!,* celebrates its management methods. Spike Lee made a famous Levi's commercial featuring the store. *Good Morning America* and MTV's *The Real World* have covered the fish market. And hundreds of businesses have come to this fish market in search of new ideas for energizing their employees.

It's not about the fish anymore (although the market does sell very good fresh fish). It's about building an exciting, creative, fun work environment where employees get to act out roles they create for themselves and feel fully energized by their work. Who would have thought that a small fish market would become the management mecca of corporate America!

ONE SIZE DOESN'T FIT ALL

While some aspects of Pike Place Fish sound appealing, none of us authors are eager to tie on an apron, step into big rubber boots, and start flinging wet fish around for the crowds. It's great fun to watch (check it out at www.pikeplacefish.com). But to do it ourselves? No thanks. It's just not us.

So what would happen if our editor forced us to dress in aprons and dance around telling jokes and tossing fish? We'd be like fish out of water . . . so to speak. And our work would probably stink as a result.

The Pike Place Fish example — even though it's an extreme one — illustrates a principle that holds true in virtually every workplace: What turns one employee on may turn another completely off. Not exactly what you wanted to hear, right? Unfortunately, those one-size-fits-all management fads that are so popular these days aren't going to work for you, especially in today's workplace, where diversity of thought, values, and demographics is fast becoming the rule.

So where does this leave well-meaning managers like you who are looking for quick and easy ways to boost employee cooperation and morale? Probably pretty dazed and confused! In fact, many managers are unaware of how their company's particular work environment fits individual employees' work styles and approaches to work.

You've no doubt witnessed the seismic clashes that can result when employees who crave excitement, individuality, and zany fun are teamed up with those who value planning, discipline, and authority (otherwise, you wouldn't be reading this book!). We'll show you how these seemingly disparate groups can work effectively together — and enjoy the experience. The key is figuring out how to bridge the substantial gap in work styles.

And that brings us to the main point of this book. Generational cohort management can help you understand what turns individual employees on (or off) and learn how to turn differences in individual values and styles into strengths instead of weaknesses for your organization.

CREATING COLLABORATION ACROSS COHORTS

The work of organizations is, after all, accomplished *by people working together.* When differences in cohort values — or differences in lifestage or any other cohort-based factor — prevent people from working together effectively and well, the organization and its people suffer. Only in the workplace do we find so many instances of cross-cohort collaboration. The cohort effect is probably the single most powerful external driver of employee relationships in organizations today. It is also the least understood and the worst managed.

For instance, surveys confirm that most employees continue to feel frustrated with the quality of communication in their workplaces and give this as a top reason for quitting a job. Yet, few companies provide any training or support for managers who must communicate to several cohorts, each of which has different affinities and values. Similarly, experts agree that teamwork, though now widespread in business, is usually frustrating and still fails to achieve its objectives. Yet few team leaders are aware of the difficulties involved in building a team consisting of people from two, three, or more distinct cohorts.

Businesses devote far more attention and resources to relatively minor factors, such as improving presentation skills, upgrading the word-processing software, or embracing the latest fad in organizational design, than they do to the fundamental issue of helping different cohorts work together. Yet cohort effects and the many cohort values–based flashpoints are the hidden smoking gun behind many of the problems and issues on the forefront of the management agenda today. Anyone who supervises others in the workplace needs to have a passing familiarity with the cohorts in his or her group of direct reports and must be aware of the distinct differences in the values held by members of each cohort. Managers often are the ones who have the burden of recognizing and working through cohort flashpoints in order to create a collaborative workplace with effective communications and teamwork. Just putting people together in teams does nothing to bridge cohort gaps. In fact, without intelligent management team structures tend to exacerbate the problem.

APPLYING COHORT ANALYSIS TO EASE FLASHPOINTS AND CREATE A CULTURE

After you have familiarized yourself with the generational cohort profiles included in Chapters 4 through 9, you most certainly will want to explore the implications of having people with different cohort profiles working side by side. This commingling of cohorts happens more often than not today — except perhaps in places like Pike Place Fish. What you get is a lot of diversity in a hidden dimension — the diversity of different cohort work styles and values existing side by side. And while managers who are unaware of cohort effects can't see the underlying cause for problems in the workplace, the problems that cohort conflict creates are all too visible: discord, low motivation, negative attitudes, dysfunctional teams, the defection of key people, ineffective leadership, and more. So we will also share insights for smoothing over these differences and defusing the flashpoints they create. In fact, when you are fully aware of the effects of coexisting generational cohorts, you can often find ways to turn that coexistence to your advantage.

You might also consider selecting a preferred profile for your specific workplace, just as Pike Place Fish did. It developed a unique strategy based on an extreme emphasis on specific cohorts' work styles (in this case, the N-Gen and Gen-X work styles). And you may well find that your organization — or specific parts of it — would benefit from specializing this way as well. For instance, if you have an operation where steady, careful work is the key, then you want to attract employees who hold the work values of the Depression Era Cohort. Even though few of these older workers are still in the workforce today, you can still find some younger individuals who fit this classic profile. As you read this book, we'll help you pick the best generational cohort profile for your specific needs.

USING GENERATIONAL COHORTS AS A RECRUITING TOOL

If you wanted to hire employees who would fit into the Pike Place Fish work environment, you would be wise to place recruiting ads in publications that reach people of the N-Gen and Gen-X age range. But when it came to interviewing and selecting candidates, you would want to look a lot more closely. You'd want to pick people who fit the classic N-Gen and Gen-X profile, regardless of age. And, of course, you'd want to remember that the law prevents you from asking candidates their age or making a hiring decision based specifically on age. When you were staffed up, you would probably find that, while you had hired many Gen-X- and N-Gen-aged employees, you had also hired some older ones who just happened to fit the same profile as your younger workers. Heck, they'd have to, or they wouldn't last very long when the other employees started throwing dead fish at them.

When you look at the ages of the Pike Place Fish employees, this type of variation in age ranges is just what you see. (Go ahead and have a squint at them on the www.pikeplacefish.com website if you want to confirm this.) Many are clearly in their 20s. But there's a smattering of older workers, too.

USING COHORT ANALYSIS TO UNDERSTAND INDIVIDUALS

Although many valid generalizations can be made using cohort analysis, all the members of a particular cohort won't have the characteristics that are common to the cohort as a whole. After all, each of us is an individual with unique experiences. Broad characterizations based on age work well for marketing, as we showed in *Defining Markets, Defining Moments* (Hungry Minds), our first book on cohort effects. But when it comes to management, a particular employee's individual characteristics hold more weight than that employee's age.

29

Here's the intriguing thing: While not everyone in the N-Gen age group, for example, fits the N-Gen profile, the profile does describe some people very well — even some people who are much older. That's because the characteristics of the N-Gen profile are produced by the impact of certain kinds of formative experiences. And whenever those experiences were present in someone's formative years, they tend to produce the characteristic profile. So the profiles that emerge from studies of generations or cohorts seem to have the power to describe individuals outside of that group as well as individuals within it.

Thus, while you may belong to, say, the Generation-X age group based on when you grew up, you may, in fact, be more like the proto-typical Leading-Edge Baby Boomer because of unique circumstances in your life — having older, indulgent parents, for example.

Exploring Work-Related Values and Attitudes

A saying in the human resources field goes "We hire on the hard stuff, but lose employees on the soft stuff." There is certainly some wisdom in this, especially when you think about how most jobs are defined — in terms of what experience, skills, and level of education are needed to do the work. This is the hard stuff. But people are a lot more than their formal qualifications, and when they actually roll up their sleeves and start working, their underlying values, attitudes, and varied approaches to interpersonal issues all come to the fore. This is the soft stuff.

As consultants and trainers, we view this not as a problem for managers but as an opportunity. It is an opportunity to improve the quality of human interactions and performances in your workplace by helping to identify and work through — and maybe even take advantage of — the many and complex aspects of what makes each employee a unique human being.

Cohort analysis offers some interesting glimpses into the underlying values and attitudes that often shape workplace behavior in subtle but powerful ways. Cohort values are among the basic variables that shape the social and emotional outlook of any human being. So it's safe to say that all of your employees do hold some of these values, and furthermore, that they hold some far more strongly than others.

The simple way to apply our work on cohorts is to look at American cohorts as defined by age — and that is a powerful way to understand the workforce in the aggregate. But as a manager, you often work with employees one-on-one. Also, you may work with some employees who do not seem to fit into the cohort that you'd expect from their coming-of-age years. Everyone takes his or her own path through life, after all!

PROFILING YOUR EMPLOYEES

In this section, we share a simple way of exploring the work-related values of an individual employee. By rating employees on the following items, you can quickly get a sense of how their values fit each of the basic cohort value profiles. Think of it as a way to translate the broad social science level analysis into a workable tool that can help you develop a better at-work relationship with individual employees.

In fact, we highly recommend that you take a few moments now to select an employee — perhaps someone who you are struggling a bit to lead at the moment — and profile this person using the following questionnaires.

DEPRESSION ERA?

1 No, 5 Yes	Does this statement describe the employee well?
1 2 3 4 5	Has a strong sense of purpose
1 2 3 4 5	Values safety and security
1 2 3 4 5	Considers social connections very important
1 2 3 4 5	Avoids waste and excess

Add the circled numbers to get a total score

WORLD WAR II ERA?

1 No, 5 Yes	Does this statement describe the employee well?
1 2 3 4 5	Highly patriotic
1 2 3 4 5	Respects authority
1 2 3 4 5	Romantic
1 2 3 4 5	Values self-reliance

Add the circled numbers to get a total score

POSTWAR?

1 No, 5 Yes	Does this statement describe the employee well?
1 2 3 4 5	Believes people will succeed and prosper by working hard
1 2 3 4 5	Values conformity
1 2 3 4 5	Values stability in both work and family life
1 2 3 4 5	Thinks self-fulfillment is important

Add the circled numbers to get a total score

LEADING-EDGE BOOMER?

1 No, 5 Yes	Does this statement describe the employee well?
1 2 3 4 5	Values personal expression highly
1 2 3 4 5	Wants to be treated as an individual but doesn't want to be alone
1 2 3 4 5	Values youthfulness
1 2 3 4 5	Values health and wellness

Add the circled numbers to get a total score

TRAILING-EDGE BOOMER?

1 No, 5 Yes	Does this statement describe the employee well?
1 2 3 4 5	Believes people need to go their own way
1 2 3 4 5	Values independent viewpoints

1 No, 5 Yes	Does this statement describe the employee well?
1 2 3 4 5	Feels family commitments are important
1 2 3 4 5	Distrustful of authority

Add the circled numbers to get a total score

GEN-XER?

1 No, 5 Yes	Does this statement describe the employee well?
1 2 3 4 5	Values friendships highly
1 2 3 4 5	Sees self as a independent free agent in the world of work
1 2 3 4 5	Takes a cynical view of the future
1 2 3 4 5	Seeks to improve own quality of life

Add the circled numbers to get a total score

N-GEN?

1 No, 5 Yes	Does this statement describe the employee well?
1 2 3 4 5	Hopeful about the future
1 2 3 4 5	Anxious about safety and security issues
1 2 3 4 5	Views diversity as a highly positive thing
1 2 3 4 5	Open to change

Add the circled numbers to get a total score

APPLYING YOUR RESULTS

Based on which table has the largest total score, you can determine which cohort your employee is most aligned with. On occasion, people might tie across two or even three of these value profiles, which simply means that they have a somewhat more diverse value profile and may respond well to a wider range of management approaches and work situations. Do not be alarmed if your analysis of an individual employee's value profile seems to suggest an affinity with the values of a cohort that he or she does not belong to, based on age.

How can you apply the information you get from the tables above? Suppose you decide that your employee fits the Gen-X profile best. With that information, you can make some educated guesses about what may turn him or her on at work. And turning people on at work is, after all, the primary responsibility of most managers. To pick one value as a starting point, a Gen-X employee (or an employee who fits the Gen-X profile, regardless of age) will probably respond well to work assignments that allow him or her to be in touch with his or her friends. This is a simple inference, since you rated friendships as being important to the person — yet it is a useful management insight. Employees with this value profile are liable to be cynical about next year's business plan and its promise of success, but they may be genuinely committed to fun work that they can do with good friends. The manager who helps that happen will win greater levels of commitment, effort, and loyalty — all of which translate into significant bottom-line benefits to the company.

As we work through a detailed look at each cohort in Chapters 4 through 9, we will make many such management suggestions based on the value profiles of each cohort.

But What About That Brewery?

You may be wondering what the right response would have been in the case of the disengaged Coors brewery workers that we discussed in Chapter 1. The middle-aged workers at that plant lacked the sense of duty and work-for-work's-sake orientation of the older workers. And the even younger workers didn't find their work at the plant interesting enough to hold their attention or get them involved in a boring project like sticking around to mop up after some equipment fails.

But if you were the plant manager, you'd want a global solution, not just an idea of how to talk with each employee individually about the incident. This is where cohort macro-analysis comes in. Specifically, the plant managers are now offering a work environment predicated on older-cohort work values of duty and the structured pursuit of wealth through a long-term relationship with the company. It's a kind of emotional partnership; the worker follows the arrows with care and pride, and the company makes sure that the arrows lead to prosperity. As long as the company continues to employ older workers, it needs to continue to manage them in this style, because it fits their cohort values well.

But it's a poor fit with middle-aged or younger workers.

For the two Boomer Cohorts, the idea of an unquestioning company man clashes fundamentally with their core values. They just don't get it, and they never will. But if the company engages their sense of individualism and desire for self-expression more fully, it can win a different but equally potent kind of loyalty. So asking them all to drop their individual after-hours plans and rush like worker ants to the call is silly. But what if the factory managers engaged them with the challenge of seeing who could come up with the best idea for how to solve the problem? This is an appeal to their need for self-expression, and would work far better than any call to duty.

Finally, let's look at the Gen-X and even younger N-Gen workers who coexist side by side with older cohorts in this brewery. Neither of the two strategies above would win their commitment to staying late and fixing a problem, at least not in large numbers. For Gen-Xers, a general appeal to their desire for excitement might work well. Their supervisors would need to present this as a wild adventure, an exciting opportunity to do something unexpected and fun. It might be as simple as mentioning that some of the workers were going to make a night of it and were calling it an Emergency Response Party — and had plans to crank up the music and maybe even to crack open a barrel once they got the problem licked.

N-Gens want to understand the big picture before making a commitment to stay late. Explain the implications of *not* fixing the problem right away, then appeal to their group orientation by letting them know you are counting on the team to come through at a critical time. Offer to bring in pizza and soft drinks while they work, then afterward make sure you thank them and recognize their effort in a very personal and meaningful way.

In Chapter 11, we detail four different work paths. Every employee has one particular work path that they will respond to best. In the brewery example, here's how the four work paths can be used (you can understand what follows without having read Chapter 11):

Structured approach: Mention that there is an emergency and that employees are welcome to stay and help fix it. This should be sufficient to engage the older cohorts.

Individualist approach: Invite individual employees to come forward with ideas and suggestions and even to point out any flaws in current work procedures that permit such accidents to happen in the first place. This should help bring both the Boomer Cohorts into the action.

Excitement approach: Let employees know you are willing to let them have fun while staying late and that it is, in fact, an exciting challenge and a chance to break out of workplace routines. This will get the attention of Gen-Xers and bring them into the equation, too.

Teamwork approach: Identify the critical issues right upfront and let employees know the company really needs their help. Show confidence that the team has the skill and the know-how to get the job done. Then, recognize their extra effort by telling them how much they are appreciated. Better yet, write each employee a personal thank-you note.

What this four-pronged strategy means, of course, is that employees working side by side to solve the problem *will be working for very different reasons.* Is that bad? Traditionally, it might have given managers some cause for concern. But today we must recognize that people do have many and varied work motives, and that unless we align their work with their work motives, we won't get their attention and commitment. Especially in the times when we need it most.

Perhaps most compelling, this four-pronged approach to the problem engages all the employees instead of only a small minority of the workers. In other words, it works.

CONCLUSION

Your workplace may never become a tourist attraction or the subject of a bestselling book the way Pike Place Fish has, but if you'd like your employees to feel greater enthusiasm about their jobs and to work together better on teams, generational cohort analysis will get you on the right track. It can help you develop a preferred generational cohort profile for your workplace. Or you can use it to explore ways to diffuse flashpoints and make the most of cohort diversity.

Keep in mind, though, that to be effective at this game you must think of your employees as unique individuals. There will be no stereotyping based on age! The four work paths, which we outline in greater detail in Chapter 11, offer the best chance of success.

The Changing American Workplace

The American workplace has undergone dramatic changes over the last 20 years. This is due, in part, to a changed corporate climate that puts more emphasis on global competitiveness. Gone are the days of the paternalistic company, with its built-in inefficiencies, that took care of its employees. Lifetime employment has become a relic. The next 20 years are sure to see even more dramatic changes.

In its 1997 study of the American workplace, Workforce 2020, the Hudson Institute identified four forces that will reshape the American workplace during the next 20 years. They are:

✦ **Continued technological change:** The pace of technological change is faster than ever before, and it will only speed up in the years to come. New industries and jobs will emerge, while others will become obsolete. Technology will create the tools to continue to allow us to do more in less time. This will no doubt put increased pressure on employees to continually improve their productivity.

✦ **Further globalization of the U.S. economy:** Advances in communications and travel will continue to make the world a smaller place. As markets and industries move toward global integration, American manufacturers will further focus on producing products for export, such as high-tech equipment. As a result, low-skilled factory jobs will be replaced with higher skilled and better paying high-tech manufacturing jobs.

✦ **Aging of the American workforce:** Americans are living longer than ever before, thanks to healthier lifestyles and advances in medical science. At the same time, the Baby Boomers — typically defined as individuals who were among the large number of babies born between 1945 and 1965 — are getting older. The oldest of this group will turn 65 in 2010. By 2020, about 20% of the population is expected to be 65 or over, compared with only 13% today. These Boomers will continue to affect the marketplace as they demand new goods and services to meet their changing needs. And they will also affect the workplace, as many will continue to work well into their 60s and 70s.

✦ **Growing diversity:** The number of women, minorities, and older people in the workforce will continue to increase in the years to come. Asians and Hispanics will be responsible for the biggest increases in the minority population. Diversity will become an even more important management issue in the years to come, as managers learn to manage employees from backgrounds very different from their own.

Source: Bureau of Labor Statistics/Hudson Institute

CHAPTER 4

GHOSTS IN THE CORPORATE ATTIC

E asy-listening music from the 1940s and 1950s drifts through the air as assembly-line workers pack tubes of Bonne Bell lipstick and other cosmetics that are popular with teenage girls into boxes. It's a job that some people might find boring. But not these workers.

The department, called the Bonne Bell seniors, includes more than 80 workers. The average age is 70. Some employees are well into their 80s, and one is 90 years old. Unlike younger workers, who often crave excitement, these employees enjoy the daily routine that the part-time job offers. They also look forward to work because of the opportunity to socialize with their peers.

Bonne Bell management created the department five years ago when Christmas orders overwhelmed the Cleveland-area company. After other temporary employees proved unreliable, management asked some of the company's retirees to help out with the Christmas rush. The experiment worked so well that managers decided to continue on with the seniors-only assembly department. (Of course, legally they can't exclude any candidates based on age, but they can create a work environment and job design that appeals to retirees, so as to maximize the chances of getting plenty of them to apply for work in this area.)

It's a move that has turned out to make good business sense. The older workers are dependable, conscientious, and eager to work. Plus, they help to fill the growing shortage of assembly-line workers. Many referrals now come through word of mouth, which only enhances the department's family atmosphere.[1]

In truth, many companies manage to exclude older workers from assembly-line positions in spite of legal restrictions against age discrimination. Bonne Bell has recognized that far from being a liability, these older workers can in fact be a real asset.

Although the stereotype of older workers is that they're inefficient, frail, and sickly, quite the opposite is often the case. Those seniors who are sick usually don't seek jobs in the first place, leaving those who are healthy and active to fill open part-time positions. The Bonne Bell seniors routinely meet production quotas, and a friendly rivalry between the morning and afternoon shifts often has the department exceeding goals.

UNCOVERING THE HIDDEN INFLUENCE OF THE GHOST COHORTS

Life expectancies have steadily risen over the last century, and today's older American is healthier and more active than ever before. At the same time, labor shortages have companies scrambling to hire dependable workers. Given these facts, it's not surprising that more and more retired Americans are finding their way back into the workforce. The Bonne Bell seniors are just one example of a growing trend that will likely reshape the American workplace in the years to come. The Census Bureau predicts that by 2020, nearly 20% of the American population will be 65 or older (compared with 13% today). These seniors will include today's Leading-Edge and Trailing-Edge Baby Boomers.

Improving the Efficiency of "Girl" Employees

World War II was the first time women entered the U.S. workforce on a mass scale. This influx of new workers created challenges for managers who were used to an all-male, or at least predominantly male, workforce.

The July 1943 issue of *Mass Transportation* magazine included an article on how managers could improve the efficiency of female workers. Blatantly sexist (and lawsuit provoking) by today's standards, these practices show just how times have changed in the American workplace. Here are some of the tips offered:

✦ If given a choice, pick young married women. They tend to be more responsible than their unmarried sisters, they flirt less, they need the work, and they still have the pep and interest to work hard and deal with the public.

✦ If you must hire older women, try to find ones who have previously worked outside the home. Older women without such experience have a hard time adapting themselves and can be cantankerous and fussy.

✦ Typically, husky girls — those a little overweight — are more even-tempered and efficient than their underweight sisters.

✦ Have a physician give each woman you hire a special physical exam covering "female conditions." This will protect you against lawsuits, and will reveal whether job candidates have any "female weaknesses," which could make them mentally or physically unfit for the job.

✦ Make allowances for feminine psychology and give each girl an adequate number of breaks during the day. A girl tends to have more confidence and is more efficient if she has a chance to tidy her hair, apply fresh lipstick, and wash her hands several times a day.

✦ Be tactful when giving instructions or offering criticisms. Women are sensitive and can't shrug off harsh words like men do. Never ridicule a woman. It breaks her spirit and makes her inefficient.

Source: Sanders, L.H. "Efficiency of Women Employees; Eleven Helpful Tips," Mass Transportation, July 1943, Volume 39, p. 244.

As Boomers reach their golden years, they are likely to work well past 65, either because they haven't saved enough for retirement and will need to work or because they'll be healthy and active and will want to work. Of course, what it takes to recruit and retain today's seniors is a lot different than what it will take to recruit and retain seniors 10 or 15 years from now. Differences in generational cohort values are the main reason.

Today's working seniors are at the forefront of an emerging trend, but their presence in today's workforce is just a very small aspect of their contribution to the American business world. The greatest impact of the Depression and World War II Cohorts on the modern workplace is the organizational structure they created, a structure that remains in place today, lingering like a persistent poltergeist. Their cohort-specific values and their views of work are built into the assumptions of modern management to such a degree that many businesses operate in a highly structured manner that appeals to these cohorts — but that may not appeal to the cohorts who now fill employee ranks.

The top-down, command-and-control management structure the Depression and World War II Cohorts put in place beginning in the postwar era reflects the values that they formed during their coming-of-age years. And the fact that these hierarchical management techniques still survive today — even though they no longer fit current business needs — shows just how much of an impact the Ghost Cohorts have on our current business culture. Despite many attempts to exorcise these old-style management practices, they keep creeping back in to haunt newer cohorts in the modern workplace.

UNDERSTANDING THE IMPACT OF THE GHOST COHORTS

The entire ethos of the big corporation, with its corner offices, middle-management ranks, and hoards of dutiful workers, stems from the Ghost Cohorts. The Depression Cohort brought to the workplace the idea that a job — any job — is in and of itself deserving of respect and something of value. That Depression Cohort employees and managers were averse to risk was a natural extension of their having experienced more than enough hard times in their formative years. Because of this past trauma, they created conservative, stable structures when they built businesses and other organizations. The military experiences of the World War II Cohort taught cohort members the value of hierarchies and respect for authority, and cohort members brought a military-influenced view of an organization to the workplace.

Combine the attitudes of the two Ghost Cohorts, and you can see why a generation of managers built strongly hierarchical workplaces in which roles were clearly defined and workers were expected to be respectful and obedient. Thinking and decision-making happened at the top, and trickled down like orders given in war. And the workers, like soldiers in the trenches, were expected to have faith in their leaders and to be happy to do whatever small part they could.

Both of these cohorts thought of information, like orders, as something to be dispersed from the top of an organization downward. Like military leaders planning an attack, Ghost Cohort managers poured over their management information, then formulated grand plans for their workers to roll out according to their instructions.

The Ghost Cohorts' organization is designed for efficiency and stability. It can grow very large and become very profitable in a relatively stable and predictable economic environment. Central planning and a top-down flow of information limits flexibility and creativity, but as long as things don't change too fast, managers can work within these limitations.

Of course, the role of the rank and file in this traditional organization is somewhat limited. There is a career path up the hierarchy for those with management potential and the "right" background to fill the traditional management role. Other employees are expected to be happy to play their lesser roles, and to be loyal to the organization and to respect and trust their seniors. A sense of duty and mutual obligation is important.

Put Me In, Coach

The emergence of career coaching as a hot new field reflects very real changes in generational cohort attitudes between Ghost Cohorts and the younger cohorts that now fill the workplace.

The Depression Era and World War II Cohorts would never have considered hiring someone to teach them how to get ahead at work. They respected authority and accepted their station in life. They didn't feel a need to fight tooth and nail for promotions. For a number of reasons, today's work environment is much more competitive, and this is precisely why good coaches are in demand. Different economic times, larger numbers of Baby Boomers, and the highly independent nature of Leading-Edge Boomers, Trailing-Edge Boomers, and Gen-Xers all make employees feel they need to compete in order to get ahead at work.

But, as has become obvious in recent years, this kind of command-and-control management style is very much out of sync with today's business needs. In fact, much of the modern history of business management is about the struggle to replace this organizational model with a new one that better addresses current economic challenges and younger cohort values. But exorcising the Ghost Cohorts has not been an easy task, and many organizations still struggle, even now, with how to break free from their influence.

Before going any farther, we need to look at the coming-of-age experiences of the Ghost Cohorts and what values emerged from these experiences. Having a historical perspective will help you devise a strategy to rid your organization of the ghosts of managers past.

MEET THE GHOST COHORTS

People who came of age during the Great Depression and World War II were ages 75 to 90 in 2002. They represent two very distinct generational cohorts, but they do share similar values. Table 4.1 gives you an overview.

TABLE 4.1: A LOOK AT THE GHOST COHORTS

Name of Cohort	Depression	World War II
Defining moment	The Great Depression	World War II
Born	1912–1921	1922–1927
Came of age	1930–1939	1940–1945
Age in 2002	81–90	75–80
Size (percent of population)	13 million (6%)	17 million (8%)
Key cohort values/concerns	✦ Sense of purpose ✦ Safety and security ✦ Social connectedness/ companionship ✦ Risk averse ✦ Waste not, want not	✦ Patriotic ✦ Respect for authority ✦ Sense of romance ✦ Self-reliance

DEPRESSION ERA GENERATIONAL COHORT

The Great Depression molded millions of young Americans who came of age from 1929 to 1939. The event shaped the Depression Era Cohort's attitudes and values well into the future, and profoundly affected the development of centralized management practices in the postwar era and beyond. Values formed during the Great Depression not only played a major role in creating the business world we inhabit today, but they're also still held by the aging Depression Cohort today. Members of the Depression Cohort tend to:

✦ **Need a sense of purpose:** This group wanted to feel like work had a clear purpose. They felt satisfaction knowing they had done a good job and completed a task. Unlike some younger cohorts, their main focus was on results, not image.

✦ **Desire safety and security:** Fear of the unknown is a major concern for this cohort. They prefer the safe route to taking a chance on something that's unproven. As a result, in the workplace this cohort wasn't known for its innovation or creativity, and its members often erected that classic business-world roadblock — the way it's always been done.

✦ **Feel an urge for social connectedness/companionship:** During the Depression, family and friends often provided a much-needed safety net. If someone needed help, members of the kin or social group pulled together to do what they could. People also relied on each other for help getting through those psychologically tough times. Members of this cohort learned firsthand the value of relationships in their private lives, and this lesson affects their actions and attitudes in the workplace. Relationship building was an important means of conducting business for the Depression Era Cohort.

✦ **Be risk averse:** This cohort preferred the safe route, and did not take many chances in business. Their aversion to risk meant that they very likely missed many lucrative opportunities, but their conservative ways also insulated them from financial crises. Also, workers tended to stay with the same job, rather than take a risk with something new.

✦ **Believe in "Waste not, want not":** Nothing was wasted during the Depression, and this thrifty attitude carried over into the working world. Money was spent very carefully, and employees were expected to stretch every dollar to the limit. A popular war slogan went "Use it up / wear it out / make it do — or do without!" Because this cohort was so concerned about their economic situation during their coming-of-age years, raises, bonuses, and promotions were particularly effective in motivating this group. These financial incentives, in turn, were how Depression Cohort members often chose to motivate their own employees when they became managers.

WORLD WAR II GENERATIONAL COHORT

World War II unified the country more than any other event had. The Japanese attack on Pearl Harbor solidified national sentiment in support of U.S. involvement in the war. Suddenly, sacrifice for the common good became a way of life. Young men joined up to fight the war, leaving their families behind to hope that they would come back alive. Women went to work in factories to produce the equipment and munitions that their husbands and sweethearts needed to win the war. Popular slogans, such as "We Can Do It!" and "You've Done Your Bit — Now Do Your Best!" reflected the need to pull together to defeat the common enemy. And people did pull together. Food and gasoline rationing, scrap drives, victory gardens, and war bonds freed up or created the materials and resources that the Allies needed to win the war. Members of this cohort learned the value of pulling together for a common cause, and they often relied on others to help get them through tough times.

The war profoundly shaped this generational cohort's values, which were carried over into every aspect of the cohort members' lives, including the workplace. World War II Cohort members tend to:

✦ **Be patriotic:** This generational cohort is by far the most patriotic of all existing cohorts. Many cohort members still tear up at the sight of the flag and the sound of "The Star Spangled Banner." After the war, their loyalty to their country carried over into a loyalty to the companies they worked for. Stand by your company, they reasoned, and the company will stand by you. In addition, most managers felt a strong sense of responsibility toward their employees.

✦ **Respect authority:** Due in part to a fear of defeat, Americans came to respect authority during the war much more than they ever had before. Soldiers quickly learned the value of following orders, and on the home front people trusted government authorities and propaganda because they feared enemy attack. When you count home-front participation, this entire generational cohort was practically trained by the U.S. military! After the war, this cohort was very comfortable following orders at work, and this top-down approach became the standard way things were done. When cohort members became managers themselves, they expected their own orders to be followed and not questioned by subordinates. It came as quite a shock to this group when, in later years, they started managing Baby Boomers — who seemed to like nothing better than to question everything.

✦ **Desire a sense of romance:** The early '40s were an emotional time, as young men left for war, uncertain whether they would ever return home again. In World War I, the average length of service was less than 12 months; in World War II, the average was nearly three times as long — 33 months. Members of this cohort felt a profound sense of postponement and a yearning for loved ones whom they had left behind during their coming-of-age years. After the war, romance flourished and the marriage rate skyrocketed as young soldiers sought an emotional anchor to home. In later years, this coming-of-age experience translated into a desire for a long-term, committed work relationship with an employer. For most, lifelong employment was their reward.

✦ **Be self-reliant:** Along with the Depression Cohort, the World War II Cohort had the discipline to delay rewards and to stay focused on a job until it was done right. Cohort members were proud of their can-do spirit. As managers, they expected their employees to have whatever level of self-reliance was needed to get the job done.

It's Tough for Executives

The new, fluid model of organizational life can be tough on executives. An expert on new organizations, Larry Hirschhorn of the Center for Applied Research in Philadelphia observes that many executives miss the comfort the old hierarchy once provided them. More and more are feeling vulnerable to scrutiny not just from their superiors, but from their subordinates as well.

Hirschhorn wrote a book, *Reworking Authority: Leading and Following in the Post-Modern Organization,* about this very topic. In Hirschhorn's terminology, we are leaving behind the old-style organization that prevailed until the end of the '50s and entering a brave new business world in which authority, hierarchy, duty, and obedience are things of the past. As Hirschhorn further observes, today's executives must *persuade* employees to do their work, rather than just tell them what work to do. The employees need to agree that the boss is on the right track and that they have appropriate, meaningful, and fairly compensated roles in the current plan of action.

Hirschhorn, Larry. Reworking Authority: Leading and Following in the Post-Modern Organization. Cambridge, MA: The MIT Press, 1997.

STRUGGLING TO CHANGE

That the Ghost Cohorts continue to profoundly shape the patterns of American business organization and management even to this day is testament to how successful these cohorts were. They did such a good job that what they built cannot easily be taken down.

A command-and-control corporate structure fit the Ghost Cohorts' values and experiences, and managers wove it tightly into the fabric of our business organizations. A sense of duty was paramount. Work was to be done because it was assigned, not because it was fun, fulfilling, or could lead to personal development. Communication flowed from the top down, just as it did in the military.

But that approach doesn't always serve us well today. The ideals of the modern organization clearly clash with the Ghost Cohorts' values and traditions. Today, you often need your business to be nimble, innovative, and flexible. The modern workplace requires faster decision-making and shorter timelines. Teams must organize and reorganize to meet challenges and to pursue new opportunities. We must learn and change, introduce new ideas and products, embrace new technologies, enter new markets, engage new customers, and rethink what businesses we are in . . . and then do it all again next week!

But the old 1950s hierarchy is durable, to say the least. It continues to haunt twenty-first-century managers, just as it haunted their predecessors. The ghosts keep reemerging in spite of new theories and programs and expensive consultants. So why is it so hard for us to give up an outmoded style of organization and abandon old patterns of management when everyone agrees that we ought to?

Well, partly because each new generation of managers has been meticulously trained in the ways of Ghost Cohorts. These top-down methods worked in the past, many modern managers reason, so they must work today. When today's managers — even Boomers and Gen-Xers — don't know what else to do, they often fall back on the tried and true methods of yesteryear. Change is scary, after all. But since these younger managers and the employees they manage have very different values than Ghost Cohorts — values that don't support the old hierarchy — a system develops by default that is different from the old one. But it's a system that no one typically is happy with. Leading-Edge Boomers, Trailing-Edge Boomers, and Gen-Xers, in particular, end up managing their people in a way that they themselves would chafe at.

A CHANGE SUCCESS STORY

Change is possible, even for older managers. Take Andy Pearson, for example, the former chairman and CEO of Tricon Global Restaurants, the owner of KFC, Pizza Hut, and Taco Bell. Now in his mid-70s and a member of the World War II Cohort, Pearson has transformed himself from an abrasive, tough-as-nails executive whose verbal thrashings sometimes brought employees to tears into a warm, friendly boss who sees employee recognition as key to the company's success.

In 1980, Fortune magazine named Pearson, then the head of PepsiCo, one the 10 toughest bosses in the country. In 2001, *Fast Company* magazine titled a feature article about Pearson "Andy Pearson Finds Love."[2]

Why this dramatic shift? After coming to Tricon, Pearson said he learned from the more progressive, people-oriented management style of Tricon executive David Novak, now the company's chairman and CEO. Novak's more personal management style resulted in bottom-line results. To Novak, emotion and the human heart are what drive the company's success, and employees' enthusiasm must be kindled through awareness, recognition, and rewards.

The company motivates employees through recognition and celebration. For example, every year, in front of the entire company, Tricon recognizes the outstanding performance of four employees with the prestigious YUM award — a huge set of false teeth that walks when wound up. This kind of silliness reflects Pearson's new approach to management.

While Pearson's hard-driving command-and-control style worked well in the past, his new warm and fuzzy approach fits in better with the values held by the younger cohorts that now comprise most of the workforce.

MEETING EMPLOYEE NEEDS

Part of exorcising the ghosts involves consciously working to meet employees' needs. In the past, people were more duty oriented and did not want to rock the boat. They tended to work right along at their assigned tasks without questioning why and what was in it for them. But times have clearly changed. Today's working cohorts have many and complex work motives. Some are in it for the money, while others are seeking a sense of accomplishment and gratification from their work. Others just need a social outlet.

As a part of giving employees what they need, you may need to change information flows so that information is exchanged in a more natural, self-generating pattern that can go up, down, and sideways as people's jobs change to fit the latest projects.

The good news is that most people's needs aren't all that complex. However, it does take time to get to know what motivates, excites, and energizes each employee. Managing by generational cohort, and thus defining moments, will help you do this.

Ousting the Chief

Jeffrey Goldstein of the School of Business at Adelphi University writes about an interesting case history of organizational change in his book *The Unshackled Organization: Facing the Challenge of Unpredictability through Spontaneous Reorganization*. Goldstein describes a hospital in dire financial straits that began to implement total quality management principles. As is so often the case when this Japanese import is used to revive rigid and ineffective organizations, the initiative began with the formation of several project teams.

Each team was given full authority to institute its own ground rules. Team members decided how to run their team to best complete their assigned projects. Empowering teams seems practical if your organization is in a hurry. But in many ways, it's a radical notion. For example, one of the teams set up rules about managing meetings that its team leader did not follow. The team impeached its leader and appointed a new leader. Believe it or not, the ousted team leader was the company's CEO! Deposing the CEO certainly illustrates what spontaneous reorganization is all about. It's not a concept that ever would have gotten off the ground 50 years ago, that's for sure.

Goldstein, Jeffrey. The Unshackled Organization: Facing the Challenge of Unpredictability Through Spontaneous Reorganization. Portland Oregon: Productivity Press, 1994.

INVITING THE GHOSTS BACK IN

Sometimes it's wise to shut down the chaotic urges of younger cohorts and run a more traditional tight ship. We do not want to make a case for eliminating the traditions and wisdom of the Ghost Cohorts from the management realm entirely. The old traditions are dangerous when they're allowed to dominate a business today — but they are still useful in some aspects of business. For instance, whenever you have a need to standardize a work process or function with the goal of making it highly stable and efficient, the old-fashioned notions of top-down authority and clearly defined tasks are still of value.

Think of it this way: Would you want a bunch of employees holding an impromptu meeting to impeach their shift supervisor on the production line instead of watching their machines and making sure the product is built correctly? Certainly not. A mass-production process needs old-fashioned management as its dominant theme. If you want to use quality improvement methods or reengineering teams in such a process, you can — but they have to be a sideshow. They won't keep the line moving. The line only moves smoothly if people are willing to work in routine ways. And whenever you have a work process that can, at least for a time, be made routine, then the high-structure approach of the Ghost Cohorts may still have a place in your organization.

The horrific events of September 11, 2001, also illustrate how the Ghost Cohorts can help companies, and our society as a whole. They have been through hard times before — think of the gold star mothers who displayed a gold star in their windows after losing a son or daughter in the war. Or those who watched their savings and their paychecks disappear simultaneously during the Depression. They can exert a calming, stabilizing influence on society in times of turmoil, taking on a role formerly held by the wise elders in more traditional societies. They can perform the same function for companies in crisis.

Sometimes this need to tap into the best traditions of the Ghost Cohorts clashes with the preferences and styles of younger cohorts — and then you need to accommodate their needs as much as is practical, while still retaining a basically traditional, high-structure approach to management. We will share ideas about how to do this in many of the later chapters.

In other cases, you will find that the traditions of the Ghost Cohorts do not serve the best interests of your organization. Sometimes you need to loosen things up, to allow teams to self-manage and employees to innovate and create, for example. And often you need to allow younger cohorts more opportunities for personal development and growth — even if this inconveniences the organization. You cannot afford to stick blindly to tradition and lose your best and brightest as a result.

A Radical Motivational Technique: The Coffee Break

During World War II, the Jewel Tea Company — one of the largest suppliers of military rations — came up with an innovative management technique to boost the morale and efficiency of its workers. The technique worked so well that the company later received recognition from the government.

What was this earth-shattering way to motivate employees? The coffee break. That doesn't sound very innovative today, but the story of its invention gives you a glimpse into the working world of the 1940s.

On the home front, preserving national security and preventing enemy infiltration were top priorities. During the war years, no talking was allowed on Jewel Tea production lines, which were staffed largely by women. The work of producing and packaging military rations was dull, tedious, and sometimes difficult. The long hours working in silence brought down morale.

Managers decided to implement a radical idea. They brewed strong coffee and allowed workers to socialize for 10 minutes twice a day in a room away from the factory floor. The coffee break gave workers something to look forward to and helped to take their minds off of their worries about the men fighting overseas.

After the coffee break was instituted, production increased 20%. The Secretary of the Treasury later recognized the Jewel Tea Company for its tremendous contribution to the war effort. Even today, government contracts often require that workers get coffee breaks twice a day.

ENDNOTES

1. Ansberry, Clare. "Averaging Age 70, Staff In This Cosmetics Plant Retires Old Stereotypes," *The Wall Street Journal,* February, 5, 1997, sec. A, p. 15.

2. Dorsey, David. "Andy Pearson Finds Love," *Fast Company,* August 2001, Vol. 49, p. 78 (7).

CHAPTER 5

UNDERSTANDING YOUR POSTWAR EMPLOYEES

S uppose you're interviewing several candidates for a part-time secretarial position in your office. One candidate is 20 years old and is fresh out of a community college's two-year secretarial program. The other is 60 years old and is reentering the workforce after having retired five years ago from her job as an executive secretary. She has decided that retirement just doesn't offer enough of a challenge, and she would like to work part time. Both women have excellent references, present themselves well in the interview, and seem to have all of the qualifications you're looking for. Who do you hire?

If you're like most managers, you will probably convince yourself that the older woman will probably be slower, more inefficient, and more likely to resist change. She also is unlikely to be up-to-date on the latest computer software, and may require higher than average health insurance costs. So you hire the younger woman.

BROKEN STEREOTYPES

The stereotype of the slow, plodding older worker who resists change and new ideas has been around for decades. You may be surprised to find out that new research is showing this stereotype couldn't be further from the truth. In fact, several studies have shown that the performance of older workers matches that of younger workers. In some occupations, including sales and clerical work, productivity actually increases with age. What's more, older workers can be more motivated and more dedicated to the job than younger workers are.[1] This means there are no practical reasons not to hire an older worker.

Typically, employers recognize that they have a legal obligation not to discriminate against candidates based on age. But employers have largely viewed these laws in the U.S. as an inconvenience and have often found off-the-record ways around them. They might disqualify the 60-year-old candidate because she lacks knowledge the younger candidate has of a specific word-processing program. That would be the official reason for not making her an offer — but in reality, the decision may have been biased by a fear that the older woman would not be able to keep up. However, the facts do not support this bias. We encourage employers to view older candidates as capable, and as even more desirable than younger workers, in some aspects.

Sure, older workers may need some specific training to do a particular job, but unlike young people, they don't need to be taught *how* to work. They have been working for years and understand the importance of appropriate dress, showing up for work on time, and customer service.

Several studies suggest that learning styles change with age, so what works when training people in their 20s may not work when training people in their 60s. For best results when training older workers, be sure to use clearly written instructions, a slower pace, faster feedback, longer sessions, and longer study periods so that they can absorb the material. Older people may take a little longer to learn new tasks, but once they learn new skills, they are likely to make up for lost time through higher motivation and job involvement. Self-paced learning, such as a training program done on a computer, is one cost-effective training option that may benefit older employees in your organization.

Doctors Head Back to Work on Their Own Terms

It's not unusual for doctors at the Samaritan House Clinic in San Mateo, California to spend half an hour talking with a patient about a backache. And most days, more doctors are in the office than are really needed. They read medical journals and discuss medical issues in the halls to pass the time.

How do these doctors have time for chitchat in our current age of managed care?

They are all retired volunteers. The founders of the clinic, which serves a largely immigrant population near Silicon Valley, are all members of the Ghost Cohorts. Many newer members of the clinic's staff come from the Postwar Cohort.

These doctors represent the new face of retirement. A recent survey of people ages 50 to 75 found that only 28% of those surveyed saw retirement as a time to take it easy and enjoy leisure activities, compared to 65% who said retirement was a time to stay active and involved.

Many members of the Postwar Cohort, especially those with sophisticated skills, such as doctors, lawyers, and accountants, want to remain active in their fields even into their 70s. But like the doctors at the Samaritan House Clinic, they want to get away from high stress and managed work environments. As a result, they look for part-time jobs or volunteer work that lets them practice their trade in a more laid-back environment.

Workers who are semi-retired provide many opportunities for businesses that are willing to provide flexible work arrangements in the years ahead. With Boomers entering retirement right on the heels of the Postwars, getting such programs started now makes good economic sense.

Source: Rimer, Sara. "Many Retirees Find It's Time to Go to Work," The New York Times, December 5, 1999, p. 1A.

AN OLDER WORKFORCE

Despite slow growth in the workforce overall, the number of older workers is increasing. In the last decade alone, the number of men working beyond 65 has increased 34%. At the heart of this trend is the Postwar Cohort. According to the Urban Institute, the median age of the American workforce was just over 39 in 2000. By 2005, the median age is expected to be 41, and it will continue to rise. A little over 48 million employees are currently over 45 years old. By 2010, that number is expected to increase to nearly 60 million.[2] Other statistics also support this shift in the workforce. The U.S. Bureau of Labor Statistics, for example, estimates that about 65% of people ages 55 to 64 will be in the workforce in 2015, up from 59% in 1998. And of those 65 and older, 14% will still be working in 2015, compared to 12% in 1998.[3]

As medical breakthroughs and healthy lifestyles continue to push life expectancies ever higher, many retirees these days expect retirement to easily last 20 to 30 years. While 30 years of relaxation may sound wonderful to some, affording such a lifestyle can present challenges. Also, golf and other leisure pursuits can get boring when they're all a person has to do. The financial burden of retirement, plus the fear of losing their purpose, has kept many older workers on the job and prompted some retirees to re-enter the workforce as temporary or part-time employees. These older workers present unique challenges to managers who are used to a very different kind of employee. They experienced different defining moments and hold very different values.

THE SEARCH FOR MEANING

Today's workplace, with its focus on leanness and competitive advantage, is very different from that of the postwar era. After World War II, consumer demand for new products and the country's economic prosperity made it relatively easy for companies to succeed. If workers did their jobs and obeyed the rules of their hierarchical organizations, they believed they were destined to rise.

In the postwar era, conformity reigned. Men typically wore dark suits, white shirts, and conservative ties to the office. Fedora hats and briefcases were also part of the de facto company uniform. If your shirts were wrinkled or worn, your boss might assume there were problems at home and give the big project to someone else. If you wore ties that were too patterned or colorful, your boss might deem you unreliable and pass you up for promotion. Women wore skirts or dresses, and made sure they always looked their best. At breaks, they powdered their noses, and they hated to be seen without lipstick. With the economy booming and demand for consumer goods at an all-time high after the war, unions helped to guarantee high wages and good benefits for manufacturing workers.

But by today's standards, work was dull and boring. Workers rarely saw the fruits of their own labor in these production-style workplaces. And with the war over and won, there was no longer any overriding cause or purpose to rally around. Collecting a paycheck did not hold the allure of collecting a paycheck *and* defending the world from the forces of evil. Many workers felt alienated.

After the war, companies used top-down management and organizational theories learned during the war to run their businesses. Workers were carefully molded into the ideal employee and followed orders from their superiors. Managers conducted business as if they were mobilizing troops for an assault at Omaha Beach. To some extent, the approach was effective. The work got done, business thrived, and profits soared. But the search for meaning continued.

Managers struggled with how to carry over the motivation, commitment, and pride that workers showed during the war years to peacetime operations (this is largely the same struggle that managers face today!). In his 1946 book, *The Concept of the Corporation,* management theorist Peter Drucker argued that workers needed more than just a paycheck. They needed meaning in their work, and they needed to be recognized for their contributions to the company and to society. Modern motivational theory traces many of its roots to this era.

In the '50s, many companies began to implement a more psychological approach to management — one designed to meet not only employees' economic needs, but also their need for deeper meaning in their lives. The company that people worked for became part of their identity. The image of the company man was born. Internal communications imparted the company line, and personality tests became popular tools for evaluating employees — and for weeding out those who didn't fit in.

Climbing the Ladder at Sears

Management trainees these days expect to start fairly high up the corporate ladder, but this wasn't always true. Sears, Roebuck & Co. offers a very good case in point.

In the 1950s, Sears management trainees started at the very lowest rungs — on the sales floor, and in some cases on the loading docks. This kind of bottom-up experience reflected the need for managers to learn every aspect of their organization. With this knowledge, they could instruct employees on what exactly needed to be done. The hierarchical management style of the Ghost Cohorts is clearly reflected in this practice.

Many employees described working at Sears, and other companies in the postwar era, as similar to being in the military. As Sears' retail network grew, the company demanded that rising executives relocate to new stores every 18 months. Constant relocation was tough on families, but it was typical of the era: The company always came first.

Source: Fitzgerald, Kate. "Sears, Wards Take Different Paths," Advertising Age, July 31, 1995, Vol. 66, no. 3, p. 27.

WOMEN IN THE WORKPLACE

The '50s have been described as a decade in which domesticity was embraced all-out, and the soaring birthrate — later known as the Baby Boom — certainly lends credence to this description. Unlike today, college-educated women in the postwar era had more children, on average, than women without a college degree. For many mothers, reliable daycare was not available, so quitting work was the natural way to go. Most women worked only as secretaries or assistants, and those who started down a professional career path typically quit when they got married and had children. For this reason, married women were not considered very good job prospects.

Single, young, attractive women, however, were another matter. They were often seen as potential spouses for male employees, and having them in the office was thought of as a way to boost morale.

From Sacred Cows to Sacrificial Lambs

Members of the Postwar Generational Cohort started out their careers with an expectation of lifelong employment, but they were the first to go when profits lagged in the late '80s and early '90s and companies looked to trim their white-collar workforce. Corporate downsizing caught this group completely by surprise, largely because they thought they had risen high enough to be untouchable. Previously, layoffs had largely been a blue-collar event. When white-collar workers had been let go, they had been young with very few years of service. White-collar middle managers were corporate America's sacred cows. But with the downturn of the late '80s and early '90s, many of these sacred cows found themselves turned into sacrificial lambs overnight.

The Postwar Cohort Today

Times certainly have changed over the past 50 years, and members of the Postwar Cohort have seen it all when it comes to the workplace — from rigid conformity and authoritarian bosses to Casual Fridays and self-directed work teams. Members of the Postwar Cohort are ages 57 to 74 in 2002. There's a 17-year time span between the oldest and the youngest — the largest such gap of any generational cohort.

The oldest Postwars are retired or semi-retired, while the youngest are looking to retire, or at least to cut back and focus on work they enjoy in the next few years. They are active and busy, and enjoy the newfound freedom that comes with being empty-nesters near the end of their careers. Some are working well into their 60s and even into their 70s, challenging long-held beliefs about the competency and reliability of older workers. Within their ranks, they carry a wealth of experience and knowledge. Their collective values are very different than those of younger cohorts.

SNAPSHOT OF THE POSTWAR COHORT

Name of Cohort:	Postwar
Born between:	1928–45
Coming of age:	1946–63
Age in 2002:	57–74
Population:	47 million (21%)

Key Cohort Values and Concerns
- The American Dream
- Conformity
- Stability
- Family
- Self-fulfillment

Current and Next Lifestage
- Divorce and remarriage for some
- Empty-nesting
- Grandparenting
- Eldercare
- Retirement

Emotions and Affinities
- Desire experiences, not things
- Enjoying life
- Nostalgia

Physiographic Profile
- Chronic medical conditions
- Aches and pains
- Changing body structure
- Vision and hearing
- Memory loss
- From looking good to feeling good

SNAPSHOT

POSTWAR DEFINING MOMENTS

The end of World War II, and the euphoria that the end of the war produced, kicked off a series of defining moments that were to profoundly shape the Postwar Cohort.

Although jobs and housing were scarce immediately after the war, the economy was racing by 1947. Prosperity reigned and Americans built new homes in the suburbs in droves, embraced consumerism like never before, and contributed to the wave of children that later became known as the Baby Boom (many of the Trailing-Edge Boomers and all of the Leading-Edge Boomers had parents from the WWII or Depression Era Cohorts). Fitting into the new consumer-driven society and keeping up with co-workers and neighbors became a top consideration.

Despite feelings of optimism, a cloud of uneasiness hung over the nation throughout the postwar era. North Korean communists invaded South Korea in 1950, marking the beginning of the Korean War. In the U.S., fear of communism led to the McCarthy witch hunts. The explosion of the Soviet Union's first atomic bomb in 1953 was a wake-up call to many Americans — suddenly it became clear that the U.S. no longer dominated the nuclear arena. The successful launch of the Soviet satellite Sputnik in 1957 only intensified worries. And fears further increased with the Bay of Pigs in 1961 and the Cuban Missile Crisis in 1962. These threatening events coupled with the booming economy created both rising optimism and creeping concern about the future.

Fears of communism and the nuclear bomb were not the only important factors shaping this cohort. The Civil Rights Movement gave blacks hope for a better future, but it angered some whites who felt threatened by integration. A series of court battles and boycotts throughout the '50s and early '60s eventually led to equal access to schools and other public places for blacks. But long-held attitudes about race proved much harder to change.

Throughout the '50s and into the '60s, the new sounds of rock 'n' roll, which had its roots in black rhythm and blues, helped to bridge the racial divide. Black artists such as Little Richard, Chuck Berry, and B. B. King appealed to both blacks and whites, giving them a common interest on which to build. The postwar era ended with the assassination of President John F. Kennedy in 1963, a traumatic event that shattered confidence and led to the formation of the Leading-Edge Baby Boomer Cohort.

Postwar Defining Moments

✦ End of World War II

✦ Good economic times

✦ Moving to the suburbs

✦ Cold War

✦ Korean War

✦ McCarthyism

✦ Emergence of rock 'n' roll

✦ Civil rights movement

POSTWAR VALUES

The defining moments of the late '40s, '50s, and early '60s created a very unique coming-of-age experience for the Postwar Cohort. This section speaks to the key values and concerns that were shaped by the Postwars' defining moments.

THE AMERICAN DREAM

Most Postwars have achieved a level of financial success at least equal to that of their parents. They experienced the rise of the middle class, and were probably the last cohort to really live the American dream. They came of age during a time of incredible opportunity, when jobs were plentiful, homes were affordable, and families were growing. At work, promotions and raises were common, as U.S. companies grew at a tremendous rate to keep up with consumer demand for new products.

Even today, Postwars still believe in the American dream, and they don't understand the pessimism of today's younger cohorts. This generational cohort found working hard to be the ticket to achieving the American dream. Postwars certainly need less coddling than other employees to motivate them to work. Members of this cohort, like members of the Ghost Cohorts, defined themselves by their job. When meeting new people, they often lead with "And what do you do?"

Because Postwars received and reflected the values of their Ghost Cohort parents, they simply accept work as a way of life and a means of achieving the American Dream.

CONFORMITY

The rise of suburbia, with its cookie-cutter sameness and mass-produced consumer goods, contributed to a growing trend toward conformity in the '50s. New technology allowed people to become more and more alike. Many Postwars saw this homogenization as something to be celebrated. Membership in country clubs and social organizations soared as people sought groups with which to identify. At work, fitting in and getting along were top considerations, and personal relationships often went further than performance in determining who advanced and who didn't. Even today, Postwars would much rather fit in and go with the flow than take a chance and risk failure.

STABILITY

The Cold War cast a shadow of uncertainty over the coming-of-age years of the Postwar Cohort. That's why Postwars still value stability today. They are comfortable with the idea of lifetime employment, and have been shaken up in recent years by the prevalence of downsizing and job hopping. This cohort tends to feel more loyalty to employers than younger cohorts, mainly because this loyalty gives them a greater sense of stability. But Postwars have had to adapt to the new business climate. Many have learned the hard way that being loyal doesn't necessarily mean you get to keep your job.

When the going gets tough, Postwars are the workers you want to rely upon to get the job done. This cohort holds dear the work-for-work's-sake mentality of the Ghost Cohorts.

FAMILY

Members of this cohort married young and had more babies than did members of older cohorts. As a result, they tend to be very family oriented. These days, most of their kids are grown, but Postwars are likely to enjoy the traditional company picnic just as much today as they once did. Picnic-type activities give Postwars a chance to interact with younger employees and their families, and provide Postwars with a social outlet for reconnecting with colleagues in an informal way. Rewards can be fashioned for this cohort around time off to spend with family, especially grandchildren. Organizations could sponsor Take a Grandchild to Work day each year to promote grandparent pride.

The Monsanto Retiree Corps

Following a wave of early retirements that coincided with the company's restructuring in the early '90s, business leaders at Monsanto in St. Louis recognized that knowledge gaps had developed.

Their solution was to create the Monsanto Retiree Resource Corps, which relies on former retirees to work part-time up to 999 hours a year as secretaries, lawyers, accountants, and in other positions. About 1,000 former employees are currently members of the organization.

Some employees, such as accountants, may work full time during tax season, then take off to enjoy themselves the rest of the year. Others work a few hours a week.

While the program initially tended to attract retirees in their 60s, program coordinators now see more people in their 50s signing up for the corps. It is a win for both the company and the retirees. Most retirees are able to step back into the company with little or no training. And the retirees like the idea of keeping busy and bringing in some income while working at a less demanding and more flexible part-time job.

SELF-FULFILLMENT

The Postwar Cohort is often referred to as the silent generation. It never had any major event to hang its hat on. It didn't rebuild America the way the Depression Cohort did or save the world the way the World War II Cohort did. It didn't even shake things up the way the Baby Boomers did. In effect, this cohort suffers from an identity crisis. By not having an economic crisis or an evil dictator or a perceived out-of-date Establishment to push back against, this cohort never achieved self-definition. For the most part, it has not produced leaders, only followers. It's almost certain to be the only cohort in modern times not to have produced a President!

As promotions and job advancement have begun to slow for this group, they have sought self-fulfillment outside of work, in leisure-time pursuits such as golf and volunteerism. Employers can appeal to Postwars by partnering with nonprofit groups to provide an outlet for employee volunteerism. Organizations can offer sabbaticals to members of this cohort to allow them to build hobbies or pursue interests they find fulfilling. Many companies are already helping ease their employees' transition into retirement, and more could do the same. Let Postwars slide into retirement by sampling a retirement lifestyle for a while, then let them return to work until they're really ready to retire.

Like Fine Wine . . .

A 1991 study by the Commonwealth Fund found that many stereotypes about older workers — that they can't be trained in new technologies, for example — are downright false. In fact, the study found numerous advantages to hiring older workers, including:

✦ **Low turnover:** 87% of older workers stay on the job for at least a year, compared to 30% of younger workers. Older workers help to keep recruitment and training costs low.

✦ **Trainability:** Older workers can be trained just as quickly as younger workers.

✦ **Low absenteeism:** Older workers are absent 1.4% of the time, compared to 3.7% for other workers. They also have a lower rate of tardi-ness (7.2% versus 7.6%).

The study also found that because older workers tended to take more time with customers, they often made better salespeople than younger workers.

Source: "The Bottom Line at 3 U.S., U.K. Firms," Productive Aging News, June 1991, Issue No. 54, p. 1(4).

LIFESTAGES

People often find that their 50s can be the most turbulent time of their lives. That's when so many lifestage changes take place. And changes such as retirement, taking care of the parents, and divorce all create stress. Others, such as grandparenting, bring great joy. The Postwar Cohort is nearly finished with their 50s, but many of the lifestages they embarked on in their 50s will stay with them into their 60s and beyond.

DIVORCE AND REMARRIAGE FOR SOME

Birth control in the postwar era wasn't what it is today, so many couples rushed into marriage partly out of sexual frustration. Many of these marriages resulted in divorce within a few years, while others lasted longer. Now, second and third marriages are not uncommon for members of this cohort. And since second and third marriages don't have a higher success rate than first marriages, many Postwars are finding themselves in the divorce and remarriage lifestage once again. Divorce can create tension and stress for them at work, as they contemplate a solitary retirement.

Postwars have been schooled not to bring their personal lives into their workplace. They will not burden managers or colleagues with their problems. But that doesn't mean that the problems aren't there or that they're not hampering productivity. At the least, businesses should be on the lookout for such issues and offer counseling and sympathy.

Many Postwars in this lifestage may choose to postpone their retirement and continue working to help pay alimony and as a kind of therapy to keep their minds off of their personal life.

EMPTY-NESTING

Some members of the Postwar Cohort have been empty-nesters for quite a while now; others are just entering this lifestage. It's not unusual for people to experience some sadness when the last child leaves home, but most Postwars look forward to empty-nesting as a time of increased personal freedom. Unless they are executives, work typically becomes a secondary consideration for people in this lifestage as they begin to explore and discover their own outside interests. They don't necessarily shirk their duties at work, but most are not looking for the same level of challenge that they once were. They are happy with routine assignments and other predictable work that allows them to leave on time and to take vacations when they want.

Don't try to pressure Postwars to compete with your young rising stars. Let them contribute in their own way, by leading and facilitating teams, mentoring younger employees, and serving as in-house consultants on various projects. For those who retired only to come back to work part time, work around their outside activities, and you will find a very loyal and dedicated group of employees.

GRANDPARENTING

Grandparents these days are on average much healthier and more active than they used to be. Most Postwars have taken on more of a fun-seeking role with their grandchildren, and so prefer to be seen as good pals. While they don't like the idea of getting older, Postwars *do* tend to feel a real fondness for the grandparenting lifestage. You can tap into this fondness for grandparenting by sponsoring a whole host of activities that are geared toward employees and their grandkids.

Coloring contests, essay contests, scholarships, picnics, bulletin boards with notes and photos about grandchildren's accomplishments, blurbs in the company or department newsletter . . . the list goes on and on. Grandparents *love* to brag about their grandchildren. Make it easy for them by giving them outlets to do so — this is one easy way to connect with employees in the grandparenting lifestage.

ELDERCARE

The average American woman spends 17 years raising children and 18 years helping aging parents or relatives. Eldercare is one of the most important issues in the workplace today. And it mainly is a woman's job — 92% of caregivers are women. Eldercare often cuts into work time and can affect an employee's performance. In most cases, empty-nesters bear the brunt of the load. Some older Postwars are on the receiving end of eldercare and are no longer employed, while those on the younger end tend to be caregivers who still work. Unlike Boomers who are dealing with the "young old," Postwar caregivers are most often dealing with parents or relatives who are in their late 80s or 90s — the oldest of the old.

This lifestage brings a lot of emotional stress to caregivers, as they begin to see their parents or elderly relatives decline in health. Many companies are starting to get the picture and are beginning to offer their employees such things as eldercare service referrals, flex time to take mom or dad to doctor's appointments, and long-term care options for parents. Some companies even offer the perk of providing eldercare help one night a week to employees who are caregiving in their own homes. This temporary rest for the employee leads to greater job productivity.

Accommodating eldercare is a smart move. With Boomers fast approaching retirement age, the impact of eldercare will only increase in the coming years. Recognize that employees dealing with ailing relatives need additional understanding and support from their managers, not a lot of questions about why they took an extra half hour at lunch.

RETIREMENT

Retirement is one of the most significant lifestages of all. It marks the end of an employee's career — something people spend a lifetime building. The average male today retires somewhere between 61 and 62 years of age. And for the Postwar Cohort, retirement remains a predominantly male lifestage. Postwar women typically have been homemakers for a large segment of their lives. Some have had part-time jobs, or may have gone to work after the children were older, but most did not have the same focus on career that their husbands had.

Some Postwars don't plan to retire in the traditional sense. Rather, they prefer to remain active doing the kind of work they enjoy on their own terms. The Senior Citizens Freedom to Work Act of 2000 paved the way in the U.S. for retirees to reenter the workforce and made it easier for people to work past age 65 if they want to — or feel they need to. The law ended caps on how much Social Security recipients could earn while still collecting full federal benefits.

Because of their advancing age and larger salaries, some full-time Postwars are finding themselves victims of downsizing and early retirement. For those who want to retire, compensation packages can be a great deal. But for those who don't have a large enough nest egg, finding a well-paying full-time job at this stage can be tough. Being forced into retirement — which is a dramatic transition, even when it's voluntary — can cause a tremendous loss of identity and self-esteem.

Although retirement often means the loss of personal identity and status, the level of stress that accompanies retirement varies, depending on how people perceive the loss and their ability to find other sources of meaning in their lives. You can help alleviate retirement-related stress by allowing older workers to phase into retirement gradually.

How Two Companies Re-recruit Retirees

Some members of the Postwar Cohort find that retirement is not all that it's cracked up to be, so they look to reenter the workforce part time in less demanding roles. Many companies have begun to tap into this pool of workers by offering generous wages and benefits to part-time and seasonal workers. At Lands' End, for example, retirees are paid $9.50 an hour to do seasonal gift-wrapping around Christmas. Other perks include:

- ✦ Year-round access to the company's activity center.

- ✦ A $25 check for working through the first season with $25 added on for each subsequent season, up to $200.

- ✦ An employee discount of about 40% off of catalog prices and 10% off outlet prices.

- ✦ A year-round benefits plan, including medical, dental, short-term disability, and term life insurance, for seasonal employees who agree to return the following year.

These are attractive benefits, to be sure. But for many of the company's seasonal workers, the biggest benefit is the chance to socialize and connect with their peers.

At Chrysler, company retirees were recruited for the Ambassadors Corps, where they assist customers their own age. They pick up new car buyers, transport them to dealers, and take them to the bank to help them get financing. Such a corps of deal-enhancing engineers is a win-win situation. Customers feel secure because they are being aided by their peers, and the Chrysler retirees find a new source of accomplishment.

Source: Maher, Kris. "How Lands' End Keeps Holiday Workers in Stock," The Wall Street Journal, December 14, 2000, p. B1.

EMOTIONS AND AFFINITIES

Some emotions and affinities become stronger as we get older. With the Postwar Cohort now transitioning into many new lifestages, thoughts about their life's accomplishments and goals with respect to career, family, and friends are common. This can result in a mid-life crisis, and it can motivate them to value their time more deeply and try to find more meaning in their lives. In this section, we present some common emotions and affinities of the Postwar Cohort.

DESIRE EXPERIENCE, NOT THINGS

Younger people typically are more interested in acquiring material possessions than are older people, and so are more focused on their work. At this point in their lives, most Postwars are more interested in rich, fulfilling experiences shared with family and friends than in acquiring material possessions. Travel, hobbies, and meaningful personal interactions top their list of priorities.

To keep them engaged at work, reward Postwars with what they want most — extra time off to pursue their interests. You can also help to make their work experience more fulfilling by letting them redesign their jobs to be more in line with their interests. For example, some Postwars enjoy working on teams and mentoring younger employees, while others would prefer to use their expertise in other ways. You might even try sponsoring interesting activities, like hot-air ballooning or horseback riding, as team-building events.

ENJOYING LIFE

Members of the Postwar Cohort are not the spendthrifts that most of their parents were. Now that they're nearing retirement or are already retired, they are looking to enjoy life. Their early years were spent saving for a home, their kids' college educations, and retirement. Now they feel it's time to start enjoying themselves a bit. While members of the Ghost Cohorts scrimped and saved to leave their children with big inheritances, Postwars are more likely to want to spend their money on themselves . . . maybe not all of it, but certainly some of it.

For those Postwars who are still working, give them plenty of opportunities to pursue their interests, and try to make work enjoyable.

In addition to letting them redesign their jobs as mentioned above, you might encourage employees to start lunchtime clubs where people with similar interests meet to plan activities or pursue hobbies or interests, such as history, bridge, chess, or walking. This taps into Postwars interest in enjoying themselves, while also reflecting their group orientation.

NOSTALGIA

The postwar era is often thought of as a more innocent and idyllic time than our current age. In many ways it was. Terrorist attacks, school shootings, and drug addiction were not worries like they are today. As time passes, people typically remember their coming-of-age years with increasing fondness. Unpleasant memories often fade, while pleasant memories become more intense. The older people get, the more important nostalgia becomes. They begin to define themselves based on favorable memories of the past. For the Postwar Cohort, this is especially true, because Postwars came of age during a time of economic expansion and opportunity.

In the workplace, you could sponsor fun activities that tap into the Postwars' fond memories of their coming-of-age years while also playing up the excitement angle for younger workers. Some ideas include hosting a '50s-style sock hop instead of a ho-hum company picnic, having a '50s day at work where people come dressed in the clothes of the postwar era, or having an Elvis look-a-like contest.

PHYSIOGRAPHIC PROFILE

Physically speaking, there tends to be quite a difference between the youngest Postwars and the oldest. Those Postwars in their late 50s and early 60s show some of the outward signs of aging, such as wrinkles and gray hair, but they feel pretty good physically. They are active and are not really slowed down by physical ailments. Beginning about age 65, though, aches and pains tend to intensify, and it becomes harder to recover from physical problems. Also, people tend to think more about their own mortality as peers begin to experience serious illness and die. In general, Postwars are now more focused on feeling good, rather than on looking good. They realize they can no longer fight Mother Nature and have accepted their gray hair and changing physical appearance with grace.

While the aging process cannot be reversed, it can be accommodated. And companies can do a lot to make sure employees' needs are met. Make older employees more comfortable at work, and they are likely to be more productive and stay on the job longer. Ergonomically designed chairs, desks, and other furniture make sitting, bending, and typing more comfortable for sufferers of arthritis and other aches and pains. Older people tend to experience changes in their body structure as they age, so furniture should be adjustable to fit employees' changing needs. Walking at lunch or participating in another form of exercise helps to alleviate some of the adverse effects of aging, so your company may want to encourage these activities.

Many people begin to notice vision problems in their 40s, but the situation only worsens in their 50s, 60s, and 70s. For internal communications, avoid using small type and colors in the blue-gray-violet end of the spectrum, which are harder to see. Instead, use at least 13-point type and high contrast colors, such as black on white or black on yellow. Use a lot of white space in your layout and avoid dense text. Also, make sure that lighting is adequate for older employees, who may need more light than younger workers. Avoid indirect lighting in the work environment, since the fluttering light it emits makes older eyes less able to take in images.

Hearing loss is a problem for people beginning in their 50s, and men are twice as likely as women to be affected. You can compensate for this change by providing on-site hearing screening, and making sure hearing aids are covered in the company medical plan.

Memory loss is another malady that increases in frequency as we get older, and the process can begin as early as our 30s. Doctors say passivity only contributes to the problem. The best way to keep memory strong is to stay active both mentally and physically. Encourage employees to learn new things by making regular training courses available, or by reimbursing tuition at nearby colleges or universities.

When these Postwars do participate in activities that enhance their mental or physical fitness, reward them. Depicting their accomplishments on plaques on the walls of the company building with "Isn't it Sterling!!" banners would be welcomed. Unlike *Golden* or *Silver, Sterling* is quite an acceptable characterization for Postwars.

Chronic medical conditions, such as high blood pressure, high cholesterol, arthritis, diabetes, constipation, and heart disease all become more common with age, and many Postwars now are living with these medical problems. Make sure to offer low-fat and low-cholesterol choices, such as fish, lean meat, and soy products, in the company cafeteria. Doing so will appeal not just to Postwars, but to health-conscious Boomers as well.

Employer investments in health and longevity pay off by keeping employees healthy, and therefore able to work longer and more productively. The costs of prevention programs are far cheaper than the costs of illness, even for part-time workers who are not on company health insurance benefits. Your Postwars are the workers whose health you should be most focused on.

UNIQUE STRENGTHS

Rather than trying to find a way to put your Postwars out to pasture, why not embrace the many strengths they bring to the workplace?

EXPERIENCE

Postwars have a wealth of experience, and often serve as the institutional memory of their organizations. They have seen new management practices come and go and return again the second or third time. They know how things work and can save less experienced employees from having to reinvent the wheel. If managed correctly, Postwars can help to improve efficiency and improve the bottom line for many organizations. And because they were trained by Ghost Cohorts, you will always get eight hours of work for eight hours of pay. They have a sense of responsibility as they go about their jobs, and don't suffer from many of the distractions that younger workers often do.

TEAM ORIENTATION

Postwars came of age during a time when most people wanted to fit in and be part of the crowd. Their collectivist nature works well with current management trends, which are focused on building effective team environments. Postwars are naturals when it comes to working on teams, and they like the camaraderie of working as part of a close-knit group. In this respect, they have a lot to teach the more individualistic Boomers and

Gen-Xers about how to work effectively with other people. Because of their group orientation and their years of experience, Postwars are often excellent people managers.

MENTORING

Because of their vast experience and team orientation, Postwars typically make excellent mentors for younger employees. And most tend to really enjoy the experience. Set up a formalized program to match Postwars with younger employees, and you will be able to capture and utilize many more of this cohort's unique strengths. Younger employees typically work better with older staff members anyway, seeing them as less of a threat than employees who are immediately ahead of them on the corporate ladder.

DEPENDABILITY, STABILITY, AND AVAILABILITY

Postwars generally are not looking to change jobs this late in the game. Rather, they look forward to finishing out their careers in their current positions. As a result, they are some of the most dependable, stable employees you could have. In addition, many Postwars are not looking to retire completely. Instead, they would like to stay active and work part time or in short-term assignments. Retired patent attorneys contracting to work on overflow cases, retired accountants working just during tax season, or seasonal employees working just to fill orders during the Christmas rush are all good examples. These types of arrangements provide opportunities for Postwars and older cohorts to stay active, while offering companies the staffing flexibility they need.

Postwar Cohort Strengths

✦ Experience

✦ Team orientation

✦ Mentoring ability

✦ Dependability, stability, and availability

THE STRUCTURED WORK PATH AND POSTWAR WORKERS

The structured work path fits the Postwar Cohort best. It offers Postwars everything they're looking for: affiliation, security, status, recognition, financial rewards, and responsibility. This cohort is very comfortable with the kind of top-down structure that the Ghost Cohorts created. This cohort appreciates authority and responds to the requests of those above them. They have always taken orders well. Unlike Baby Boomers, they do not feel the need for strong participation in the company's decision-making process.

You need only look at their coming-of-age years to discern how they became so amenable to the top-down chain of command. Looking for stability on the job and in their lives as they pursued their careers throughout the late 1940s and 1950s, they embraced an "I'll be happy to do what you tell me to do" attitude in their work style. And the Ghost Cohorts loom over them with sufficient influence to further push Postwars toward the structured work path. (More information on work paths is in Chapter 11.)

FUTURE OUTLOOK AND CONCLUSION

Postwars are expected to remain in the workforce longer than their predecessors — not necessarily because they need to work, but because they want to. This will help to ease the growing scarcity of skilled workers in the years to come. But not all companies or managers will see the value in keeping older workers around. With higher salaries and costly benefit packages, Postwars, and Leading-Edge Boomers for that matter, are likely to fall victim to the corporate axe. But we think it's short-sighted to cut veteran employees. We feel that keeping Postwar workers is important for a number of reasons:

+ **Postwars have the wisdom of years on the job:** Tapping into their vast experience can save money and improve efficiency.

+ **Postwars are dependable:** They work because it is part of the fabric of their being. They are much more loyal, devoted, and involved with their work performance than younger generational cohorts.

✦ **Having older workers around adds another important element of diversity to the workplace:** This can lead to heightened creativity and innovative solutions. And they can certainly offer mentoring for younger cohorts.

According to the Hudson Institute's *Workforce 2020,* both employers and employees will need to find ways to integrate older workers into tomorrow's workplace.[4] This poses several major challenges that must be addressed:

✦ Workforce planning will become more difficult as human resource professionals find retirement much less predictable.

✦ The ongoing presence of higher-level managers may create dissension among younger subordinates looking to move up. Employers may need to get creative and come up with off-line or part-time positions for senior managers so that younger workers will have opportunities for advancement.

✦ Benefits must change to meet the needs of older workers. Expanded coverage for things such as hearing aids, vision testing, prescription drugs, and long-term care will be in demand.

✦ The link between health insurance and employment must be revised. The number of people covered by employment-based insurance is on the decline as more and more people work for small firms that are not required to provide health insurance. To attract and retain skilled workers, smaller firms must be able to make sure that their employees are covered by health insurance. This will require a coordinated effort at the national level, or some other broad-based approach to address this important issue.

Recent retirees can be a gold mine for many businesses. If you'd like to focus on hiring older workers, try sources other than want ads and other mainstream vehicles. For example, tap into your company's retiree network, or place posters at senior centers and community centers. Word of mouth is another excellent source for referrals, as are local or regional magazines and other publications aimed at older people. Keep in mind, though, that because of good planning and conservative spending in years past, many of these older employees won't *need* to work, but will *want* to. So the job has to offer them more than just a paycheck. You might as well start focusing on older workers now, because Postwars are just a dress rehearsal for the coming tidal wave of retiring Baby Boomers.

ENDNOTES

1. Sullivan, Sherry E., and Edward A. Duplaga. "Recruiting and Retaining Olders for the New Millennium," *Business Horizons,* Nov/Dec 1997, vol. 40, p. 65 (5).

2. Welch, Sarah J. "Boomers and Beyond," *Successful Meetings,* August 2000, Vol. 49, p. 63 (5).

3. Author listed as anonymous. "Senior Workers on the Rise." *The Futurist,* September/October 2000, Vol. 34, p. 19.

4. Judy, Richard, and Carol D'Amico. *Workforce 2020: Work and Workers in the 21st Century.* Hudson Institute: Indianapolis, Indiana, 1997, p. 105–106.

CHAPTER 6

UNDERSTANDING YOUR LEADING-EDGE BABY BOOMER EMPLOYEES

More so than the members of any other cohort, both the Leading-Edge and Trailing-Edge Baby Boomers have a very real awareness of being part of a generational group. Because of their large numbers, they were targeted almost from birth by savvy marketers. They have continued to play a major role in trends affecting the American marketplace and workplace ever since. And there is no sign that their importance is going to change anytime soon.

The most pressing issue facing managers of Leading-Edge Boomers is the coming wave of people leaving the workforce as they hit retirement age. Baby Boomers will begin to turn 65 in 2010, but many consultants predict a skilled labor shortage as early as 2005. Benefits consulting firm Watson Wyatt Worldwide estimates that by 2006, the number of people 55 to 64 years old will increase by 54% from 1996 levels, while the number of workers ages 25 to 34 will drop by 8.8% during the same time frame.[1]

These numbers certainly point to a coming labor force crisis as Baby Boomers, who have always dreamed of retiring early, leave the workforce in droves to pursue their search for inner meaning. But wait a minute — while the coming labor shortage is real, we think it will be offset somewhat by one critical factor: Baby Boomers have never been savers and are ill-prepared for retirement. As a result, many are likely to work quite late into their lives, either because they want to or because they have to. This demographic change will impact the workforce, as older workers begin to stake out more and more room at the company picnic.

This demographic shift has tremendous implications for executives, who in recent years have tended to think of older workers not as a source of vast experience, but as a drain on resources.

In this chapter, we look more closely at the Leading-Edge Baby Boomer Cohort. We attempt to understand what generational cohort values they bring to the workplace, and how to best retain them in order to avoid the labor crisis that so many experts and demographers predict.

TWO SEPARATE BABY BOOM COHORTS

The 76 million people born between 1946 and 1964 have historically been lumped into a single group, the Baby Boomers. But our work clearly shows two distinct generational cohorts within this classification.

- ✦ Leading-Edge Boomers came of age between 1963 and 1972, during a time of social protest, idealism, and a good economy.

- ✦ Trailing-Edge Boomers came of age between 1973 and 1983, during a time of cynicism, oil shortages, and rising inflation.

The fundamental attitudes of these two groups are different in a number of ways. Older Boomers tend to be more optimistic and idealistic, while younger Boomers tend to be more skeptical and often feel cheated. In this chapter, we're just concerned with the Leading-Edge Boomers. In Chapter 7, we write about Trailing-Edge Boomers.

The Newer, Gentler Workplace

When the Leading-Edge Boomers began entering the workforce in the early '60s, the postwar tradition of the authoritarian boss was just beginning to give way to a new trend — the sensitive manager. Remember the self-help book *I'm OK — You're OK?* A touchy-feely approach began slipping into management. Sensitivity training, encounter groups, and group dynamics facilitation became common training approaches, but rather than train people on how to value differences and work together better, they primarily focused on ways to change the behavior of individuals to make them more cooperative with management. Managers were taught to be friendly and caring, and they were told to appear to be interested in and value the views of the people they managed. But there was the unspoken understanding that management still knew best.

At the same time, workers began to expect that their jobs should provide them with more than just a steady paycheck — work should be meaningful as well. The concept of meaningful work gained ground in the '50s, but it didn't really take off until the '60s. The work of psychologist Abraham Maslow and his hierarchy of needs became prominent during this time. Maslow thought that people are motivated by their unmet needs, which can be arranged in a pyramid fashion. At the lowest levels, people are motivated by their most basic physiological needs for food and shelter. From there, they move up to a need for safety, social interaction, and self-esteem. Only after these needs are met can people reach the apex of the hierarchy, self-actualization. Self-actualization is what Leading-Edge Baby Boomers have been seeking from their work ever since they entered the workforce. Some have achieved it, but most have not.

Disappointment and Change

During the long postwar expansion in the '50s, '60s, and '70s, Leading-Edge Boomers saw companies adding more and more management layers at ever higher pay levels. They equated success with promotions and raises, and they began to expect that they would achieve at least as good a career as their bosses. During the '70s and '80s, Leading-Edge Boomers paid their dues, working their way up the corporate ladder. But then in the early '90s, everything changed. Corporations began peeling away the layers and cutting costs. As mid-level managers, many Leading-Edge Boomers fell victim to the first waves of downsizing. Those who survived quickly learned the lingo of the lean organization and realized they would have to be happy plateauing, or else be prepared to leave.

Independent by nature, some Boomers decided to strike out on their own, starting up new companies or becoming independent contractors and consultants. Others made the conscious decision to focus on other areas that offered greater promise for self-actualization — things like family, hobbies, and volunteerism.

The Leading-Edge Baby Boomers Today

The Leading-Edge Boomers are 48 to 56 years old in 2002. Many have risen into the ranks of middle and upper management, and they have entered their peak income years. They will remain there throughout their 50s. At 31 million strong, they represent about 14% of the population and are a sizable force in today's workplace.

As we noted earlier, the first wave of Baby Boomers will begin to turn 65 in 2011, and retirement now looms large on the horizon for this cohort. Having always valued self-indulgence, many Leading-Edge Boomers have not put away much money for retirement. Many studies have shown that a sizable number of Boomers aspire to retire early, but the reality is that most have little hope of ever doing so. In fact, they are likely to work longer than members of any previous cohort did.

Leading-Edge Boomer Defining Moments

To fully understand Leading-Edge Boomers, you have to understand the defining moments that shaped them and the values and other motivating factors that have resulted from those defining moments. The coming-of-age years of Leading-Edge Boomers began with the assassination of President John F. Kennedy in 1963. The event shocked all Americans, but it had an even greater impact on the young adults who were coming of age at the time. For them, it signaled the end of childhood innocence, and marked the dawn of a new era in which everything was questioned.

Robert F. Kennedy's assassination in 1968 and Martin Luther King's in 1969 further marred Leading-Edgers' coming-of-age years. The Vietnam War became a rallying point for protestors, and social turmoil raged. Young people rebelled against the Establishment and experimented with drugs, sex, music, politics — you name it. Self-indulgence, personal fulfillment, and new experiences were the name of the game.

Despite the social unrest of the '60s, the stock market continued its upward climb and the economy skipped along at a rapid pace. In fact, the carefree attitudes and experimental nature of the era were supported by the booming economy and a low unemployment rate. Neil Armstrong's 1969 moonwalk only enhanced American feelings of optimism, pride, and technological superiority.

These events made a lasting impact on the Leading-Edge Baby Boomers, shaping values that remain with them to this day.

Leading-Edge Baby Boomer Defining Moments

✦ Assassination of John F. Kennedy

✦ Vietnam War

✦ Assassination of Martin Luther King, Jr.

✦ Assassination of Robert F. Kennedy

✦ First man on the moon

SNAPSHOT OF THE LEADING-EDGE BOOMER COHORT

Name of Cohort:	Leading-Edge Boomer
Born between:	1946–54
Coming of Age:	1963–72
Age in 2002:	48–56
Population:	31 million (14%)

Key Cohort Values and Concerns
- Personal/social expression
- Protected individualism
- Youth
- Health and wellness

Current and Next Lifestage
- Empty-nesting
- Childrearing
- Some grandparenting
- Second career
- Divorce

Emotions and Affinities
- Nostalgia
- Challenge authority
- Social justice
- Sexually experimental
- Generational community

Physiographic Profile
- Vision problems
- Weight changes
- Hypertension
- Arthritis
- Gray hair and hair loss
- Menopause

LEADING-EDGE BOOMER VALUES — A DRAMATIC SHIFT

Postwars and Leading-Edge Boomers have dramatically different values. This shift is far greater than the shift between any other two contiguous cohorts. Postwars are much more group oriented than Boomers, and far more willing to accept authority. Boomers, however, want to do everything *their* way. In this section, we present a summary of the key cohort values and concerns of Leading-Edge Boomers.

PERSONAL AND SOCIAL EXPRESSION

Prioritizing personal and social expression is a key element of both Boomer Cohorts' value systems. In the '60s and '70s, this trait emerged as part of the anti-war protests. These days, Leading-Edge Boomers are more likely to be focused on personal, rather than social, expression. But the value still remains.

In the workplace, give Leading-Edgers an outlet for personal expression. Let them help design their own workspace, for example. And Leading-Edgers will want to join in on all decision-making. They are not ones to be told what to do; they want to participate in designing their work.

And remember that 77% of Boomer women work today. Having a dual-career family adds many demands on the household, and these are reflected in how Leading-Edgers define their personal expression, or even their social expression. Leading-Edgers will need flexibility to integrate their personal and professional lives. Childcare at work, flexible hours, telecommuting, even four-day workweeks can be very helpful in working through the pressures that come of having both partners in a relationship work. Anything you can offer to help your Leading-Edgers at home can be a powerful motivator and reward.

PROTECTED INDIVIDUALISM

Leading-Edge Boomers won't be talked into doing things out of guilt or for the greater good of the group. If you want them to take on a big project or work on a team, don't try to persuade them with stale platitudes such as "We're all counting on you." Leading-Edgers will be much more motivated by appeals to their individualism.

87

Tell a Leading-Edger that he's the only person for the job because of his unique skills, offer to provide extra vacation days if the project comes in on time, and so on. Participatory management and team approaches, which allow for greater individual input, help to enhance Leading-Edgers' job satisfaction. Another way to indulge Leading-Edgers' sense of individualism is by offering cafeteria-style benefit plans, which give employees a wide range of choices, and by offering flexibility in work schedules and work locations (home, office, or satellite commuter center). These types of programs will be popular not only with Leading-Edgers, but also with younger employees.

YOUTH

The youth culture of the '60s warned Leading-Edge Boomers not to trust anyone over 30. When the inevitable happened and Leading-Edgers began to turn 30 themselves, they immediately began to change the rules about aging. Aging wasn't something to accept, but to fight. As they moved into middle age, their obsession with youth prompted many Boomers to dye their hair, start working out at the gym, and even undergo plastic surgery in an attempt to maintain their youthful looks and stay competitive at work. Cosmetic surgery increased 173% between 1997 and 2000. Forty percent of that was performed on the two Boomer Cohorts. Many procedures are to maintain a youthful appearance in the workplace to retain a position or get ahead on the job.

At work, your company could host fitness seminars and offer referrals for spas, retreats, even plastic surgeons and hair replacement. Remember company Christmas-club savings programs? Today's Boomers might prefer a similar savings program, in which money is put aside for anti-aging purposes, such as aromatherapy, acupuncture, and even cosmetic surgery. You could call it the Fountain of Youth Club, or something similar. Check it out with your employees. You might be surprised how much interest the concept generates!

Or, how about Outward Bound–type trips to bring Boomer workers together and to appeal to their desire to retain their youthful sense of adventure? You can come up with so many ideas for innovative incentives for this generational cohort. You could provide noontime challenges like scaling company-installed telephone poles and standing upright 25 feet above the ground! Your Leading-Edgers will want to participate just to prove that they can do it. (Of course, each person would be secured by ropes or bungee cords for maximum safety.)

HEALTH AND WELLNESS

Leading-Edge Boomers' focus on health and wellness ties in with their obsession with youth, but it also relates to their individualistic nature. While older cohorts trusted doctors with their health, Boomers tend to want to take a more active role. Health- and wellness-related programs are likely to go over big with Leading-Edge Boomers. Your company can appeal to Leading-Edgers by offering:

✦ A corporate fitness club.

✦ On-site walking trails.

✦ Inclusion of alternative medicines, such as chiropractic care, in company healthcare plans.

✦ On-site massage.

✦ Low-fat meals in the company cafeteria that are labeled with calorie, saturated fat, and carbohydrate content.

LIFESTAGE

It used to be that people followed very linear lifestages. After graduating from high school, they looked to either go on to college or start working. Once employed, they often married fairly quickly and began raising a family, eventually retiring to enjoy hobbies and their grandchildren. These days, however, people are more likely to jump from one lifestage to another and back again. This is due in part to the more liberal attitudes of Leading-Edge Baby Boomers, who turned the traditional lifestage path upside down, particularly when they began entering middle age. For example, second marriages, second families, and second careers are all very common and mainstream now.

Lifestage plays an increasingly important role in the workplace. If someone is a new parent or grandparent — or both! — it often affects the way that person approaches his or her job. The employee may, for example, be looking for more stability and less travel if he's a parent, and more time away from work to visit grandchildren if she's a grandparent.

Although Leading-Edge Baby Boomers are in a number of different lifestages right now — some still have children at home, while others are grandparents and starting second careers — the following are some common lifestages that apply to this group. These lifestages have a real impact on workplace performance.

EMPTY-NESTING

Once upon a time, when the last child left home, mothers often grieved for their sudden loss of identity. They had spent their entire lives raising children and then, literally overnight, they no longer seemed to have a purpose. These days, however, Leading-Edge Boomer parents are not lamenting their loss of identity as the kids leave home, wondering how so many years could have passed so quickly. Rather, they're jumping for joy!

The difference is that these days many more Leading-Edge Boomer mothers work outside the home, and those who don't often have volunteer or other outside activities to keep them active and engaged apart from the family. To them, the empty-nesting lifestage marks the end of day-to-day family responsibilities and opens new opportunities for self-indulgence and fulfillment. As the need to support the family dwindles, older Boomers are focusing their attention away from work and are looking to achieve a better balance between their professional and personal lives.

In their younger days, Leading-Edgers sacrificed family and personal time to climb the corporate ladder. Some have made it to the top, but the vast majority has not. So now they're looking to find some kind of meaning in life. Instead of climbing the corporate ladder, they are much more likely to want to climb Mt. Everest, backpack in the Andes, walk the isle of Crete, or kayak Alaska. In other words, empty-nesting often brings with it a change in attitude. Instead of providing for the family, Leading-Edgers are now meeting their own needs.

Unless they are actively looking to move up the ladder, don't reward empty-nesters with more responsibility and opportunities for advancement. Rather, offer them time off to explore their interests or sponsor a company-wide or department-wide adventure, such as rock-climbing, sky-diving, or kayaking. Also, make sure that they have some mountains (or at least hills) to climb in their work. Most of them will not be able to squeeze through the promotion bottleneck to make it to executive levels, but they can be challenged with opportunities to lead project teams or generate entrepreneurial new ventures, or they can simply be put in charge of solving any one of the many urgent problems that arise in the life of a company.

CHILDREARING

Many Leading-Edge Boomers had children later in life than their own parents did, so even in their late 40s and early 50s, many Boomers are still very much involved in the childrearing lifestage. And because divorce has become so commonplace, many Leading-Edge Boomers are now starting second families or raising children alone as single parents or as stepparents. By 2007, more than half of all families will be blended, where children live with one biological parent and one stepparent. While it used to be unthinkable for a man in his 50s to father a child, today it is fairly common. The childrearing lifestage pulls at employees in two different directions:

- ✦ They realize they have a responsibility to support their family, so they tend to take fewer risks.

- ✦ They want to spend more time with their children, and so want more time away from work.

You can keep employees in this lifestage engaged by sponsoring family activities, encouraging participation in Bring Your Child to Work Day, or rewarding employees by giving them a day off to spend with their kids. Also, recognize that Boomers who do start second families are going to appreciate and respond strongly to flexible work arrangements, even though you may not guess, based on their age alone, that they need such accommodations.

SOME GRANDPARENTING

Although grandparenting does not fit with the traditional Boomer affinity for youth, more and more Leading-Edge Boomers are nonetheless entering this lifestage. In fact, due to their large numbers, Leading-Edgers have already begun to fuel a grandparenting boom. And just like they have done with every other lifestage, the Leading Edgers are redefining grandparenting. Rather than being stern disciplinarians, they see themselves as fun-seeking companions to their grandchildren. Some feel that they missed out on raising their own children, and do not want to make the same mistake with their grandchildren, so making time for grandkids is a priority.

To appeal to employees in this lifestage, institute a Grandchild at the Office Day, for example, during which grandchildren can shadow their grandparents. It could be called Hold My Hand Day, or even Hold My "Plan" Day. Grandparents buy 25% of all toys, so you may want to place toy catalogs in break areas if you have a Leading-Edge heavy workforce. Or maybe you can add a place on the walls of the office where grandparents can put pictures of their grandchildren. Your company could even sponsor a scholarship for your employees' grandchildren who have special accomplishments, or it could sponsor a contest for grandchildren and reward college-education money to the winner.

These types of activities help busy grandparents indulge their grandchildren without costing them much of anything. Now, these grandparent-friendly activities are not likely to be motivators by themselves, but they can be used to help retain Boomers or as rewards. Promoting such unique perks could help in recruiting as well.

SECOND CAREER

The popularity of second careers took off with the corporate downsizing of the early '90s — a wave of layoffs that effectively killed job loyalty forever. It also prompted many people to embark on second careers as they came to realize that the career path they chose at 20 didn't necessarily fit at 50. "Meaningful work" became their battle cry. Rather than waiting around to be downsized, Leading-Edge Boomers are striking out on their own, going back to school, and looking for new job opportunities in completely different fields. Many Leading-Edgers in the corporate world see smaller companies as an appealing option, mainly because these companies seem to offer greater flexibility and a more personal management style.

Members of the Postwar Cohort were looking for stability at this age. But Leading-Edge Boomers are realizing that midlife career redirection is yet another way to achieve self-fulfillment. And it is also a way to redefine middle age and start over. So don't neglect these second-career Boomers in your recruitment efforts. You may be pleasantly surprised with the level of experience and skill they can bring to your organization.

And consider this possibility. You know that Leading-Edge Boomers tend to embrace the notion of a new career relatively late in their working lives — many of them have not done so to date. You can think of this as an opportunity and seek employees who are willing to rise to the challenge and take on a new kind of work that lets them bridge into new career areas. When you find someone who is enticed by the opportunity to work in a new field, you can often negotiate lower pay and even part-time working arrangements, since many Leading-Edgers consider learning a new skill to be valuable in and of itself!

DIVORCE

Since the '70s, about half of all marriages have ended in divorce. This grim statistic correlates with the Leading-Edge Baby Boomers' ascent into adulthood. Not that they are to blame completely, but their self-indulgence has carried over to the rest of the population. Although it's true that there are some benefits to the increased acceptance of divorce, the rise in divorce has forever changed the American family. Divorce as one enters the empty-nest lifestage is becoming quite common. These days, second and third marriages are not uncommon either, further changing the structure of blended families.

While divorces and remarriages do not have obvious implications for management, employers need to show understanding, and perhaps some flexibility as well. Recognize that members of this cohort, even though they're in their 50s, may be going through major transitions. Be ready to provide flexibility and, if needed, emotional support.

EMOTIONS AND AFFINITIES

At this stage in their lives, Leading-Edge Boomers have developed a unique set of dominant emotions and affinities that clearly distinguishes them from other cohorts. As people age, different priorities come into play and then diminish. Cohort values interact with these aging effects and dictate how they are carried out in life. For example, Leading-Edge Boomers' youth orientation makes them put a much greater emphasis on the nostalgic icons of their youth than older people do. That youth value pervades interpretations of these emotions and affinities.

NOSTALGIA

Middle age is typically a time when people start to reminisce about the past like never before. Music, movies, fashions, and so on all become cues that conjure up youth. No cohort is more nostalgic than the Leading-Edge Baby Boomers. They were going to be young forever, and so look back to their youth with even more fondness than most cohorts do. To engage this affinity at work, sponsor a Wild '60s Day or Bellbottom Day, in which people wear their favorite clothes from the late '60s and early '70s. Or instead of playing canned music at work, why not play classic Leading-Edge Boomer music for a week? If that doesn't appeal to you, find some other creative way to tap into this group's fondness for the good old days.

REBELLIOUS

The protests of the '60s and '70s reflected and amplified a blatant mistrust of authority that many Leading-Edge Boomers still carry with them today. While they have learned over the years that there are times to toe the line, many still have a rebellious streak. At work, they tend to question authority and fight for programs or projects they believe in. Trying to quell their rebelliousness was never easy in the '60s, and it still isn't today.

SOCIAL JUSTICE

Social justice fell out of vogue somewhat during the '80s as Leading-Edge Baby Boomers became career-driven yuppies. Donating to charities became an acceptable substitute for protesting. But now that most older Boomers have plateaued in their careers, social justice is back and is part of the great search for meaning. Look for Leading-Edgers to get more involved in causes, such as helping the poor and homeless and aiding battered women. In the workplace, they are excellent choices to lead charity fundraising efforts.

GENERATIONAL COMMUNITY

Leading-Edge Baby Boomers have had a sense that they were part of a larger generational community from the time that they were children. It didn't have a name then, but advertisers clearly had this cohort in their cross hairs. In later years, the Boomers formed their own youth subculture and vowed never to trust anyone over 30. Even today, because Boomers have always felt like a part of a group, they feel a kinship and a sense of connectedness with other Boomers. In the workplace, such terms as *Woodstock, revolution,* and *commune* could be used as a bridge to their communal spirit. For example, exhort Leading-Edgers to "revolution-ize" their work plans. Or, you could designate teams as communes rather than teams.

When a group of employees that is comprised predominately of Boomers is working over a weekend, dub it a Woodstock Work Weekend and promote greater freedoms during that work period. Let them come to work at their leisure and pipe in the songs of Janis Joplin, Crosby, Stills, and Nash, or some other classic rock. Such an idea is clearly revolutionary, but it's worthy of testing. And by the way, only prescription drugs would be permissible.

PHYSIOGRAPHIC PROFILE

Now that the Leading-Edge Baby Boomers have hit middle age, the physical effects of aging have begun to take their toll. Sure, this cohort will fight aging every step of the way, but some things are unavoidable. Many physiographic changes have little or no impact on the workplace (gray hair and hair loss, for example). Others, such as vision problems and arthritis, can have significant consequences. Leading-Edge Boomers may not want to admit that they are having trouble reading the overhead slides or that their hands are stiffening up with so much typing. But these changes are very real. Menopause is another physical change now affecting Leading-Edge Boomer women. And work stress may contribute to high blood pressure.

Taken together, these physiographic changes can account for a large number of lost days of work. By acknowledging the very real bodily changes affecting the oldest Boomers, your company can take steps to address these problems. You could develop a health and wellness program that's targeted to meet the needs of this specific cohort. For example, your company could offer fitness training to increase the flexibility of employees who suffer from arthritis.

Because older eyes have trouble reading small type and colors in the blue-gray-violet end of the color spectrum, make sure internal communications use at least 13-point type and high contrast colors, such as black on white or black on yellow, which are easier for older eyes to see. And make sure office lighting is adequate for older workers, who may require more light to read comfortably.

Also, as Boomers age, convenience and comfort will become increasingly more important to them. For some Leading-Edgers, convenience and comfort may become critical factors in whether they stay with your company. Errand services that pick up and drop off dry-cleaning, for example, or on-site banks and medical offices can score big points. Ergonomically designed office space and furniture that make working more comfortable will appeal to aging Boomers in the years to come. One company in Minnesota even has an automobile service station at its corporate headquarters, which allows employees to save time and get their cars fixed at reasonable rates while they work. Other companies offer on-site massage and health clinics for their employees. And some pharmaceutical companies, including Eli Lilly and Pfizer, even provide employees with free company-made prescription drugs. This includes both Prozac and Viagra.

UNIQUE STRENGTHS OF LEADING-EDGE BOOMERS

Leading-Edge Baby Boomers are individualistic and like to challenge authority, but they also tend to be good at working on their own and coming up with new solutions to vexing problems. Their years of experience are another strength, although some companies are trimming the ranks of older Boomers to save on the higher costs of their salaries and benefit packages. In the long run, we think that companies will find that Leading-Edge Boomers' experience will more than pay for itself, although, of course, it's hard to quantify the cost or benefits of such an intangible.

Boomer skepticism can also be a great strength. Because Boomers question managerial decisions, better decisions often result. Postwar managers find it difficult to accept anyone challenging their directives — that's not the way they were brought up! But they must be more accepting of Leading-Edge Boomers' drive to express themselves. In the end, it often leads to a more effective company.

THE INDIVIDUALIST WORK PATH AND LEADING-EDGE BOOMERS

Typically, members of this cohort are not eager to play a role defined by tradition. This is a broad generalization, of course, but it's often accurate. That's why the individualist work path fits most members of this cohort so well. Encourage employees who are on this work path to come forward with their own ideas and suggestions — even to point out flaws in current operating procedures. Being able to give input helps engage Leading-Edgers in their work and makes them feel that their contributions are important. If you offer them a promotion to a leadership position, you better let them write the job description, rather than try to hire to the standard position. What their position should be called, where and when they should work, what their workspace should look, feel, sound, and smell like, who should report to them — every detail should be on the table for negotiation so that they can truly individualize their role.

If you value individualism as much as most Leading-Edgers do, you want your advancement in an organization to coincide with more opportunities to express yourself uniquely and individually. Yet in many companies, there is greater pressure toward conformity as people move higher up in an organization. So the career path toward the top often turns members of this cohort off instead of turning them on. Some Boomers will not even consider advancing to top management positions, simply because they don't want to have to wear traditional, formal business attire! We're talking about a very strong urge toward individualism here — one that needs to be accommodated in order to keep these employees motivated and engaged with their work.

It is also wise to appeal to this cohort's vitality. Taking on a leadership role is unappealing to them if doing so means filling the shoes of the wise elder statesmen or women who came before them. Leading-Edgers

see this as selling their soul and allowing themselves to become old like
"them" — and remember that "they" were the enemy in this cohort's
formative years.

Help this cohort grow old while staying young at heart. Fun, youthful
ways of being a leader are far more appealing to most of them than the
traditional approach to leadership. On the individualist path, employees
need to be able to feel they are staying fit and rekindling their youthful
enthusiasm through their work. Retreats to spas, opportunities to learn
new sports or hobbies, and perks like personal trainers are all going to
appeal to this cohort. But because Leading-Edgers are individualists,
they will want to select their favorites perks and not simply be given the
standard ones.

FUTURE OUTLOOK AND CONCLUSIONS

To offset the coming labor shortage and to retain Leading-Edge Boomers
as they age, you need to make sure there is a career path that comes
much closer to meeting their daily needs and underlying values than is
usually the case today. Offer them one-foot-in options, whereby they
work part-time or as intermittent leaders and advisors and mentors rather
than in traditional full-time positions. Some companies have begun giving
older employees the opportunity to "rehearse" retirement. They can work
reduced hours, take a different part-time job, or take unpaid sabbaticals
to explore post-retirement opportunities. These options make work more
appealing and less of a grind. Other companies, realizing that many
people start new careers after retirement, offer money for tuition reimbursement in the two or three years before and after retirement. These
are all excellent ways to help retain older workers.

Boomers with enough experience to be promoted to leading positions in their workplaces are also reaching an age and lifestage where
they are eager to turn their backs on the 24-7 executive lifestyle and
start enjoying themselves. That urge to pamper themselves often conflicts with the demands of life at the top. Companies need to find ways
for them to step up to more senior roles without necessarily becoming
traditional executives. Can your company, for instance, have a younger
executive director who is counseled by a team of senior advisors or a
leadership committee? One of the perks of being on the committee could
be that the members make their own work hours and only work part time.

Replacing Leading-Edge Executives

While many Boomers dream of retiring in their 50s, most do not have the financial wherewithal to pull this off. The rare exception is the Leading-Edge Boomer executive or consultant who has quickly risen through the ranks and bankrolled enough money through salary, stock options, and individual investments to live the new version of the American dream.

Some studies show that by 2005, many large, older companies will see as many as 40% to 50% of their executives leave.

Executives from older cohorts would rarely have considered jumping off the treadmill early, but Leading-Edge Boomers have a completely different value system. The Boomer exodus from the executive suite has some companies scrambling to fill the void with qualified managers. A large number of companies, obsessed with cost cutting, effectively downsized the successors of today's executives — the middle managers of yester-year. And they now have no formalized programs for replacing today's aging executives.

But some companies are trying to rectify this in a hurry. The U.S. Postal Service, for example, is in the process of rebuilding its system for identifying top talent. The agency's top officers are required to identify successors for their own positions and for any of the executives under them. That begins a formal process in which potential candidates are interviewed, tested, and evaluated for leadership potential. When an opening occurs, a list of qualified managers is ready for review.

Other companies, including Deloitte Consulting, are encouraging older executives to stick around longer by offering perks such as allowing spouses to go on business trips for free, or by allowing executives to redesign their work to make it more interesting and rewarding. This kind of job restructuring is appealing not just to execs thinking of retiring, but to those who may succeed them down the line.

The bottom line is that organizations have to be prepared to fill the shoes of older executives with younger workers from less populous cohorts. As you will see in subsequent chapters, there are ways to change the workplace to make it a far better fit for younger cohorts, including the valuable Trailing-Edge Boomers and Gen-X up-and-comers who are poised to assume leadership roles. Your company may need to accelerate their development.

One key way to develop a new generation of business leaders to step into the Leading-Edge Boomers' shoes is to help bridge the gaps between this cohort and younger ones, especially Generation X and N Gen. It is important to encourage mentoring relationships and stimulate collaboration. The knowledge of the older cohort must be transferred to the younger ones. Otherwise, too much knowledge will be lost through the defection of the Boomers.

ENDNOTES

1. Miner, William J. "Ask a Benefit Actuary: Importance of Workforce Management," *Business Insurance,* June 1, 1998, v32, p. 17 (1).

CHAPTER 7

UNDERSTANDING YOUR TRAILING-EDGE BABY BOOMER EMPLOYEES

Surveys in recent years have indicated that employees have increasingly less faith in their workplace leaders. More and more employees are skeptical of their leaders and uncertain that they can be trusted to make the right decisions. In fact, a growing number of employees say that they're not even sure that their leaders are honest with them. Other areas of American life are similarly affected with a distrust toward leadership.

So what's going on?

This is an excellent example of a cohort effect in the workplace. Leading this trend toward distrust in the workplace, and in society as a whole, is a group we call the Trailing-Edge Boomer Cohort. This cohort came of age during a time of economic turmoil, political scandal, and social upheaval, so the members of this cohort learned early on not to put their faith in leaders, but to rely on themselves.

The Benefits Conundrum

When employers survey Trailing-Edge Boomers to ask them what they want, good benefits often top the list. Remember that the members of this cohort experienced a lousy economy when they were in late adolescence and early adulthood, and so they prize financial security. Employers with sufficiently deep pockets are trying to satisfy this desire. But what if a company keeps these employees on the payroll for years after the employees wish they could have retired? Will they be productive, or will they prove a hidden drain on the company?

A *Workforce* magazine analysis of this problem observed that "by providing benefits, employers may be unnecessarily keeping boomers tied to them — while boomers may grow increasingly resentful that they have to work at all. Will employers really be getting the best out of them in this scenario? Probably not."

We think that rather than worrying about retaining every employee from this cohort into old age, employers should focus on identifying the individuals whose

There are similarities between the Leading-Edge Baby Boomers and the Trailing-Edge Baby Boomers — individualism and self-indulgence are two that come to mind. But, as we point out in Chapter 6, there is a fundamental difference in attitude between these two generational cohorts. This is due mainly to differences in their coming-of-age experiences. Leading-Edge Boomers internalized the hope and idealism of the '60s, optimistic times that were fueled by a booming economy. Trailing-Edge Boomers, meanwhile, were shaped by the cynicism and fear that came with Watergate, a plunging economy, and the fall of Saigon.

Trailing-Edge Boomers' experience of economically trying times and traumatic political events created a greater tendency in this cohort to withdraw or hold back out of fear of being hurt. In the workplace, this trait can translate into an unwillingness to put themselves at too great a risk.

expertise, enthusiasm, and commitment make them exceptional employees — and then offer them more money so that they can afford to take care of any gaps in their healthcare or retirement planning on their own.

Providing lifetime security for all employees of this cohort would be nice, but if doing so means doubling the costs of retirement and healthcare benefits for the entire workforce, then it's not going to pass the bottom-line test. Better to figure out which of your Trailing-Edge Boomers are really key and want to step up to the next level, then work on keeping them around long after that age-55 retirement goal by giving them meaningful work and a good salary.

Plenty of younger employees are coming up through the ranks who are willing to take on more responsibility and who can replace any Trailing-Edge Boomers who don't want to be there, but are just hanging on to take advantage of the benefits.

Source: Jennifer Laabs, "What If They Don't Retire?"
Workforce, Dec. 1997 v76 n12, p. 54.

Trust is always an issue for any cohort that experiences bad events in its formative years — especially if these events take people by surprise or are shocking. Although Trailing-Edgers are often described as cynical, keep in mind that they arrived at their cynicism through anxiety or a fear of being undercut by bad events.

In this chapter, we explore many aspects of this cohort. Their cynicism and their underlying concern that the institutions and leaders they rely on may break their trust is, in our view, perhaps the most important issue when it comes to managing this cohort. Also, the members of this cohort are poorly prepared economically for retirement, and are now facing, or soon will be facing, a crisis in this aspect of their lives that cannot help but affect employers in fundamental ways.

UNMET EXPECTATIONS

Trailing-Edge Boomers began to enter the workforce in 1973 and were soon met with bitter disappointment. They were children during the '60s and so had seen the Leading-Edge Boomers living the good life. They expected and were promised that things would be very much the same for them. But that's not the way it turned out. Oil shocks sent the economy reeling, inflation reached new heights, and many people became pessimistic about their prospects for the future. And none were more pessimistic than the Trailing-Edge Boomers, who had come of age with great expectations, only to have them dashed.

The search for job satisfaction that had begun in the '60s continued into the '70s. People wanted interesting work, but because of the bad economic times, most were willing to settle for a paycheck. Worker participation, or workplace democracy, began to take hold in a few companies. This was the precursor to empowerment. Worker participation advocated workers having a say in how their work was done. Some companies experimented with this new concept, but most stuck to the old, established, hierarchical way of management.

Women began entering the workforce in greater numbers during the '70s and '80s. Many of these were young Trailing-Edge Boomers intent on having it all. They were Supermoms on the fast track. But they found that being all things to all people was not easy. They experienced great stress in their lives.

The economy improved in the '80s, and Trailing-Edge Boomers felt it was time to make up for lost time. They became young, urban professionals, or Yuppies, a new term that represented all of their materialism and self-focus. The '80s also brought a flurry of new management fads that promised bottom-line results. Managers were to become more lovable, and workers got more of a say in how their jobs were done. Japanese-style quality circles became popular, and developing the right corporate culture became the obsession of many executives.

But the Trailing-Edgers ran into more hard times in the early '90s downsizings. Those who weren't downsized became painfully aware of the concept of *plateauing,* which we'll talk more about later. Because of their large numbers, they were told not to expect much in the way of future promotions or advancement. It was déjà vu all over again for this cohort. They felt they were slapped down again just as they were starting to enjoy the lifestyle they had always wanted.

THE TRAILING-EDGE BOOMERS TODAY

At 49 million strong, Trailing-Edge Boomers are the largest generational cohort group. They are ages 37 to 47 in 2002, and some are now in the ranks of middle management. A few have even advanced to upper management. But promotions have not been as forthcoming for this cohort as they have been for older workers. One major factor is the large size of this cohort — supply and demand dictates that opportunities for advancement are hard to come by. And the relatively large size of the Leading-Edge Boomer Cohort doesn't help matters much. This older group has slowed, and in some cases blocked, the advancement of younger Boomers.

This demographic bottleneck has helped to stymie wage growth. Annual raises fell from 5.2% in 1990 to 4.2% in 1999. Variable pay, however, such as stock options and bonuses, increased from 4% of payroll to nearly 10% during the same time frame. Trailing-Edge Boomers tend to value money, so these types of one-time variable awards are one way to motivate and retain them when promotions or big raises aren't possible.[1]

TRAILING-EDGE BOOMER DEFINING MOMENTS

This cohort came of age from 1973 to 1983 — a decade of scandal, social unrest, and skyrocketing inflation. In 1973, President Richard Nixon set aside hopes of ever winning the Vietnam War and arranged for U.S. soldiers to begin returning home. Most Trailing-Edge Boomers were too young to have actually served in the war, but they clearly remember the negative reaction these returning veterans received. And they remember the fall of Saigon in 1975 — an event that etched images of U.S. failure on the minds of this cohort.

When President Richard Nixon resigned amid scandal in 1974, many Americans completely lost faith in government and public officials, but none more so than Trailing-Edge Boomers. Because they were in their impressionable coming-of-age years, Nixon's involvement in Watergate forever made them suspicious of public officials and authority figures.

The energy crisis, coupled with high inflation and rising unemployment, only worsened matters. After two decades of prosperity, America was in recession. Trailing-Edge Boomers had seen the prosperity and optimism that had met their older brothers and sisters as they entered adulthood, and they felt ripped off. This feeling of having missed out remains with them today.

Trailing-Edge Baby Boomer Defining Moments

+ Watergate

+ Nixon resigns

+ The fall of Saigon

+ The energy crisis

TRAILING-EDGE BOOMER VALUES

Even now that they are approaching middle age, many Trailing-Edge Boomers still feel bitter about what they missed out on in their youth. To Trailing-Edge Boomers, the deck was stacked against them from the start, and they still carry much of this cynicism. It hasn't helped matters that their large numbers have diminished opportunities for job advancement in the workplace. The promotions bottleneck has tended to make them a very competitive lot. In this section, we present their key cohort values and concerns.

LONELY INDIVIDUALISM

Because of the uncertainty in their coming-of-age years, many Trailing-Edge Boomers seek control over many aspects of their lives. Delegating authority or trusting others to get the job done is tough for them — a trait that often creates problems in the workplace. Many have gotten the reputation for being control freaks or micromanagers.

SNAPSHOT OF THE TRAILING-EDGE BOOMER COHORT

Name of Cohort:	Trailing-Edge Boomer
Born between:	1955 to 1965
Coming of Age:	1973 to 1983
Age in 2002:	37 to 47
Population:	49 million (22%)

Key Cohort Values and Concerns

- ✦ Lonely individualism
- ✦ Cynicism and distrust, especially of government
- ✦ Health and wellness
- ✦ Family commitments

Current and Next Lifestage

- ✦ Home ownership
- ✦ Childrearing into teenage years
- ✦ Divorce and remarriage
- ✦ Career changes

Emotions and Affinities

- ✦ Casual
- ✦ Politically ambivalent
- ✦ Overt materialism
- ✦ Sexual freedom

Physiographic Profile

- ✦ First markers of aging
- ✦ Acute health conditions

SNAPSHOT

If given a choice, Trailing-Edge Boomers would almost always prefer to do the job themselves and not rely on other people. This kind of lonely individualism tends to undermine the effectiveness of teams. As a manager, you can accept the anti-team instincts of the Trailing-Edgers and avoid putting members of this cohort into team situations. But not placing these individuals on teams is difficult to do. A more attractive option may be offering remedial training on how to work together on a team and backing this up by rewarding team-oriented, rather than individual-centric, behavior.

CYNICISM AND DISTRUST OF GOVERNMENT

This cohort's cynicism and distrust of government is relevant in the workplace because it extends to anyone in a position of authority. Trailing-Edge Boomers made the cartoon character Dilbert, with his irreverent look at management, a popular icon in the American workplace. To many, Dilbert says and does things they can only dream of. Managers must work extra hard to win the trust of this cohort. Don't promise more than you can deliver, because good intentions will get you nowhere with this group. In talking about new corporate initiatives, for example, stick to the facts. Don't try to embellish reality with rosy scenarios about what the future *might* hold.

HEALTH AND WELLNESS

Trailing-Edge Boomers tend to be very health conscious — a side-effect of having come of age during the fitness craze of the '70s and early '80s. As with Leading-Edge Boomers, they are likely to appreciate a company gym, company-sponsored fitness activities, such as a 5K run or softball tournament, and having low-fat choices in the company cafeteria. These kinds of perks help with employee retention, but don't forget that they are unlikely to counter a bad working environment.

FAMILY COMMITMENTS

This cohort is looking to balance work life with family commitments, even more so than the Leading-Edge Boomers. The older group tried to have it all, and their attempts to be rising stars at work *and* Ward and June Cleaver at home largely failed. Women, in particular, found out that the Supermom ideal was largely unattainable. Younger Boomers later learned that having a stellar career often meant sacrificing family. Many were not willing to do that.

Their decision to simply have an okay career and to put family first was made easier by the fact that their large numbers made it difficult to get ahead anyway. Younger cohorts also value family commitments, a fact that makes flex time, work-at-home options, and part-time opportunities even more popular today.

LIFESTAGE

Trailing-Edge Boomers are maxed out on a lot of fronts these days. They are in the midst of several lifestages — childrearing and career changes, in particular — that often are at odds with each other.

Unlike members of the Ghost and Postwar Cohorts, most members of this cohort are part of dual-income families. This cohort has seen opportunities for women expand dramatically, and mom isn't always at home to pick up the slack so dad can work late every night. Somebody has to leave work on time to pick up the kids from daycare. This can create tension at work when employees are expected to work overtime. All the more reason for managers to know what is going on in their employees' lives. At the same time, being part of a dual-income family provides an economic cushion against hard times, although many consumption-oriented Trailing-Edge Boomers are spending practically every dime that comes in.

HOME OWNERSHIP

Having missed out on some of the fun when coming of age, the Trailing-Edge Boomers are now very much into living large. For many, their home is not just a haven from the stress of the outside world, but a major status symbol as well. Remember, members of this cohort were financially deprived as they came of age. For them, money talks . . . and so does the status associated with their houses. As they have risen up the ranks at work, they have tended to buy bigger and bigger houses. Larger and larger mortgage payments have effectively locked many into their current jobs.

Living paycheck-to-paycheck makes it tough to take a risk and try something new. And as they approach retirement, this cohort's high living expenses mean that they have not saved as much as earlier cohorts did. Combine a lack of savings with increasing pressure on employers to reduce the costs of funding employee benefits and retirement plans, and you have the makings of a serious problem on a national scale. How will members of this cohort afford to retire? Many of them believe they cannot stop working — yet many employers eventually expect this cohort to step aside in favor of the next. We will look at this problem more fully at the end of this chapter when we make some recommendations about this cohort's future in the workplace.

CHILDREARING INTO TEENAGE YEARS

Many Trailing-Edge Boomers have teenagers at home, while others are becoming parents for the first time. This is quite a change from older workers, who rarely had children in their 40s, unless by accident. Because most of this cohort's children were planned, they want the very best for their kids. And with the number of divorces and blended families on the rise, quality time with the kids is becoming a hot commodity. Managers can no longer assume that employees will automatically work overtime. If children are involved, parents may need to pick them up from daycare, attend their soccer match, or make sure they get to ballet lessons on time.

To motivate and reward Trailing-Edgers, make sure you first get to know their individual situation to see if they are able to, or want to, work extra hours. If they are single parents with small children, for example, don't expect them to stay late. Reward them and other parents with time off to spend with their kids, and you may find that their productivity during regular work hours rises dramatically. Also, seek ways to involve their families in the workplace. One company creates a corporate calendar featuring art done by employees' children. Others sponsor youth sports teams, hold company picnics in local parks with games for the children, and operate on-site daycare centers.

And as this cohort's children age, we expect to see the focus of such programs change in age-specific ways. For instance, it would be appropriate to hold a college placement day on a Saturday morning at the office, inviting in experts to do workshops and even getting representatives from local colleges to come and speak about their programs and admission processes.

Divorce and remarriage

These days, nearly one out of every seven 40-somethings is divorced. This is twice the ratio from 1975. This group also has high rates for remarriage and stepparenting. In fact, by 2007, blended families are expected to outnumber traditional nuclear families for the first time. This means you can expect many of your employees from this cohort (and younger cohorts) to be facing challenges associated with divorce, single parenting, social pressures over their nontraditional relationships, or other lifestyle-oriented stresses. Although these situations may not seem relevant to work at first glance, a person's emotional status certainly can affect his or her work performance. Something as simple as difficulty sleeping at night — a common result of stress — is a major but seldom-recognized cause of poor workplace performance.

Employers and managers simply need to be sensitive to such issues and to help employees cope with stresses that may linger for months or years when, for example, they struggle through a difficult divorce.

Career changes

With company loyalty a dusty relic of the past, Trailing-Edge Boomers are now pursuing their own self-focused career paths. This often leads to career changes, as they find they have better opportunities in other companies than in their current company.

Like many workers from younger cohorts, Trailing-Edgers are willing to climb the corporate ladder until they find a better deal. Because of their large numbers, they have heard the plateauing speech more than once. Plateauing calls for employees to be satisfied with where they are and to not expect anything more than lateral job moves for the rest of their career. This may be fine for some employees, but Trailing-Edge Boomers are competitive, and most of them are not about to roll over and accept that it doesn't get any better than this. And so the exodus of Trailing-Edgers looking for the promised land — or at least a better job — has begun.

But it is not always easy for them to find better opportunities, and some feel the urge to go but are trapped by a vested retirement or pension plan that loses some or all of its value if they leave. The need to stick with a job for another three or five years in order to qualify for retirement compensation isn't enough to motivate workers on a daily basis, and Boomers who stick around for that reason are increasingly disillusioned and down about their work — and in danger of spreading their negative attitude to others.

EMOTIONS AND AFFINITIES

Like the older Boomers, this cohort is very much into self-indulgence. But they are a bit more conspicuous about it. Their emotions and affinities reflect this focus.

CASUAL

The Trailing-Edge Boomers welcomed more casual dress codes at work, and this reflects their attitudes in other areas. They prefer informal exchanges of information to sitting through a formal, two-hour meeting. They also tend to prefer more casual and friendly relationships with their bosses. They want to be able to joke around and not worry about the formal codes of conduct that were big with the Ghost Cohorts.

The Trailing-Edge Boomer manager's emphasis on casualness can be confusing to the younger Gen X and N Gen Cohorts. For example, if the boss routinely goes out for a drink after work with the employees he or she supervises, they begin to see the boss as just one of the guys. This is wonderful, if it helps build rapport. But if employees don't observe some professional boundaries with their supervisor, they can put themselves into a very difficult situation when it comes time for a raise or promotion.

POLITICALLY AMBIVALENT

This cohort came of age in the midst of Watergate and the fall of Saigon, a time when trust in authority hit rock bottom. As a result, they tend to be ambivalent when it comes to national politics and ideological issues, such as school prayer and flag burning.

However, when it comes to issues that affect them or their families directly, such as school reform or the company health plan, Trailing-Edgers tend to take a much more active role. The same is true for office politics.

Younger workers criticize them for the inordinate amount of time they seem to spend posturing for more status at work. But this is all part of their competitive nature, and they are doubtful that the established political process will serve their interests. In managing them, make sure to include them in the decision-making process, when feasible. Obviously, if an immediate response is needed, you cannot afford to permit lengthy politicking. But if there is time to consider options, let the members of this cohort design a process that will generate and evaluate those options.

OVERT MATERIALISM

Trailing-Edge Boomers feel they missed out on all of the prosperity that older Boomers enjoyed during their coming-of-age years, and they are now trying to fulfill their unmet needs. To tap into this affinity, reward members of this cohort with things like first-class plane tickets and luxury hotels for business travel. Financial rewards and status symbols are great motivators for this group. They respond well to bonuses, higher commission rates, and the old standby — salary raises. These are a means to the end of improving their social position in relation to their older Boomer counterparts.

SEXUAL FREEDOM

Trailing-Edge Boomers came of age before AIDS and after the pill, so they had greater sexual freedom than members of any cohort before or since. This group also came of age during the women's movement, which contributed to a growing trend toward sexual equality. Times have certainly changed, but Trailing-Edge Boomers still have liberal attitudes about such things as premarital sex, living together, and adult themes on TV. Many of them also have a permissive view of affairs — both extra-marital and intra-office. This attitude towards sex can lead to behavior that generates complaints of sexual harassment and, even when no charges are leveled, to tension and uncomfortable situations for others in the workplace. It is important to establish clear limits to sexual behavior in the workplace, and to make sure these are understood and respected. A clear sexual harassment policy is needed, and it should be communicated in multiple ways and at multiple times to make sure that the message stays fresh in employees' minds.

PHYSIOGRAPHIC PROFILE

As they reach their 40th birthdays and beyond, physiographics are beginning to be a factor for this cohort. These physical changes still aren't the strong drivers of behavior that they are for older cohorts, but as Trailing-Edge Boomers age, look for their physical condition to have more and more impact.

And look for rising benefits costs, too. The large number of people in this cohort are going to spend healthcare dollars at record levels in the U.S. in the coming years. Anything employers can do to help Trailing-Edgers manage their health wisely will pay off dramatically in healthcare savings. Poor health affects the bottom line directly through benefits, lost days, and the premature loss of expertise, as well as indirectly through the portion of state and federal taxes that has to go to healthcare-related expenses.

Your company can take actions now to reduce future costs. For example, wellness programs aimed at helping employees reduce smoking, lose weight, increase exercise, and shift their diets away from indulgently high levels of fat are likely to reduce the amount of heart disease — which is the most important health threat for this cohort in the coming years and the one that will cost them and their employers the most money.

FIRST MARKERS OF AGING

The earliest signs of aging typically start to become apparent some-where around the mid-30s. That's when hair begins to gray and fall out, weight begins to accumulate around the middle, hearing declines start to become noticeable, and vision continues to degrade. Most physiographic changes will not affect a person's work at this point, but in years to come they will have more of an impact.

Having come of age during the fitness craze of the late '70s and early '80s, Trailing-Edge Boomers tend to be very health conscious. They are much healthier than their parents were at the same age. Deaths from heart disease and cancer have dropped dramatically, and this cohort is less likely to smoke and drink than older cohorts.

This group also wants to look good to stay competitive in the work-place. There is an unspoken understanding at many companies that older people just aren't keeping up with the latest technology or ways of thinking. While this perception is often completely false, it remains. As a result, no one wants to be seen as "the old fart" or the old lady.

Hair dyes, liposuction, face lifts, and other cosmetic procedures are popular with both male and female members of this cohort. Members of this cohort want to stay young as long as possible. Looking their best is also a way that the Trailing-Edgers can stay competitive with those Leading-Edge Boomers in front of them in the promotional pipeline.

One simple way to help harness this pro-youth sentiment in the workplace is to have members of the Trailing-Edge Boomer Cohort work on or lead teams of younger workers. While they may need a little leadership training, they will enjoy the chance to "hang" with younger workers and will feel younger themselves.

Trailing-Edge Boomer Strengths

- ✦ Openness
- ✦ Creativity
- ✦ Individualism
- ✦ Innovation
- ✦ Focus on health and welfare
- ✦ Entrepreneurship

UNIQUE STRENGTHS

Trailing-Edge Baby Boomers have a lot to offer businesses today. In this section, we write about the strong points that characterize many Trailing-Edgers.

OPENNESS

This cohort grew up at a time when women and minorities had more opportunities and were more likely to encounter positive role models in the workplace. As a result, more of this cohort participates fully in the economy than earlier cohorts, and it is much more open than older cohorts to people of different cultures and backgrounds. In particular, this cohort is a leader in bringing women and minorities into prominent roles in business and making opportunities available to them. This cohort has generated record numbers of women- and minority-owned new businesses. Trailing-Edgers also have run into many glass ceilings, and indeed put this term into our vocabulary, so there is still an unfinished agenda for later cohorts to take up.

CREATIVITY

This cohort's strong bent toward individualism, coupled with its willingness to question authority, contributes to this group's highly creative nature. If you're looking for an answer that is outside the box, letting a member of this cohort lead efforts to find a solution gives you a good chance of success.

INDIVIDUALISM

Their early experiences with the failure of government leaders made Trailing-Edgers at least a little suspicious of all leaders. They are not likely to trust their business leaders blindly. As a result, they have helped usher in many changes in business, and have been open to new ideas, such as total quality management, which was at first strongly opposed by senior executives in the '80s, but which appeals to Trailing-Edge Boomers because it takes power out of the hands of a few executives.

TECHNOLOGICAL INNOVATION

Younger cohorts are often credited with being computer whiz kids, but Trailing-Edge Boomers are the ones who first showed widespread enthusiasm for using new technologies in key business processes. As a result, these younger Boomers are the real innovators in the technology revolution. From the start, Trailing-Edge Boomers have been open-minded about the introduction of new technologies, particularly those that give individuals more freedom, choice, and access to information. This is consistent with their core values. The rise of e-mail, for example, has made it possible to have more dispersed organizations that can coordinate daily, even by the hour or minute, for fast response. The Internet has been integrated into business life in large part because middle managers from this cohort have seen its value.

FOCUS ON HEALTH AND WELLNESS

This cohort's focus on health and wellness has been important in refocusing compensation and benefits practices to a more holistic model. Employers are far more likely today to offer flexible, broad-ranging benefits aimed at improving employees' quality of life and general welfare. Alternative healthcare is becoming mainstream, thanks in good part to Boomers. Companies in some areas of the country might offer spa memberships or on-site day spas that offer massage therapy/reflexology, hypnotherapy, dance and humor therapy, and therapeutic touch therapy. Yoga and Tai Chi are also relaxation activities favored by Trailing-Edge Boomers. Maybe these offerings seem unusual, but they might be embraced in seemingly unexpected, more conservative parts of the country.

Things like eldercare, maternity/paternity leave, daycare referral programs, on-site fitness clubs, and so on are all becoming more mainstream. This is largely because the Trailing-Edge Baby Boomer Cohort has always put such issues high on their own agenda, whether as employees seeking jobs or as managers designing them.

ENTREPRENEURSHIP

Some Trailing-Edge Boomers have proven to be great innovators in technical and marketing areas, and, as a result, have turned out to be brilliant entrepreneurs. Entrepreneurism suits Trailing-Edgers' individualism. If you want to retain them and keep them engaged, create some kind of *intrapreneurial* option for them. Intrapreneurship is letting employees act like entrepreneurs, but within the same company and with fewer restrictions on their work behavior. It frees them from the bonds that many company policies impose. Trailing-Edgers like the idea of working on cutting-edge technology or projects, so lure them with this bait, then back off and give them room to work. They, like Gen-Xers, don't want the boss constantly looking over their shoulder.

THE INDIVIDUALIST WORK PATH AND TRAILING-EDGE BOOMERS

To attract, retain, motivate, and reward Trailing-Edge Boomers, make a conscious effort to appeal to their core values. The individualist work path suits them the best. Individualists don't join a company or stick with a job because they believe in the company. They aren't strongly motivated by affiliation. Yet, companies traditionally emphasize their overall reputations and rely on their reputations in recruiting.

Trailing-Edge Boomers are often willing to turn down an offer from a company like IBM and take one from an unknown high-tech startup if the latter seems to offer more opportunities for individual expression and the potential for personal achievement and future growth. Name recognition is nice, but this competitive cohort wants to know "What's in it for me?" In this regard, they are similar to Gen-Xers.

To recruit Trailing-Edgers, focus on what they can do to make individual contributions and to make a difference through their work. Also, address the chronic problem this cohort faces—a lack of clear pathways to career development and promotion. Between the flattening of organizational structure (a response to the economic need to make businesses more flexible and responsive) and the clogging of middle-management ranks due to the large size of this cohort and the one that precedes it, formal advancement opportunities are hard for Trailing-Edgers to find. They need to be given other sorts of opportunities.

Teams provide a good vehicle for giving Trailing-Edgers new opportunities and can fit in well with the individualist work path, if formed correctly. Develop charter teams to do innovative things, and let members of this cohort lead the team. But make sure the team has real autonomy and is not micromanaged to death, or else its members will quickly get discouraged.

This cohort sees training as a vehicle for the pursuit of individual interests and the development of unique capabilities. The ever-popular, one-size-fits-all job orientation isn't going to cut it with this group. In fact, they are likely to see this kind of watered-down overview as completely useless.

Members of this cohort really like being able to select what training topics, courses, or workshops they get to take. They like being able to rate their trainings afterward and have their views truly shape future offerings. They are forcing corporate training departments to create university-style curricula and to treat them like customers. Training can't be "done" to them. Instead, they want it to be meaningful and to provide a valuable experience that meets their individual needs.

FUTURE OUTLOOK AND CONCLUSION

Over the next decade, Trailing-Edgers will come to their peak earnings period and reach their pinnacle corporate positions. They will be looking for more ways to enjoy their new lifestages of empty-nesting and grand-parenting. Their financial and family obligations will increasingly be reduced, and they will indulge themselves to a greater degree than in recent years. Trailing-Edgers' managers will need to take into account these new life roles. Leadership of this cohort will be a new challenge.

Getting past their cynicism and finding ways to build their trust in your leadership is the key to working effectively with this cohort. By understanding that trust has two separate dimensions — rule keeping and caregiving — you can better anticipate what events or actions will undermine employees' sense of trust, and then take appropriate action. Managing trust involves defining unwritten and unspoken rules and creating shared expectations. Building and maintaining trust with Trailing-Edge Boomer employees should be a top priority for all managers. Too often, trust is violated in the workplace because of poor communication and unrealistic expectations.

Managers must provide sufficient structure to their Trailing-Edgers, but also must make sure their emotional side is attended to. Trailing-Edgers must be made to feel that "they're OK." Just telling them what's expected is not sufficient. Also tell them how well they're doing.

Keeping Your Trailing-Edge Stars Shining

Don Hutcheson and Bob McDonald are the founders of a company, called The Highlands Program, that special-izes in employee development and training. Their ideas about how to manage employees are particularly well-suited to the challenges of managing Trailing-Edge Boomers. They argue that "when people do the work of carefully lining themselves up with their companies, they don't feel like jumping ship."

Their approach is to make sure employees are doing what they do best. Aligning an employee's interests and expertise with important work creates a strong com-mitment to that work and a higher level of motivation than any benefits package or salary can.

With Trailing-Edge Boomers, this goal of self-actualization may have to be combined with a customized approach to balance work and family life. But if you are providing flexibility for your star employees at the same time that you're tapping into their greatest strengths and skills, then the trouble of doing so is certainly justified.

We might sum up this strategy as follows:

1. Find out what your employee is best at.

2. Align their expertise with a meaningful challenge to maximize their contribution and commitment.

3. Give them the flexibility to pursue this challenge in their own way and on their own schedule as much as possible.

These steps work well with the individualist work path. The solution to the conundrum of how to keep Trailing-Edge Boomers committed to their work (and not just their benefits) is to track them into an individual-expression path.

Those who have special skills that match company needs should be engaged in the three-step process described above. If the three-step process is followed, employees will be aligned so as to provide maximum benefit to their employer. This should make them worth their weight in gold, thereby making it practical to retain them through both compensation and work alignment.

Source: Hutcheson, Don and Bob McDonald, "Employees Desire More Than Money and Perks," Business Journal, Sept. 29, 2000, v17 i18 p. 34.

ENDNOTE

1. Conlin, Michelle and Peter Coy. "The Wild New Workforce," *Business Week,* December 6, 1999, p. 38 (6).

CHAPTER 8

UNDERSTANDING YOUR GENERATION X EMPLOYEES

Typically, when employees are given an opportunity to choose their own job titles, most come up with something very close to what they already had — Senior Account Manager, for example, or Technology Consultant. But when managers at InteQ, a management service provider based in Bedford, Massachusetts, told a senior graphic designer to come up with her own title, she chose one she felt truly described her work overseeing the company's graphic design needs: She now calls herself a Crayon Evangelist.[1]

Of course, she is a Gen-Xer, one of those quirky kids who have turned the workplace upside down in recent years. A slew of articles have been written about how to recruit, retain, and motivate this generational cohort. Some of the conventional wisdom on Gen-Xers is helpful, but some of it has unfortunately spread negative stereotypes that tend to stimulate conflict and discord. In this chapter, we try to sort out fact from fiction, as the saying goes.

The hardest part about managing Gen-Xers is that they're not Boomers. And at this point in their careers, most of their bosses are either Leading-Edge or Trailing-Edge Boomers. Gen-Xers disdain the long hours, office politics, and time away from family that Boomers took for granted during their climb up the ladder. This backlash against the Boomers often makes for a difficult working environment. But managers can get beyond this by taking time to really understand and get to know their Gen-X employees, setting up an appropriate work path to meet their needs, and developing mentoring programs to bridge the cohort gaps.

From McJobs to Reengineering

When they were children, their parents typically worked full-time, leaving Gen-Xers to their own devices as latchkey kids. As a result, Xers assumed many adult responsibilities, such as shopping, making dinner, and watching younger siblings, at a much younger age than members of previous cohorts did. Gen-Xers early household responsibilities were even greater in cases where their parents were divorced — and there was an increased rate of divorce among their Postwar and Leading-Edge Boomer parents.

When it came time for them to enter the job market in the late '80s and early '90s, Xers were largely met with disappointment. *Reengineering, downsizing, right-sizing, lean organizations,* and *delayering* were just a few of the buzzwords that welcomed Gen-Xers into the wonderful world of work. These were lean times for corporate America. The difficult job market, a declining economy, and a huge national debt sapped Gen-Xers, who were at the brink of adulthood, of much of their hope for the future.

Many young workers found getting a decent-paying job in their field difficult, at best. When Xers began looking for the on-ramp to a career path, many found themselves headed down a dead-end road. They started working at *McJobs* instead. These were jobs with little future — secretarial work for temp agencies, for example. Gen-Xers were under-employed on a massive scale.

Unable to support themselves on what they made, many had no choice but to live with Mom and/or Dad. In fact, they were the largest group of young adults to live with their parents since the Great Depression. To make matters worse, some of their parents, loyal

Postwars, found themselves suddenly out of a job after 20 or 30 years of service. This experience left Gen-Xers with a lingering antipathy toward corporate America.

In the midst of all this upheaval, many companies focused on building new corporate cultures. Because most of the middle managers were gone, there was a greater need for employees to do more with less. Reengineering focused on using new technologies to coordinate tasks so that one person could do them. Reengineering was not only supposed to make employees more efficient, but it was also supposed to make their jobs more varied, and thus more interesting. It was the opposite of scientific management, which had been popularized earlier in the twentieth century with the rise of the assembly line. Scientific management broke complex tasks apart and assigned each to workers who repeated the same tasks over and over again. Reengineering grouped tasks together and empowered employees to make decisions on their own.

But as is often the case with new management theories, managers didn't fully embrace the concepts. They used all the right buzzwords (*empowerment, teams, self-directed workforce*), but in practice many found it hard to change their mindset away from the hierarchical system of the Ghost Cohorts. "I'm the boss, and you do as you're told" was their default style of managing. While this approach had worked in the past, it did not work at all with Generation Xers. When faced with such a boss, Xers either quit to do something totally different, or they jumped ship and went to work for someone else. They saw no reason to stick around and take what they perceived as abuse.

In many cases, cross-functional reengineering teams succeeded in redesigning work flows and coming up with significant cost and quality improvements. And in many cases, the employees working on such teams were highly engaged in the challenges of the work and proud of the results. However, these projects culminated in efficiency gains that often led directly to layoffs — sometimes of the very people who had staffed the reengineering effort. It is easy to react cynically to layoffs, and many Gen-Xers did.

Technology was an area in which Gen-Xers clearly excelled from the start. When e-mail and the Internet first started to appear in the office, most Xers already knew how to use them. The same is true with cell phones and pagers. They were right there teaching Boomers how to log on, surf the web, and use their wireless communications tools. They, along with the N Generation Cohort that follows them, have continued to stay ahead of the technology curve. No wonder that they were at the center of the dot.com bubble. Gen-Xers' comfort with technology sometimes puts them at odds with Boomers, particularly Leading-Edge Boomers, who are often not as comfortable with technology as the young people they supervise.

THE GENERATION X COHORT TODAY

Today, members of the Generation X Cohort are working at real careers and are an integral part of the American workplace. They have moved out of Mom and Dad's house, and are beginning to put the slacker image behind them. Today, they are "knowledge workers in the new information economy!" (At least many are, if they didn't get laid off by a failed dot.com.) They are hard working (when they want to be — more on motivation later) and have a driving entrepreneurial spirit. In fact, they were behind many of the dot.com success stories of the late '90s and early 2000s. Times have since toughened, but Xers have nevertheless made a lasting impact on the workplace.

Their smaller numbers have finally begun to work to their advantage, opening up more opportunities at a younger age. While Xers have matured, they still see themselves as free agents, and tend to put their own interests ahead of the company or team. This attitude might more clearly be expressed as a feeling that the company is not going to look after them very carefully (any more than their parents did) and that they had better take responsibility for themselves. Given the work climate they have experienced, with frequent job hopping and waves of layoffs, this attitude has been reinforced in many cases by work experiences.

Gen-Xers also tend to see their interests outside of work as being more important than their work. A Gen-Xer might view herself, for example, as a windsurfer or a mom who also happens to be an accountant. They have a strong sense of self that helps them be resilient in times of stress — they are less likely to be depressed when they lose their jobs, for example, than the Boomer Cohorts are. But because work is only one aspect of their lives, they can run into trouble with their bosses— Leading-Edge and Trailing-Edge Boomers who expect them to be dedicated to their work to the exclusion of all else. This difficulty is compounded by the fact that employers don't want Gen-Xers to expect too much from them too soon.

Convincing Xers to Trust

We feel that employers need to work harder to convince Xers to develop greater interdependence with their working group. Xers need to be convinced that trusting others and working together on a team is safe and will produce results.

This could be accomplished by making unbreakable promises of care and security — but that is unrealistic for employers today. We recommend that managers articulate honestly and clearly what employees can and cannot expect from their employer — what the limits of the compact binding them to their employer and vice versa really are. When someone is distrustful, full disclosure is the only way to do business! And Xers in survey after survey report that they don't trust their managers, don't think their employers trust them, and *want much better, more open, and more honest communication* with their employers.

But Xers are impatient. They don't want to wait around for 10 years for a good assignment — they want it *now,* or they will leave and try to find it somewhere else. They will never be the loyal subjects their parents were. They are more likely to jump from one job to another, piecing together marketable skills that they can sell down the line to the next employer.

GENERATION X DEFINING MOMENTS

The defining moments that shaped Generation X were largely a series of good-news events turned sour. As a result, this cohort lacks the optimism and idealism that bonds other cohorts together. But Gen-Xers are also more self-reliant than members of other cohorts.

When he took office in 1981, President Ronald Reagan implemented a plan to cut taxes and spending on social programs, while increasing spending on defense in an effort to jumpstart the stalled economy. Reaganomics, as the plan became known, did help to reduce interest rates and inflation and create new jobs, but the middle class and the poor largely felt left behind. The rich got richer and the poor got poorer under Reaganomics, and at a rate unprecedented in recent U.S. history. By the early '90s, the national debt had reached $4 trillion, and homelessness had become a new social issue. There seemed little hope for the young Gen-Xers just entering adulthood, typically a lifestage filled with anticipation and optimism about the future.

The AIDS epidemic was the fallout from the free love of the '60s and the sexual revolution of the '70s. The public became aware of this deadly new disease in the mid-'80s — just as Gen-Xers were coming of age. AIDS changed attitudes about sex among this cohort away from the promiscuity of the older Boomer Cohorts and toward a more cautious approach. *Safe sex* became a new buzzword, and most Gen-Xers came to expect free condom distribution in high schools and on college campuses. Interestingly, condom usage by this cohort was higher than among previous cohorts, but still not as high as one might think, given the high risk of STDs.

Many Gen-Xers watched the 1986 explosion of the *Challenger* space shuttle live on TVs in their classroom. It was a not-so-subtle reminder that, despite more than 20 successful shuttle missions, space flight still had its risks. The mission, which included the first ordinary citizen to be on a space mission — Christa McAuliffe, a social studies teacher from New Hampshire — was to include live broadcasts beamed to schools around the country. The failed mission affected Gen-Xers by making them realize there were no guarantees in this world, and that nothing should be taken for granted. The disastrous events of September 11, 2001, in which terrorists hijacked four planes and crashed them, killing thousands of people, were seen by Gen-Xers as a confirmation of this no-guarantees mentality, even though their core values were defined long before September 11.

On October 19, 1987, the stock market lost 22.6% of its value in a single day, marking a dramatic end to a high-flying bull market. The crash, along with earlier scandals involving insider trading, fraud, stock manipulation, and other securities violations, helped make Xers cynical and pessimistic about their future. They felt the rug was being pulled out from under them at a time when the red carpet had been rolled out for other cohorts.

One of the few positive events that shaped Generation X's coming-of-age years was the fall of the Berlin Wall in 1989. The image of East Germans pouring over the wall into West Germany gave Generation

Xers cause for optimism. It also made them feel part of a wider global community. Here was a glimmer of hope in an otherwise gloomy series of defining moments.

To many Gen-Xers, the 1991 Gulf War seemed more like a video game or a movie than a real war. While many Gen-Xers served in the military during the war, most Xers were not directly affected by the confrontation. Most stayed home and watched the war on CNN from the comfort of their living rooms. Yet the war did shape Gen-X attitudes about war and violence, contributing to an even greater cynicism about government and the role of oil in our modern world. But the unique circumstances of the Gulf War made it unlike any previous war. It was much shorter, fewer lives were lost, and no draft was required. To Generation X, the war seemed like it was happening to *other* people, not to them personally. They saw the Gulf War as if it were a major television event rather than a major societal event.

GEN-X VALUES

The difference in values between the Baby Boomers (both sets) and Gen-Xers is so pronounced that it's no wonder these groups have trouble getting along in the workplace. Boomers have paid their dues and now feel they deserve some deference and respect from underlings. But Gen-Xers are not likely to do as they're told without a lengthy explanation of why it's important and what's in it for them. In this section, we address their key cohort values and concerns.

FREE AGENCY AND INDEPENDENCE

Many Gen-Xers had parents who were divorced and/or both working full-time when they were growing up, so members of this cohort learned early on to be independent. In the workplace, their free agency and independence tends to get them into trouble with Boomer managers and supervisors. Gen-Xers tend to focus on their own achievements, and don't possess much team loyalty. This pioneering spirit makes Gen-Xers excellent entrepreneurs. To harness this value, don't assign them to a traditional team and expect them to thrive. Give them some autonomy and room to be creative, and you may be surprised by what they come up with. They, like Trailing-Edge Boomers, may also benefit from a booster shot of training in how to work effectively on a team.

SNAPSHOT OF THE GENERATION X COHORT

Name of Cohort:	Generation X
Born between:	1966–76
Coming of Age:	1984–94
Age in 2002:	26–36
Population:	42 million (19%)

Key Cohort Values and Concerns
- Free agency and independence
- Friendships important
- Cynical about future
- Street-smart
- Pursuit of quality of life
- Acceptance of violence and sex

Current and Next Lifestage
- Graduate school
- Career search
- Cohabitation/First child
- Marriage
- Home ownership

Emotions and Affinities
- Environmental concerns
- Social, sexual, and ethnic diversity
- Sexually cautious
- Global community

Physiographic Profile
- Invincible
- Earliest signs of aging

SNAPSHOT

While not wanting to be told directly what to do by supervisors, Gen-Xers tend to crave lots of feedback. They want to know how they are doing at all times. So don't wait until a project is done to offer praise or share information on performance. Touch base with them regularly and reinforce what they are doing right. Redirect Gen-Xers if they are not getting it right.

FRIENDSHIPS IMPORTANT

Because so many Xers are children of divorce, they put a lot of importance on friendships. In the workplace, they tend to value personal relationships and people more than corporate goals and job advancement. They prefer bosses who take a personal interest in them to bosses who keep things on a purely professional level. Take time to get to know the Gen-Xers on your staff, but do so only if you are genuinely interested in them. Xers are quickly turned off by phony managers and corporate game playing. You can also encourage friendships in the workplace by organizing after-work activities for the staff, such as intramural basketball or softball.

CYNICAL ABOUT FUTURE

Xers are cynical about what the future holds for them, mainly because of the dire events that marked their coming-of-age years. Xers feel they have been cheated by history, and they're not about to be duped again. As a result, many tend to distrust politicians, corporations, or anyone in a position of authority. This trait can make it tough for their managers to motivate them to do their best work. But, while self-reliant, they do like a challenge. In fact, issuing challenges is the best way to motivate them. Give Xers engaging work, and don't make promises you can't keep.

STREET-SMART

Gen-Xers grew up barraged by TV commercials, so they're very aware of being sold to. This makes them extremely savvy when it comes to advertising hype and rah-rah corporate initiatives. They are turned off by corporatisms such as *right-sizing* and *plateauing,* and want to avoid playing the corporate game as much as they can. Instead, they prefer straightforward internal communications that focus on how changes or new initiatives will affect them personally. Focus on communicating openly and honestly and without a lot of corporate positioning.

129

That Was Then, This Is Now

In the past, employees tended to defer to their bosses. That was how the game was played in the old hierarchical system. But today, as working relationships have grown more informal, employees tend to assert themselves more and often are empowered to make decisions without management approval.

At the same time, the level of respect that surrounded positions of authority in the past has been greatly reduced. In the '50s and '60s, it was unthinkable for junior employees to call their boss or a high-level executive by their first name, but today it's commonplace. Also, obedience was valued over independence, but today it's just the opposite.

Words like *boss* and *president* were once symbols of success and respect, but today's managers and executives often feel uncomfortable flaunting such titles. Why? Because they are members of younger cohorts who, unlike the Ghost Cohorts, do not tend to value authority.

While members of the Ghost Cohorts looked for stability in a job, today's Xers are looking for something completely different — a balance between work and private life, a chance to work independently, opportunities to use new technology, and workplaces that are more like communities.

Source: Conger, Jay A. "How Gen X Managers Manage," Strategy & Business, Issue 10, October 1988, p. 21 (8).

PURSUIT OF QUALITY OF LIFE

Gen-Xers' tireless pursuit of quality of life is probably the biggest difference between them and the Trailing-Edge Boomers. Trailing-Edge Boomers have tendencies toward workaholism, but Xers have been accused of having a heightened sense of entitlement that rivals that of the very rich. Xers learned long ago that work is just a paycheck, and that the things that really matter in life (family, friends, hobbies) are much more fun than work.

Gen-Xers want to enjoy life, and they don't want their work to get in the way. This trait can cause problems when the job requires overtime to get a project done. As a manager, if you can make the task interesting and exciting and give Xers some autonomy in how it gets done, rest assured that Xers will get the job done. Xers tend to embrace efforts to improve the quality of their work life, such as flex time, telecommuting, casual dress, and unpaid time off. To them, quality of life is important, and many would gladly trade money for free time. So reward them with extra vacation days and the freedom to spend time with their family, pursue a hobby, or do absolutely nothing.

Gen-Xers are the first cohort to expect work to be fun. They don't want to toil away in a miserable work environment for years with their only hope being that someday they will get to retire. If the work isn't fun, many Xers will quit and try to find a job that they can enjoy. Accentuate the fun by focusing on matching people with challenging projects and rewarding exceptional performance. And do fun and spontaneous things like bringing in ice cream, party hats, and noise makers when an important milestone is met. Or better yet, put the Xers on your staff in charge of such celebrations.

Feedback Tips for Managing Xers

In general, most employees need and want the most feedback when they are in the midst of working on a task, not after it is done.

This is especially true of Gen-X employees. Do not let them work in isolation (even if they seem to want to) and then zap them with negative feedback at the end. Instead, give them an information-rich flow of performance feedback along the way, and also make sure to note and praise effort and commitment when they are exhibited.

Many managers complain that their Xers aren't trying hard or don't seem committed — but these same managers have never taken the time to give positive feedback when they do see it. The easiest way to nurture a desired behavior among Gen-Xers is to encourage it when you see it. Positive feedback is a powerful tool for managing this cohort (as it is in general).

Buy a Harley and See the Country

In the late '90s, managers at one automotive manufac-
turer were delighted when they realized that a large
number of their new hires for production jobs were
college educated. It seemed to them that such a highly
educated workforce would give them a competitive
advantage.

Further investigation, however, revealed that this
college-educated segment had a high turnover rate. The
reason? Most were Gen-Xers. They were working long
hours at a time when wages were high to make just
enough money to quit and do something really exciting.
For example, one employee said he was working just long
enough to buy a Harley Davidson motorcycle, and then
he planned to take off and see the country.

Source: Smith, Brett C. "The Labor Gap and Meeting Gen X," Automotive
Manufacturing and Production, Nov. 1998, v. 110, p. 14.

LIFESTAGE

Gen-Xers are settling into many of the same lifestages that older cohorts
have already gone through. The primary difference is that Xers are
waiting longer to get married, have children, and buy a house than older
workers did.

CAREER SEARCH

This is the first cohort for whom the career search may never be completely over. Gen-Xers are always on the lookout for a bigger and better
opportunity. Rather than staying with one company for life, many Xers
are looking to build marketable job skills quickly, then move on to the
next opportunity. During their coming-of-age years, they saw their
parents downsized after years of being loyal to the company, and Xers
are not about to let that happen to themselves. Most realize that corporate loyalty will get them nowhere, so corporations are going to have to
focus more attention on attracting and retaining this group of employees.

For many Xers, learning new job skills through training is high on their list of motivators. This is true because they are looking ahead to the next job, but the desire to learn new skills can be used as a valuable retention tool as well.

Marriage, home ownership, and the first child

Generation X has delayed getting married and having kids longer than previous cohorts, but many Xers who are now in their 30s are looking to settle down, buy a house, and start a family. In many ways, this makes them more stable employees at work. They are less likely to be out all night partying with friends and accidentally oversleep. In fact, they are likely to be more dependable than ever, especially after having a child and buying a house. Suddenly the yoke of parental responsibility hangs on them, and this is a cohort that takes parenting seriously.

While these lifestages make Xers more stable employees, this cohort also wants time away from work to spend with spouses and children. They grew up as children of divorce and know the devastation that divorce can cause, and they want to avoid it at all costs. So unless there is a darn good reason, they won't be sticking around the office any later than 5 p.m. They are not interested in socializing with clients or colleagues after work hours, because they would rather have that time to spend with their family or in leisurely pursuits. One recent study showed that many highly skilled Gen-X engineers would choose lifestyle enhancement over career advancement, if given the choice.

Also, since most are part of dual-income families, moms *and* dads will sometimes need to take off work to care for a sick child. Don't hassle Xers about this, or they will find a more family-friendly boss or company to work for. On-site childcare centers or childcare referral programs help to attract and retain Xers who are in the new parent lifestage.

Emotions and Affinities

Gen-Xers came of age at a time when international travel and instantaneous global communication were making the world a smaller place. As a result, many of their emotions and affinities reflect this globalization.

ENVIRONMENTAL CONCERNS

Key events that took place during Gen-X's coming-of-age years, including the Exxon Valdez oil spill, the Chernobyl nuclear disaster, discovery of holes in the ozone layer, and a greater emphasis on the need for recycling, heightened this cohort's concern about the environment. Xers are likely to remain more loyal to a company that demonstrates a genuine concern for the environment and implements programs to, say, reduce greenhouse gases or reduce landfill waste. Another way to tap into this affinity is to reward Xers by encouraging them to volunteer one day a month at the local recycling center or with a favorite environmental group. Or, put them in charge of planning the company's Earth Day activities.

SOCIAL, SEXUAL, AND ETHNIC DIVERSITY

Except for the N Generation, this cohort is the most diverse of all. Most Gen-Xers grew up with kids of different races and backgrounds, and so they think of ethnic and social diversity as no big deal. By the time Xers came of age, women, minorities, and homosexuals were all fairly well established in the workplace. So Xers do not tend to get hung up on diversity the way some older workers have. Most have never known their communities to be anything except diverse.

GLOBAL COMMUNITY

Gen-Xers tend to see themselves as part of a wider global community. The Internet, the ease of international travel, growing diversity within their peer group, and the prevalence of foreign movies and music has helped to foster this feeling. As a result, they are good at building cross-cultural and diverse coalitions — provided they are given opportunities that excite and motivate them.

PHYSIOGRAPHIC PROFILE

Physiographics have little or no affect on Gen-Xers at this stage in their lives. They see themselves largely as invincible, as do most young people. While many Xers feel that they are in the prime of life, some are just beginning to notice the earliest signs of aging, including a few extra

---

What Gen-Xers Want

- ✦ Challenge
- ✦ Excitement
- ✦ Feedback
- ✦ Recognition
- ✦ Time off
- ✦ Training
- ✦ Fun at work
- ✦ Meaningful work
- ✦ An end to politicking

---

pounds around the middle and a few gray hairs. On-site health clubs, health and fitness programs, and other activities that emphasize physical fitness are likely to attract and help retain Xers. Locating work sites near trails suitable for jogging, biking, or walking provides a strong incentive for Xers to work hard and stay with an organization. Given a company's investment in training, along with Xers' sense of job mobility, retaining Xers should be a major aim, but it can be a difficult row to hoe.

UNIQUE STRENGTHS

Even though Gen-Xers have gotten a bad rap in the workplace, they have some very powerful strengths. In fact, some analysts have concluded that Gen-Xers are just the kind of employees that managers say they need — flexible, self-reliant, and up-to-date on current technology.

SELF-RELIANCE

Because so many of them were latchkey children of divorce or had friends who were, Gen-Xers learned at an early age to be self-reliant. When they brought this characteristic into the workplace, older managers were initially taken by surprise. They were used to telling subordinates what to do, and then holding their hands along the way. But Gen-Xers didn't want any hand-holding.

FLEXIBILITY

Flexibility is another attribute of Gen-Xers. Most don't expect to stay in the same job, or even work for the same company, for more than a few years. Their whole career is built around being flexible enough to seize new opportunities when they come along. This works out well for companies that are trying to change the mindset of employees away from expecting lifetime employment. Of course, flexibility may mean that Gen-Xers leave to work for someone else after a few years, but that's just part of the game these days. Gen-Xer flexibility also includes the desire and ability to work anywhere at anytime. Let Xers have some latitude in when and where they work, and you are likely to find much more dedicated, productive employees.

COMFORT WITH TECHNOLOGY

Compared to older workers, Gen-Xers have always been ahead of the technology curve. They practically grew up with computers, and have continued to assimilate new technologies, such as instant messaging, palm devices, and new computer programs, into their everyday lives. Typically, they are able to learn how to use new technology much quicker than older cohorts, and are very interested in keeping their skills up-to-date. Most Xers see learning new skills and participating in training programs as a real perk. Use this to your advantage by rewarding them with opportunities to learn new technologies.

MULTITASKING

In part because of their early exposure to technology, Gen-Xers, as well as N-Gens, are good at multitasking. These younger cohorts have always had a shorter attention span than most older cohorts. Growing up, they were constantly being entertained by music videos, video games, computers, the Internet, cable TV (especially MTV), the radio, CDs, and other distractions. As a result, they became adept at doing multiple things at once. In the working world, this makes them incredibly valuable employees because they can often work on multiple projects at once, and not lose time transitioning from one to the next.

OPENNESS TO DIVERSITY

Gen-Xers grew up with people from different races, religions, and sexual preferences, and so typically do not have any trouble accepting diversity in the workplace. To them, a diverse work environment is preferable to one where everyone is the same. They thrive on newness and difference, and have come to see diversity as a valuable stimulator of creativity.

ENTREPRENEURIAL SPIRIT

Entrepreneurial spirit runs deep with many Gen-Xers. Their willingness to take risks and to change jobs every few years made them a hot commodity during the dot.com boom of the late '90s and early 2000. But while the economy has slowed since then, the spirit of entrepreneurism still thrives among Xers, even if they work for an established company. Give them an opportunity to work on emerging hot projects, or set up a special team for entrepreneurial types to pursue new ideas apart from their regular job duties. Hewlett-Packard has set up *garage teams,* for example, in which small, independent teams of employees work on new ideas and are funded as venture capitalists by the company. This is just the kind of work environment many Xers are looking for.

Gen-X Strengths

- ✦ Self-reliance
- ✦ Flexibility
- ✦ Technology
- ✦ Multitasking
- ✦ Acceptance of diversity
- ✦ Entrepreneurial spirit

THE EXCITEMENT WORK PATH AND GEN-XERS

For Generation X, the excitement work path makes the most sense. It offers Xers the variety of challenges they need to stay highly engaged with their work and their workplace. In fact, if you are not a Gen-Xer yourself and have trouble visualizing ways of making the excitement path real in your workplace, just ask a Gen-Xer or a small team of Xers to figure it out for you. Just about anything that Gen-X employees might put on their wish list or complaint list is a source of inspiration when it comes to building an excitement path.

For instance, Gen-X employees often feel that their work is too dull and not important enough to hold their attention for long. Rather than disagree with them, why not assume that they're right? Challenge them to come up with an innovation and figure out ways to make the innovation work. Ask them to rotate jobs with other employees who feel underchallenged — job exchange programs are a staple of the excitement path.

Also, spend a little time (but not too little — half an hour is about right) talking over each Gen-Xer's short-term performance and development goals. Do this at least once a month. Most managers don't check in with their Gen-X employees nearly that often, and that is why the employees feel ignored, underappreciated, and out of the information loop. In these meetings, go over specific tasks, prioritize them, set performance goals (in an open style that shares decision making), and then ask your employees to keep you up-to-date on how they do against their goals.

Make sure that employees understand what the priorities are, and why they are priorities. A clear line of sight from each task to a big-picture objective makes the Gen-X employee's day seem meaningful and prevents cynicism from creeping in.

Finally, use those monthly one-on-one planning meetings to work on a simple personal development plan. For every three business goals, for example, the employee might want to have one personal goal (like gaining the experience needed to become a division manager). The manager then can help the employee plot a course that maximizes the opportunities for personal advancement.

Many managers complain that they do not have the time to talk one-on-one with each employee regularly. But monthly half-hour meetings require only six hours per employee per year. When there is a problem that requires correction, discipline, or replacement and retraining, managers end up spending a great deal more than six hours on remedial efforts. A half hour of prevention is worth many hours of cure when it comes to managing Gen X.

FUTURE OUTLOOK AND CONCLUSION

In many ways, the future of the Gen X Cohort in the workplace is defined by its past, and not just the defining moments that shaped its values. More recently, Gen-X employees have found themselves working hard to get ahead in workplaces where, by and large, they were treated as substandard material and discussed in derogatory terms. This negative atmosphere needs to be fixed.

FIXING A BAD START

Who would feel good about being labeled a slacker by the business press? Who wants to be accused by the boss of not caring and being lazy? Or of being a whiner? We feel that the Gen X Cohort hit the ground running backward when it entered the workplace, and that some work still needs to be done to make up for this negative start and get things on a more positive level.

It is interesting to go back and look at the authoritative voices on Generation X when it first entered the workplace, with a little hindsight to aid us. Many experts went to great lengths to insult this cohort. Here is a typical example, from *Training* magazine, a leading voice on workplace issues:

> *Baby-boomer executives are constantly at odds with their Generation X subordinates. . . . They see Xers as indolent, cynical and illiterate complainers.*[2]

Ouch! *Indolent?* That sort of language can really hurt. And a more recent description of this cohort from another leading authority, *Manage* magazine, uses another string of negative adjectives that are no less painful:

> *Bored easily. Short attention span. No long-term affil-*
> *iation. Zilch corporate loyalty. Impatient. Want all the*
> *perks without the dues.*[3]

We need to get away from this litany of complaints about Gen-X employees. Even when it's followed by advice on how to manage them to overcome these faults, the approach focuses on negatives — whether real or imagined.

What we find in our work on employee motivation and management styles is that managers get what they see. If they think of their employees in negative terms, they tend to look for evidence of problems and faults. When they find something, they have to go into corrective mode, giving negative feedback, blowing their tops, maybe even warning or terminating employees. This is a destructive way to relate to employees, and it tends to create a lot of resistance and negative feeling toward the manager in return. When this approach is used with Gen-X employees, it usually gets an even stronger and quicker negative response than when it's used with other cohorts. Then managers' worst suspicions are confirmed, the disagreements and conflict escalate, and soon Gen-X employees and their managers start to trash each other. Before you know it, their working relationships are characterized by mutual suspicion and distrust.

Why is a criticism-heavy approach to employees especially likely to escalate into employee resistance with Gen-Xers? We think it is because of Gen-Xers' need for a sense of security and their often-cited need for an interested, caring, almost parental manager. Their tough exterior misleads many managers, who think that Xers need to be treated like spoiled children. Not so. What they need is to be given excellent management, characterized by support, skill-appropriate challenges, and plenty of ongoing performance feedback, including a preponderance of positive feedback.

Boomers and Xers are often at odds, but they shouldn't be. A bad relationship puts a lot of wear and tear on managers, and it alienates Gen-Xers, perhaps irreconcilably. The most important thing is to recognize that this intercohort effect, this major flashpoint, is much more a matter of style than substance. As a manager, you can make this flashpoint vanish. There is nothing inherently negative about Gen-X employees. They are simply different, and with good hands-on management by managers who use solid people skills, Xers can and do perform very well.

As Gen-X employees move up into the ranks of management in many organizations, their ability to provide good supervision for N-Gens is determined largely by the kind of role models they have had over the last five or ten years. If the new Gen-X managers were constantly at odds with older managers who seemed to distrust them and tried to catch them doing something wrong at every opportunity, then these Gen-Xers will not know any other management style. They will replicate a negative style of managing characterized by a combination of benign neglect and periodic policing and zapping to correct perceived errors or bad attitudes.

A CLASSIC SOLUTION TO MANAGING GEN X

Interestingly, the fundamental issue in managing Generation X employees was perhaps best articulated some time ago in the best-selling management book of all time, *The One Minute Manager* (Kenneth Blanchard and Spencer Johnson, Berkley Books, 1981). The authors described a common but ineffective management style they called *leave alone — zap,* in which the manager ignores employees much of the time, then jumps all over them when something goes wrong. This alienating pattern unintentionally damages motivation and is especially destructive with Gen-Xers. Blanchard and Johnson's prescription in *The One Minute Manager* is also particularly appropriate with Gen-X employees. They emphasize participative goal-setting, combined with regular check ins and positive feedback as the foundation of the manager-employee relationship. We think it is vital that Gen-Xers have a relationship of this sort with their managers and that Gen-Xers are encouraged to continue this tradition when they become managers. It is a far more positive and engaging way to relate to employees than the combative relationship that too often dominates in Gen-X workplaces.

CUT THE CONTROL, BUT MAXIMIZE THE MENTORING

Unlike older workers, Gen-Xers don't tend to be driven by authority figures. That's not to say they don't care what management and senior colleagues think. Rather, they crave meaningful feedback, participation in the decision-making process, the knowledge that their work is making an impact, and recognition for a job well done. To help bridge the gap between senior employees and younger Gen-Xers, implement a mentoring program that not only addresses the technical or practical components of a job, but that also deals with the personal and social aspects as well.

Gen-Xers like the unpredictable, whether it comes in the form of fast-changing assignments or an up-in-the-air career path. They are easily bored with repetitive tasks and highly structured work. They want challenge and empowerment. And unlike Boomers, who tend to play office politics at the highest levels, Xers view politicking as dumb and a huge waste of time.

TURNING A NEGATIVE INTO A POSITIVE

The Gen-X desire for excitement is best viewed as a positive rather than negative attribute. Workplaces *need* to be exciting. They are probably far too boring and static right now. Businesses must change and innovate and be strategic leaders. Too many businesses either slip into the purgatory of selling a commodity or slip even further into the hell of technological antiquation. You do not want to compete on the basis of slashing costs and profits and offering the cheapest price. And you certainly don't want to go the way of the typewriter — driven out of the market by new innovations that make your offerings seem old-fashioned or unnecessary.

But who is going to lead the organization of tomorrow, the organization that has a fast-changing, irreverent, flexible culture that finds and refines exciting new ideas quickly? We think the executive-level leadership in such organizations will come from Gen-Xers, the same Gen-Xers who the business press has characterized as ignorant, impatient illiterates with short attention spans who expect rapid career development and exciting work. Great! That list includes many of the characteristics that organizations need to keep them ahead of the game. Good thing an up-and-coming cohort understands how to think and work this way.

ENDNOTES

1. Canabou, Christine. "Job Titles of the Future," *Fast Company,* August 2001, vol. 49, p. 36 (1).

2. Filipczak, Bob. "It's Just a Job: Generation X at Work," *Training,* April 1994, vol. 31, no. 4, p. 21.

3. Marston, Judy and Cam Marston. "Leading the Younger Worker," *Manage,* July 1999, vol. 15, p. 12.

CHAPTER 9

UNDERSTANDING YOUR N GENERATION EMPLOYEES

C an you imagine ever putting your company training manual on your coffee table as a conversation piece? Well, that's just what some young employees of the Hard Rock Cafe did with the company's fun and visually enticing staff-training handbook.

Hard Rock's training manager said the company realized that to appeal to the "green-haired, mohawked, unshaven, tattooed and body-pierced freaks that seem to be running our cafes," Hard Rock needed to be able to communicate with them in a way they could understand. So the company developed a training manual in the spirit of rock 'n' roll, complete with comic book–style photographs, bullet-point text, workbook responses, and employee drawings. The training program that goes along with the handbook does away with written tests and includes performance-based exercises and activities.[1]

This is just the kind of training that appeals to the youngest of our generational cohorts — the N Generation. We call them this because the Net has been a defining factor for them. And, they are the engine (n gen) of growth over the next 20 years. This cohort is still in its formative years, yet it has begun to emerge as a dominant new force in the American workplace. While still not totally defined, N-Gens are the children of the Baby Boomers and are expected to be an even larger group than their parents were.

LIFE IS A BEACH

When N-Gens began entering the workforce in the late '90s, they found themselves in the enviable position of being in the midst of a very tight labor market. Companies were so desperate for employees that they began hosting job fairs on Florida beaches, making it easy for potential recruits to interview while on spring break.

Other companies, particularly dot.coms, were so intent on retaining employees that they offered tremendous perks, such as dog-walking services, on-site saunas and massages, and huge signing bonuses. It was a seller's market, and N-Gens happened to be in the right place at the right time.

In 2000, though, the job market began to change. As the economy slid into a recession, companies no longer had to bend over backward to attract top talent. Many companies began laying off employees, which contributed to a glut of qualified applicants for many job openings. The tables had been turned. N-Gens knew deep down that the good times couldn't last forever, but that didn't stop them from hoping.

THE N GENERATION COHORT TODAY

How large this cohort will eventually be is still not clear. In 2002, the oldest *adult* members of this cohort are ages 18 to 25. In all, there are about 26 million of them as this book goes into print, but that number will no doubt expand as more and more youth come of age. Older N-Gens are now working in their first or second job, while others are still in college or high school.

As children of the Baby Boomers, this cohort grew up protected by car seats, bicycle helmets, and their parents' own economic good fortune. Many N-Gens have grown up in two-income households (with parents or stepparents) and so, like Gen-Xers, have learned self-sufficiency and self-reliance from an early age. Unlike Xers, though, who were largely left on their own, N-Gens were the first cohort to need their own day planners. They received more parental attention than Xers and participated in a steady stream of after-school activities from elementary school on.

N Gen is much more diverse than other cohorts, and about a quarter of N-Gens come from single-parent households (compared with an eighth of young people in 1970). They have never known life without CDs, computers, answering machines, or cell phones. As employees, they are truly wired and technologically savvy.

Like Generation X, however, they have a strong sense of entitlement, and many carry unrealistic expectations about how fast they will advance in the workplace. Many disdain starting at an entry-level job and expect to start much farther up the ladder.

N-Gen Defining Moments

It's really too soon to say what defining moments will ultimately be most influential in shaping the N Generation. Cohort values evolve over time as the influence of defining moments sinks in. That said, a handful of events have already made a significant impact on this emerging cohort.

Like December 7, 1941, when Pearl Harbor was bombed, September 11, 2001, is a day that will live in infamy for many Americans. When terrorists hijacked four commercial airliners, slamming two into the World Trade Center and one into the Pentagon while another crashed in an empty field in Pennsylvania, life as we knew it changed forever. These attacks took many Americans by surprise, but for young people just coming of age the event was particularly traumatic because they were not able to look back on years of peace. Whether September 11 was such a defining moment that a new cohort will have begun or whether it was just another galvanizing event for N-Gens is impossible to say right now. What we know for sure is that the attacks were a tragic defining moment for *some* cohort.

Many N-Gens coped with this tragedy by logging onto the Net and sharing their feelings and grief with their peers. This is the first cohort to grow up with the Internet. To N-Gens, it is not the special, new technology tool that older cohorts see, but something they take for granted and have integrated into their very existence. They use the Internet for just about everything, including looking for jobs, shopping, keeping in touch with friends, and even meeting potential mates.

The oldest members of the N Generation came of age in the last half of the '90s, when the economy was stronger than ever and dot.com-mania took the stock market to new highs. From 1995 to 1999, the S&P Index increased an average of 28.6% per year. Everybody, it seemed, was making big money in the market, and N-Gens came to expect that this would always be the case. There seemed no end to the optimism. Things began to change in 2000, however, as the dot.com bubble burst and the economy started its slow, steady decent into recession. This downturn was the first taste of economic hardship for many N-Gens, who grew up in dual-income families and who had come to think of 20% annual returns on investments as ordinary and perfectly reasonable. If the recession is deep and long, it can be expected that N-Gens will value financial security as a generational cohort value. Remember, we often value most that which we don't have when coming of age.

The April 1999 massacre at Columbine High School in Littleton, Colorado, capped a decade in which school violence escalated dramatically to become almost commonplace. Metal detectors, security guards, and emergency readiness plans became part of N-Gens' high school experience. These events had a very real impact on this cohort, making them more fearful of their personal safety than members of older cohorts. N-Gens never got to experience carefree youth like their parents did. The September 11 terrorist attack intensified N-Gen anxiety even further.

President Bill Clinton's impeachment in 1998 for lying under oath about his relationship with White House intern Monica Lewinsky stunned the country. But it also had a lasting impact on N-Gens, who were just coming of age. The event caused them to lose faith in politicians, to be sure. But it also prompted two different responses from N-Gens. One group became cynical about government, in general, and withdrew from the political process completely. For other N-Gens, the event spurred them to political action and prompted them to try to reform the system. At this point, we can't say which group will dominate in the years to come.

SNAPSHOT OF THE N GENERATION COHORT

Name of Cohort:	N Generation
Born between:	1977–1984
	(ages 18–25 only)
Coming of Age:	1995–present
Age in 2002:	18–25
Population:	26 Million (12%)
	(ages 18–25 only)

Key Cohort Values and Concerns

- ✦ Tempered hopefulness about future
- ✦ Respect for institutions
- ✦ Team players
- ✦ Heightened fears about personal safety
- ✦ Enthusiasm for change
- ✦ Tolerance and diversity
- ✦ Intense patriotism

Current and Next Lifestage

- ✦ High-school graduation
- ✦ College
- ✦ First job
- ✦ Dating
- ✦ Early marriage

Emotions and Affinities

- ✦ Brand conscious
- ✦ Retro and eclectic styles
- ✦ Socially and environmentally aware
- ✦ Street-smart

Physiographic Profile

- ✦ Physical peak

SNAPSHOT

147

N Generation Defining Moments

✦ The Internet

✦ Good economic times

✦ School shootings

✦ Clinton's impeachment

✦ Terrorist attacks on September 11, 2001

VALUES AND CONCERNS

The value system of the N Generation is quite different from that of Generation X. N-Gens tend to be less cynical, more idealistic and altruistic, and far more optimistic than Gen-Xers. Ironically enough, one common bond that ties members of the N Generation Cohort together is their rejection of their Boomer parents' liberal and anti-establishment values. N-Gens are just doing what comes naturally to them — and to all youth at the brink of adulthood, for that matter. They are rejecting the values espoused by their parents. In fact, N-Gens often seem to have more in common with the World War II Cohort — respect for institutional values, conservatism, and the feeling of having been unified by a national crisis — than they do with either Leading-Edge or Trailing-Edge Baby Boomers. Their key cohort values and concerns include the following.

HOPEFUL ABOUT FUTURE

The tremendous economic success of the late '90s helped to shape N-Gens' expectations for the future. With the stock market flying and companies desperate for talented employees, N-Gens found themselves in demand. Job fairs everywhere, hefty stock options, on-site fitness centers, and even pet-sitting services were just a few of the perks that awaited them in the job market. As a result, N-Gens are very hopeful about their prospects for the future.

In a 1997 poll of 2,000 high school students conducted by Drexel University, 8 in 10 respondents said they will be better off financially than their parents; nearly 1 in 3 thought sexual harassment for women will diminish; and 38% strongly believe that Social Security will still be there when they retire.[2] For the most part, N-Gens see the recent downturn in the economy as a temporary setback. They are hopeful that things will improve. If the recession continues for a long period, companies will find their N-Gen workforce dismayed by the level of pay they receive. Companies should think of low-cost rewards to compensate and motivate N-Gens — allowing them more flex time in their work schedules, opportunities for enhancing their social interactions with other workers, and greater leeway in designing their work environment, for example. But in the end, money talks for this cohort.

RESPECT FOR INSTITUTIONS

N-Gens respect institutions, but they don't have the same feeling of absolute, unquestioning deference to the company, the family, the church, the school, or the government that Ghost Cohorts did. At work, they are more likely to work through the system to change something that bothers them than are the Boomers and Xers, who are more likely to raise hell. Because they respect institutions, they are much more likely than Xers or Boomers to remain loyal to the company. This is good news for managers who do not wish to lose their investment in training N-Gens.

TEAM PLAYERS

Gen-Xers tend to be free agents, but N-Gens are more likely to be team players. They tend to relate to people in a cooperative, collaborative sense, and they believe that teamwork can achieve more than they can as individuals. This is just the attitude that managers are looking for! Of course, N-Gens have to work with Xers and Boomers, most of whom have never really embraced the team concept. Unlike the cynical Gen-Xers, the N-Gens also may respond well to the requests of their Gen-X and Boomer managers.

HEIGHTENED FEARS ABOUT PERSONAL SAFETY

Compared to members of older cohorts, N-Gens tend to have heightened fears about their own personal safety. The rising level of school violence throughout the '90s and into 2000 challenged their youthful notion of immortality. Suddenly, teenagers and even younger people were being killed in school, a place formally considered a safe haven for learning.

The September 11, 2001, terrorist attacks only intensified fears. Many companies are still feeling the psychological effects as employees feel that they're working in a climate of fear and anxiety. Bomb threats, anthrax scares, and other threats of terror — both real threats and hoaxes — are putting workers on the defensive. A few weeks after the September 11 attacks, more than 30% of Americans polled said they were less willing to enter skyscrapers.[3] Others are trying to vary their workday routines to avoid high-profile buildings at peak times. Again, it's too early to know the long-term effects of September 11, but certainly in the short run getting on airplanes for business trips will not be something N-Gens desire to do often. Teleconferencing, faxing, e-mailing, and phoning will be preferred to having face-to-face meetings.

N-Gens are likely to feel greater anxiety about their personal safety than older cohorts. That's because they don't have a lot of other experiences with which to compare the tragedy. They may not be as eager as they once were to go on business trips or to transfer to the company headquarters in Manhattan. In fact, we can expect N-Gens in particular to seek employment in rural areas deemed safer from terrorists' attacks. Companies contemplating building new office complexes would be well advised to keep them low to the ground. While no other attacks such as the ones on September 11 may be forthcoming, the vivid image of the twin towers in rubble will be deeply ingrained in the minds of N-Gens. This image will likely deter many N-Gens from applying for jobs in tall buildings.

To allay N-Gens' fears, your company should take terrorist threats seriously and put measures in place for spotting suspicious packages and for beefing up security. Develop an emergency readiness plan, which should include such things as a telephone tree and emergency evacuation procedures. And most of all, in the face of such a tragedy, give employees a chance to express their feelings and admit their fears.

ENTHUSIASM FOR CHANGE

Having grown up with ever-changing technology and the Internet, this cohort sees change as something positive and beneficial. Unlike older cohorts, who tend to resist anything new, N-Gens are very comfortable with new technology and see embracing it as part of being on the cutting edge. They like to be on the forefront of new trends, so if you position change this way, younger employees are likely to buy in a lot quicker.

Terrorist Attacks Have
Ripple Effect at Work

Following the September 11, 2001, terrorist attacks, President George W. Bush encouraged Americans to go about their business as usual. Most people found this to be easier said than done.

The attacks have had a tremendous impact on the workplace, triggering what some are calling the largest mental health challenge ever faced by American companies. Television and the Internet turned the attacks into a live event — something experienced by millions of Americans. Following the attacks, 7 out of 10 Americans polled by the Pew Research Center for the People and the Press said they experienced some level of depression about the event.

News articles predicted a drop in productivity and increased absenteeism at work as people suffered a wide range of physical symptoms brought on by stress, overeating, insomnia, and drinking.

Companies — even those not directly affected by the attacks — hired grief counselors to talk with employees and their families across the country. Other companies made the decision to loosen up restrictions on the number of mental health visits allowed by their health plans.

In the wake of such tragedies, managers need to encourage people to express their feelings and to be open about their fears. Open discussions are critical, not just for younger workers, but for all cohorts. But because N-Gens are at that highly impressionable late adolescence/early adulthood time, the impact of September 11 will have a greater importance in creating core values that will last a lifetime.

Source: Appleby, Julie, and Stephanie Armour. "USA Begins to Deal with Grief Over Attacks," USA Today, September, 20, 2001, section: Money, page 1B.

After all, they are best suited to the excitement work path, and change plays a large role in keeping things new and fresh. To make the most of this key cohort value, put N-Gens in short-term assignments and let them explore other kinds of work. If they don't know what to expect next and are learning new skills along the way, N-Gens will stay energized.

You can also keep N-Gens excited about their work by providing them with regular training in areas such as new technology, project management and working with people from other cohorts. Like Gen-Xers, they see their careers as largely their own doing, and they are eager to pick up skills to make themselves more valuable in the long run.

TOLERANCE AND DIVERSITY

One-third of N-Gens are from minority groups, compared to one-fourth of the general population. N-Gens are very comfortable with diversity. They grew up with people from different races, religions, and so on, and so are very tolerant of people's differences. In fact, they tend to see diversity as something to value. Play to this value by making sure your work environment is as diverse as possible. Diversity includes a mix of cohorts, as well as people from different races, religions, and genders. N-Gens are so accepting of diversity that well-developed policies that embrace diversity in all its forms can even be used in recruiting.

INTENSE PATRIOTISM

Following the September 11, 2001, terrorist attacks, patriotism surged throughout the country. Members of every cohort group, even cynical Gen-Xers, were seen putting flags out on their homes and rising with their hands over their hearts to say the pledge of allegiance. Because N-Gens are at such an impressionable stage in their lives, they were particularly affected by this revival of patriotism. In high schools across the country, N-Gens organized via the Internet to wear red, white, and blue clothing to school on September 13. Traumatic events tend to magnify and intensify core values, and the September 11 attacks clearly served to instill an intense feeling of patriotism in the N Gen Cohort.

The length of time that patriotism will be top of the mind is dependent on what happens as America's war on terrorism goes forward.

Although the general workplace offers few opportunities to demonstrate love of country, those actions will have a great impact on N-Gens. Companies can use flag decals on company vehicles, allow flags on desks, and certainly they should fly old glory outside the company facilities. While these efforts affect everyone, they will be most appreciated by N-Gens. Remember, to N-Gens, Vietnam is just a story.

The Trouble with Being 25

You've heard of the midlife crisis, when middle-aged people suddenly realize that they've lived half their lives and wonder what it's all for. They do crazy things like have affairs and go climb Mt. Everest in an effort to rekindle their youth. But have you heard of the quarterlife crisis?

The quarterlife crisis is the period of angst that often accompanies the transition into adulthood, typically in the early to mid-20s. The concept was described in a recent book by Alexandra Robbins and Abby Wilner called *Quarterlife Crisis: The Unique Challenges of Life in Your Twenties.*

Your 20s are supposed to be the best times of your life, but for many young adults they're a difficult time filled with disappointment and temptation — thus the crisis. Most difficulties stem from the contrast between how most young adults are seen by the outside world (typically as kids) and how they feel (overwhelmed by choices and opportunities and fearful of making a mistake).

Most older people would love to have such problems! And understandably, they don't have much sympathy. But for some N-Gens, transitioning to adulthood can be a difficult experience, especially when they realize at age 25 that they are halfway to 50.

Source: Carter, Kelley L. "The Trouble With Being 25," The Detroit Free Press, June 3, 2001, p. 1K (2).

Lifestage

N-Gens are just now becoming adults. For them, it's a time of anxiety and insecurity, as well as excitement and new opportunity. N-Gens are experiencing a wide range of lifestages right now. The following list includes those lifestages that are most relevant to the workplace.

College

The N Generation is expected to become the most highly educated cohort of all. Many N-Gens are now in college, and are due to graduate in the next few years. Because college costs have risen so much in recent years, and because requirements for student grants and loans have gotten stricter, this cohort is expected to have a very high debt ratio when they do get out of school. As a result, they are very focused on getting high-paying jobs and starting out on a career path as soon as possible. At least for starters, cash awards are likely to be highly motivational for this cohort. Signing bonuses offer a real enticement to N-Gens with college debt on their hands.

Some educators have complained that N-Gens are more interested in getting a *degree* than in getting an *education*. To N-Gens, higher education is the means to an end. As a result, they have become somewhat disengaged from the learning process. As entry-level employees, though, they are likely to want to make a good impression and will be open to suggestions. Training in areas such as advanced computer technology, management, and how to work with members of older cohorts is of particular interest to them.

First Job

Like Gen-Xers before them, N-Gens are not interested in letting work consume them and define who they are. They are looking for a balance between work and life right from the start. As a result, 1 or 2 weeks off and a standard benefits package are not going to wow many in this cohort. They are more likely to respond to such perks as flexible scheduling, the ability to take unpaid leave, and permission to work from home — perks typically not offered to entry-level employees. Another benefit that is particularly valued by younger workers is tuition reimbursement. Taking college courses and getting advanced degrees, such as a master's, doctorate, or MBA, allows them to advance in their careers while continuing to work for you.

N-Gens see working in cubicles as akin to solitary confinement. They prefer team environments and look for a steady stream of challenges. Many expect to skip over entry-level jobs because they feel they are already trained. These kinds of unrealistic expectations need to be managed right from the start.

In general, younger workers expect to be paid for performance, so seniority-based advancement will not motivate them to stick around. Rather, it is more likely to drive them away.

N-Gens also want freedom to be creative and to manage their own time. Because the Internet plays such a prominent role in their lives, N-Gens are sometimes accused of crossing the line when it comes to acceptable use of the web at work. They expect to be able to e-mail friends and family and buy tickets for Madonna's latest world tour, for example, before they start their workday. If your company has strict rules about Internet use, make sure N-Gens, in particular, are clear about what is and is not permitted. N-Gens, and Gen-Xers too, for that matter, prefer to have open, unfettered access to the Net. At a minimum, they will abide by restrictions that put off limits racially, sexually, or religiously sensitive material, but see other restrictions as overly totalitarian.

Loosening up the reins on personal Internet use can help to energize and motivate younger employees. After all, they are the masters of multitasking. And giving them unfettered Internet access shows that you trust them to get the job done. Policing employee Internet use can backfire and demoralize your workers, so unless people are looking at highly offensive material, let it go, and spend your time worrying about something else.

EMOTIONS AND AFFINITIES

N-Gens are now trying to develop their own identities and make their mark in the world. Everything is new to them, and they are in the process of figuring out their emotions and affinities. The following sections address some of the emotions and affinities that may affect the work environment.

Early Marriage

Neotraditionalism, or the return to more old-fashioned values, is a new trend among N-Gens. They are marrying earlier than Gen-Xers, and they're having children earlier and more often. In addition, they have an expectation that one parent should be home with the kids. This attitude is a throwback to earlier times, but with a new twist: Instead of Mom staying home with the kids, this cohort feels it is just as acceptable for Dad to stay home — just so one parent is always there. With a large number of N-Gens having grown up in daycare and having experienced their parents' divorce, this cohort is looking for stability. We often most value what we lack when coming of age, so it makes sense that N-Gens are looking to settle down. Early marriage is one way for them to find stability in an uncertain world.

In the workplace, N-Gens who tie the knot and start families early are likely to be attracted by flexible work options, such as job-sharing, telecommuting, and part-time opportunities. Summers off to be with the kids can be extremely attractive. Some companies, particularly those in healthcare, have made dramatic changes to meet the needs of younger workers. For example, some hospitals now offer increased flexibility in scheduling to attract workers who don't want to start out working nights and weekends. And when it comes to retirement benefits, most young people are interested in the transferability of pensions and 401(k) savings, so some companies are trying to come up with more flexible options there, as well. Note too that financial benefits, such as savings plans, will fit well with the financial expectations of N-Gens, because many witnessed their parents getting downsized during the 1990s.

SOCIALLY AND ENVIRONMENTALLY AWARE

N-Gens tend to be more concerned about social and environmental issues than Generation Xers. They are more idealistic than Xers and tend to think that they can make a difference and bring about change. When Nike was accused of relying on sweatshop labor to produce its shoes and athletic apparel, the company fell out of favor with N-Gens and a boycott was ensured. If all else is equal, N-Gens are more likely to work for a company that has a history of supporting social and environmental causes. In trying to recruit this cohort, emphasize your company's role as a good corporate citizen.

N-Gens are also good choices for developing or working on programs that link your company with charity groups that are focused on social or environmental causes. This cohort is cause oriented, so provide them with outlets for their idealism and activism. Money alone is unlikely to offer enough allure to attract and retain them for long.

Ben & Jerry's has risen to prominence in the super-premium ice cream business with two unique and creative business principles: 1) If it's not fun, why do it? (more on this in a minute); and 2) Business has the responsibility to give back to the community. Ben & Jerry's donates 7.5% of pretax profits to charitable causes. This is exactly the kind of company that N-Gens like to work for.

STREET-SMART

This cohort is probably the most marketed to of all time, surpassing even their Baby Boomer parents, so they are very aware of hype. They prefer honesty and authenticity, and are turned off by extravagant exaggerations of reality. In the workplace, corporate communications must be simple, straightforward, and without a lot of public relations spin. Otherwise, this cohort will lose their belief in management, and motivating them will become even more of a challenge.

PHYSIOGRAPHIC PROFILE

At this stage in their lives, N-Gens are not at all concerned about the effect physiographics has or will have on their bodies. They are at their physical peak, and expect to stay that way forever. Their primary physical concern at this point is staying in shape to attract a mate. Companies that have on-site workout facilities or that offer free or reduced rates at an off-site gym can use these perks to help attract and retain fitness-conscious N-Gens.

Because they are at their physical peak and don't need healthcare very often, many N-Gens don't see the need for company health plans that have low deductibles. They would prefer to have a higher deductible and see such things as contact lenses, prescription drugs, and dental visits covered by the company health plan. They would also like to see alternative medical care, such as acupuncture and herbal supplements, covered by their health plan. As a result, cafeteria-style health plans that offer flexibility and a wide range of coverage will be the most appealing to this cohort.

UNIQUE STRENGTHS

You may not have very many N-Gens among your direct reports — yet. But you soon will. Here is a preview of some of the unique strengths this cohort brings to the workplace.

TEAMWORK

Because they have a more collectivist nature, N-Gens work well on teams. They learned teamwork skills early on, having been shuttled by their parents to and from soccer, T-ball, hockey, and other team activities. They like the camaraderie that comes from working closely with a diverse group of people. Unlike Generation Xers and older workers, N-Gens typically are more interested in being part of a team, rather than in *leading* the team. One challenge in working with this cohort is creating team goals that balance team performance with individual initiative.

TECHNOLOGICALLY SAVVY

For N-Gens, the computer is the hot rod of the new millennium, and they expect to have the fastest, sleekest equipment available to them. They consider having up-to-date computer equipment, along with high-speed access to the Internet, as one of life's necessities. Their technological savvy can be a real strength for the companies that employ them. For many N-Gens, the Internet has become a way of life, and using it for practical purposes is second nature to them. Cell phones, pagers, instant messaging, and more have also become a way to communicate with people in far-flung locations in real time. N-Gens are good at multitasking, and like to be on the cutting edge of the latest technology.

In providing them with technology training, make sure the material you are offering is absolutely the most up-to-date technology around. If it is outdated, N-Gens will start looking elsewhere for work that is a little more challenging and cutting-edge.

ALTRUISM

This cohort's altruism stems in part from its affinity for teamwork and cooperation. N-Gens look out for one another and will stand up for what they think is right. This is just the kind of attitude companies need to make teams work effectively. More N-Gens in the workplace will help to diffuse the competitiveness of Boomers and Gen-Xers. While N-Gens do tend to be somewhat authority driven, they will fight the system if they think leaders are not acting fairly or are lacking in integrity.

THE TEAM WORK PATH AND N-GENS

The team work path is typically the best one for N-Gens. They want their work to be meaningful, and they want it to foster relationships that extend beyond the workplace. They want to be able to feel that their work is meaningful, and that they are contributing toward the accomplishment of a larger goal, be it corporate or societal. Because they are not loners, in it just for themselves, they want other people to notice. And they want to be given the responsibility for achieving lofty goals — unlike Xers, N-Gens are not likely to say, "Not my job, man!"

Some companies may find that creating a culture that fosters teamwork and larger goals is difficult, but if you work at it, you can come up with innovative ways to create such a culture. As we mentioned earlier, ice cream maker Ben & Jerry's has done an excellent job making itself a must-work-for company. In addition to devoting 7.5% of profits to social causes, it has created a group of unusual and engaging activities that keep employees coming back for more. For example:

✦ During a particularly busy time, top managers put on production uniforms and helped out production workers however they were needed. They also cooked dinner for the staff, ordered pizza, and even hired a masseuse to give free massages. This created a bond between workers and top management.

✦ The company's normal benefit package includes such things as healthcare, dental care, profit sharing, tuition reimbursement, an employee stock purchase plan, free health club membership . . . *and three free pints of ice cream every day!* The company also has a compressed 7 to 1 salary ratio, which prevents top executives from making more than 7 times what the lowest-paid worker receives.

✦ The Joy Gang is an employee committee that meets several times a month to help boost employee morale and to make sure that everyone is having fun. Some of the gang's activities include hosting an Elvis look-a-like and sound-a-like contest; throwing a late-night party for the second and third shift, complete with food, prizes, and a disc jockey; and holding a Halloween costume contest in which the president/CEO once wore a pink tutu and danced in front of the entire company.

Another way to keep N-Gens engaged is for managers to do things like take younger employees to high-level meetings, not as participants, per se, but as spectators. Doing so exposes employees to interesting discussions about the company and gives them a taste of what they could be doing in the future. It also keeps them engaged in their day-to-day activities and helps to give them a greater commitment to the company.

FUTURE OUTLOOK AND CONCLUSION

Our understanding of the values, attitudes, and preferences of the various generational cohorts we have profiled in this book has come about through the work we've done for clients. As we studied various age groups, scanned the literature others have written about these groups, reviewed what the media has said, moderated a multitude of focus groups, and conducted surveys, we found similar patterns that differentiated age groups based on their values, their attitudes, and their preferences. But cohorts' characteristics were not apparent when the various generational cohorts were coming of age. They only manifested themselves later.

Most N-Gens are still coming of age. The full array of values and attitudes that will remain stable over their lives cannot be known *with certainty* as we write this book. However, we've given you what information we *can* discern at this point. And some points *can* be made with certainty.

We have noticed a definite shift, starting about 1996, in people's approach to life. The economy changed for the better at that time, and the Internet burst onto the scene. We strongly believe that an inflection point was reached in 1996 in the mindsets of those coming of age.

How to Keep Younger Workers Happy

✦ Give them opportunities to work in small, peer-related teams.

✦ Turn projects into entrepreneurial endeavors.

✦ Let them choose their own hours.

✦ Find out their skills and interests and help them become self-fulfilled.

✦ Find ways to make work meaningful, beyond just a paycheck.

✦ Create ways for them to spend time with upper managers.

✦ Have them work for ethical leaders.

✦ Set up a mentoring program.

✦ Be generous with rewards and recognition.

Also, the terrorist attacks of September 11, 2001, changed forever the way we live. As this book goes into production, we are still reeling from the effects of those attacks. N-Gens will be more influenced by September 11 than any other cohort. We cannot know whether the events of September 11 and their aftermath will create an inflection point that is strong enough to form yet another cohort or if they will be a galvanizing event for those who we define here as the N Gen Cohort. Only time will tell. We may well find new cohorts forming as the children of Baby Boomers thread their way through their coming-of-age years. It all depends on what defining moments occur over the next 10 to 15 years. We can only hope that these defining moments are happy ones.

ENDNOTES

1. Knight, Jim. "Generation Y: How to Train It and Retain It," *Restaurant Hospitality,* May 2000, vol. 84, p. 88.

2. Wellner, Alison. "Get Ready for Generation Next," *Training,* February 1999, v. 36, p. 42 (5).

3. Armour, Stephanie. "Fear Still Permeates Some Workplaces." USAToday.com, 9/27/01.

CHAPTER 10

MANAGING COHORT FLASHPOINTS

W hen we talk about the differences between generational cohorts, many people's first reaction is, "Aha!" The cohort effect helps them understand various frictions and disagreements they have seen or experienced in their own workplace. Everyone seems to have a story to tell! You may even have a few of your own.

Over the years, we've noticed that there are common threads in many of these stories. Managers and employees from different cohorts often tend to disagree or clash along predictable lines. Leading-Edge Boomers and Gen-Xers, for example, often disagree about what is appropriate behavior at work. Should employees disagree with their boss in public? Boomers say, "No way," while Xers say, "Why not?"

These value-level differences are very real, and they can be a huge source of conflict between managers and the people they supervise, or between members of the same team. In fact, we've found that cohort differences, while far less visible than many other factors, are actually much greater drivers of interpersonal conflict than differences in gender or race. Different generational cohorts hold very different values, and most people take their values *very* personally.

Left unresolved, cohort conflicts, or flashpoints, can severely undermine team and individual effectiveness. The good news is that differences in cohort values don't always have to produce negative results. Flashpoints can produce light as well as heat.

Many managers are uncomfortable with conflict. To them, an effective meeting is one that ends quickly after everyone agrees. But conflict often plays an important role in helping businesses achieve their potential. That's why we encourage managers and leaders in every organization to view inter-cohort conflicts and differences as a potential strength, not just as a potential weakness.

An Expanded View of Diversity

The majority of U.S. employers view diversity as something they have to worry about and invest in because the legal costs of not doing so are prohibitive. We see diversity in a much more positive light. To us, it's a major but little understood source of strength to organizations. In fact, the more different the members of a group are, the more potential that group has to achieve difficult goals.

These days, stable, long-term market niches are impossible to find. Businesses need to be fast on their feet. And that means they need to do the kinds of creative problem solving and opportunity seeking that diverse groups of people are good at.

In most companies, diversity initiatives are focused on differences in race, religious background, gender, sexual preference, and other factors. But we feel that these initiatives need to be expanded to consider generational cohorts as well. We believe that the healthiest organizations are the most diverse, and we like to see lots of different cohorts struggling to coexist. As long as organizations that embrace diversity are managed sensitively and well, they can accomplish a great many things that less diverse groups might not.

Tales from the Consultant's Beat

We were called into a dot.com company recently to help defuse a major problem. A team of highly valuable top-level programmers were mad at their supervisor and threatening to quit. They seemed to hate everything about this manager, describing him as controlling, aloof, unfriendly, and inconsiderate. The company's executives didn't want to fire the manager because he was one of the few older and highly experienced engineers.

When we met the people involved, we were at once struck by the fact that the programmers were all members of the N Gen Cohort, while the manager hailed from Generation X. This small difference in actual ages was enough to put them on different sides of a cohort divide.

The manager typified the free-agency ideal of Gen-X, and was very self-sufficient and emotionally independent in his approach to work. He came to work and did what he saw needed doing, and he did it well. He assumed his employees would operate the same way. If they needed something from him, then they would just have to get in line and advocate for it. His approach was something along the lines of "life's tough, but if you're tough enough you can get ahead!"

His employees, however, expected their manager to create a warm, supportive environment for them and to take at least a little interest in them as people, not just as technical elements of the project equation.

To remedy the problem, we worked with this manager to teach him to use more people-oriented leadership styles (which we go into in Chapter 12). We helped him come up with a list of his employees' needs and wants based on a profile of their cohort. And we encouraged him to think about what they might need to be happy and productive — recognizing that his employees might need different things than he needed at their age.

Why Diversity Works

Diversity is helpful in a turbulent business environment because it:

✦ Creates a wider variety of experience and knowledge for the group to draw upon

✦ Produces more varied views of problems and decisions, thereby making a broader and more open-minded approach feasible

✦ Provides multiple, often complementary, temperaments and personalities for the group to draw upon

---

Differing viewpoints are a wonderful source of insight, but, as we've seen, they're also a potential source of friction. Yet, we still view the diversity of cohorts and the potential for friction between them as a wonderful source of strength. It comes down to our differing view of diversity.

Although cohorts are age-related, we need to reiterate that we're not in favor of specifically selecting candidates for any role or position on the basis of age. This would be a misreading of the cohort approach — not to mention discriminatory and illegal! However, we do advocate the creation of workplaces and jobs that are accessible to and appropriate for people of many cohorts and people of every background. This means taking a proactive approach to diversity.

DIVERSITY AND THE DOT.COM DEBACLE

The need for diversity is perhaps best illustrated by the flameout of many dot.com companies in 2001. We watched these companies rise and fall with particular interest because a high percentage of them were mono-cohort cultures. That is, they were dominated by just one cohort, usually N Gen or Gen X. Still others were a mix of both of these younger cohorts, but lacked any balancing presence of either of the Boomer Cohorts or of Postwar or Ghost Cohort mentors.

The dot.com firms did not consciously create these work environments. Instead, they simply staffed up to fill new technical positions in a hurry, not really thinking about anything but the technical requirements of the work. And because the technology was new, they got a narrow group of younger workers pretty much by accident.

As a result of their mono-cohort cultures, these workplaces had very little creative friction. Everybody got along, in our opinion, a little *too* well. Nobody stopped to look around and question the business model, or ask whether they were doing the right thing spending all their venture capital on fancy equipment and facilities before they had any customers to speak of. Not enough contrary voices were raised in those weekly staff meetings or quarterly budget and planning sessions. And so these firms' employees all ran off the cliff together, like so many lemmings.

When you mix people with differing cohort values — who are also typically in different lifestages — you are guaranteed a greater cross section of viewpoints. If you can ensure that people are willing to speak out and contribute their ideas, you will have lively, even aggressive, discussions instead of thoughtless agreement.

We like to see a mix of cohorts and a wide range of ages in any group that is doing anything important and at all risky or difficult. You won't see a mixed herd of many different types of animals topple over the nearest cliff together. There is too much stopping to sniff the wind, question the leaders, and wonder where the group is going.

A certain amount of healthy distrust and disagreement ensures a more open-eyed approach!

MANAGING FLASHPOINTS

The suggestions above are aimed at creating a working environment that is communication rich and sensitive to individual differences. Such a workplace helps to forge strong teamwork (whether there are formal teams or not) and to tap into the potential strengths and advantages of a diverse group more fully. But it is also important for managers to recognize generational cohort–related interpersonal problems when they arise so as to be able to respond effectively to them. Prevention practices will reduce the incidence of flashpoints, but not eliminate them altogether, so sometimes managers need to practice intervention as well.

Ice Cream, Anyone?

We were visiting the company that publishes this book a couple of years ago on a Friday afternoon. In the middle of a serious meeting, the publishing staff all looked at their watches, jumped up, and said, "Come on! We're going to be late for the Ice Cream Social!" Well, this behavior was met with a certain degree of skepticism at first. Interrupting a serious meeting to eat ice cream? Come on!

But once we saw what was going on, the value of the ritual was clear. A large room was filling up with employees, some of whom knew each other, but many of whom were obviously barely acquainted. A lot of "Oh, you work in the such-and-such department? Do you know so-and-so? Oh, she left last month? Who does her job now?" sorts of conversations were taking place. That there was a real need for this sort of informal interaction was obvious. If nothing else, it was a way for employees who worked on the same plans and projects to at least know each other by sight.

In every organization, these sorts of informal get-togethers need to take place, particularly now that e-mail, phone conferencing, and telecommuting take away many of the face-to-face interactions that used to be part of the workday. It's easy for the mad rush of events to make informal exchanges less frequent than anyone would like. We strongly recommend making room in the monthly schedule for at least one casual get-together, be it an ice cream social, a dance, a brown-bag lunch, or any other informal gathering of employees.

If you can't think of a good idea, try holding a brown-bag lunch or coffee at which you ask employees to suggest ideas for future gatherings. Someone is bound to have a good idea!

Keep in mind that awareness is always the first and most powerful step in handling such issues in any workgroup. Sometimes it is enough in and of itself to simply recognize, acknowledge, and show appropriate respect or empathy for another's issues. As a manager, you can't always solve everyone's problems, but you certainly can show consideration toward those who are experiencing problems! We think of this as the *consideration cure,* and it is about the closest thing to a silver bullet that any manager can have when it comes to handling people problems in his or her organization.

Now we look more closely at a number of specific flashpoints, starting with several that arise when managing N-Gen employees.

FLASHPOINT: N-GEN EXPECTATION OF QUICK SUCCESS

A tight labor market and good economic times in recent years have given N-Gens an unrealistic expectation of work, which often frustrates older managers who had to pay their dues along the way.

To handle this flashpoint better, managers need to both manage expectations and provide more opportunities for short-term successes. On the managing expectations side, discussing expectations openly and often is a good idea! Don't assume that your N-Gen employees understand that there are relatively few opportunities for a major promotion in the first six months of work. Ask them what they think and tell them honestly what's feasible. Exploring expectations early and often keeps the gap between expectations and reality from getting too wide.

Even after N-Gens understand that career advancement takes time, managers and organizations need to provide more frequent opportunities for recognizing success and for giving employees a chance to step up to higher levels of responsibility and challenge. This does not mean adding new layers to the organization chart — they were taken out for very good reasons. But short of creating new titles, what can be done to provide more frequent opportunities for N-Gen employees to step up?

First, seek ways to break down big steps into little ones. Responsibility and status can be conferred in smaller bits that are doled out more frequently. Instead of having an employee wait two or three years for a step up to a supervisory level, break some of those supervisory responsibilities into assignments that the employee can take on every six months or so. Some firms, for example, use team leadership or even team membership assignments as stepping stones.

Second, use recognition to help scratch N-Gens' itch for success and progress. Because this cohort shares some similarities with the Ghost Cohorts, formal award ceremonies with public recognition of achievements are often a good thing. Certificates of appreciation can work wonders too. Let N-Gens know that the organization feels they've achieved a certain level of success. Doing so gives them a feeling of momentum.

Some companies have used storytelling as a vehicle for lauding particularly effective employees. At company-wide gatherings, workers are told tales in detail, sometimes by customers, of how certain employees achieved greatness in some area of the company. Rewards include applause and recognition from co-workers or framed pictures that include detailed explanations of their actions that are hung on corporate walls. N-Gens will respond well to this kind of attention.

Also, you simply must do individual development planning with each of your N-Gen employees. You probably should do this sort of planning with all your employees, for that matter, but if you have N-Gens, it is doubly important to introduce this practice right away. Spend some time, perhaps once a quarter, sitting down with employees to discuss their interests and needs. Help them plan to achieve their career development goals. Make sure the meeting produces at least a few simple action steps for each quarter — even if it's something as simple as a one-day job rotation to expose them to another department's work or participation in a half-day workshop. Getting the employee a subscription to a professional magazine or an association membership is also a quick and easy action item. The things you do need not be expensive or time consuming. The point is that N-Gen employees will feel better and perform better if they feel they're doing *something* to move their careers ahead.

FLASHPOINT: N-GEN NEEDS FOR SECURE COMMUNITIES

We expect N-Gens to have a more lasting response than older cohorts to the terrorist attacks of September 11, 2001. Specifically, it is likely that their needs for a sense of caring and community in the workplace and for a feeling of security may not be fully recognized by older managers.

Remember that the September 11 tragedy happened while many N-Gens were coming of age. We think that, as a result, a sense of community and security are likely to be high on the list of things they value. Managers and organizations need to continue to talk about security issues and take visible, reassuring steps to make employees feel safe in their workplaces. Even something as simple as hanging extra fire extinguishers and first aid kits in the workplace is helpful — not only for practical reasons, but also because they increase people's peace of mind. Safety drills, buddy systems, and phone trees are good ideas anyway, and implementing them will certainly help this cohort feel more cared for and comfortable.

This cohort's need for genuine caring and consideration in the workplace may be harder for managers to meet. N-Gens are likely to resent impersonal management more keenly than other employees. For example, if a layoff is announced coldly and terminated employees are given little time to say goodbye and pack up, you can expect that your N-Gens left behind will take this personally. They will likely view the incident as a traumatic one, and it may shake their faith in their employer and lead them to question their commitment to their work.

Managers and organizations may not be able to get away with the insensitive behavior they've gotten away with in the past — at least not without risking the dissatisfaction, demotivation, and possible defection of this important new cohort.

The mantra for managing this cohort is "Try not to look like a jerk to them or to the people they consider part of their working community!" Easier said than done, of course, given the tough management style we've inherited from the Ghost Cohorts.

FLASHPOINT: GEN-X INFORMALITY, INCIVILITY, CYNICISM, AND STREET SMARTS

The Gen-X mentality may offend older supervisors, leading to accusations of poor attitude and insubordination, which employees feel are unjustified. Gen-Xers' communications with their managers are usually quite poor.

Many managers and co-workers from older cohorts are likely to be put off by Gen-Xers' style. The key to working with this cohort is the same one that parents of teenagers need to learn: Focus on the substance, not the style! You're not likely to agree on style, but you probably can see eye to eye on substance if you avoid style issues right from the start.

For instance, many managers get tired of holding staff meetings with Gen-X employees and stop doing so altogether. When asked why, they say that the meetings didn't work because the employees were often late and sometimes skipped the meetings altogether, and when they did come, they weren't willing to stick with the agenda and were often impolite, spoke out of turn, or disagreed openly with the manager.

Those are *style* issues. The Trailing-Edge Boomer, Leading-Edge Boomer, or Postwar manager who thinks he or she can "teach these kids some manners" is wrong. Gen-Xers simply have a different set of social mores, and while individuals who are eager to acquire corporate success skills may adapt their behavior, expecting every Gen-Xer to do so is unrealistic and unnecessary.

A staff meeting that has an air of informality and some blunt language is still a meeting. It still gets people together and allows them to rub shoulders, get to know each other better, and exchange progress reports and problems. It's still a valuable exercise in communication and overlap, even if it makes the manager cringe a bit!

FLASHPOINT: GEN-X NEED FOR EMOTIONAL AND FINANCIAL SECURITY, COMBINED WITH A DESIRE FOR INDEPENDENCE

Managers often misread the independence value as indicating that Gen-X employees resent direction and do not want attention. Gen-X employees do not know how to elicit the desired emotional support and reassurance/security from their supervisors.

Managers and employers need to make sure to provide as much structure as employees need, not just as much as they ask for. Structure can take the form of specific instructions, clear goals, and accurate feedback — the most important types of structure on a daily basis, because they clearly define the tasks that employees must execute.

When it comes to feedback, Gen-X employees do much better with *informative* feedback than with *controlling* feedback. In other words, instead of telling the employee what you think of the work ("Good job!" or "I'd prefer you did it this way"), give the employee access to enough information to form the same judgment independently. For instance, instead of telling a Gen-X employee that she needs to be more polite to customers, ask her to keep track of how polite other employees think she is. Give her a form or measurement method of some sort to record her progress on a politeness scale. Let her keep her own score. She's able to pursue a goal independently, but you're structuring her work by providing her with a clear goal and making sure that she's pursuing it.

FLASHPOINT: TRAILING-EDGE BABY BOOMERS' TENDENCY TOWARD LONELY INDIVIDUALISM AND DESIRE TO BE PART OF THE INFORMATION FLOW

Older managers often fail to recognize that Trailing-Edge Boomers resent being excluded from information flows and need to be given a chance to express their opinions. Many employees actually quit their jobs over this issue.

When you ask employees, especially Trailing-Edge Baby Boomers, why they quit a job, they often say that they felt excluded from communications and key information. Trailing-Edgers may act and look like they don't want to be fully involved, but they do. Open communication and participatory decision making are *very* important to them.

When possible, try to include these employees more fully in decision making. Even if you must make a dictatorial decision, the best way to sell it to this cohort is to share information about it and report on it fully. The more information loops Trailing-Edgers are in, the better. Information is the glue that holds them in place and keeps them committed.

FLASHPOINT: TRAILING-EDGE BOOMERS' LEANING TOWARD OPEN SEXUALITY

Trailing-Edgers tend to be more open to sexuality and explicit sexual language or behavior than other workers. Without sensitivity training and proper coaching in sexual harassment issues, these Boomers generate many harassment claims and problems when they become managers. This characteristic is especially problematic because they may not realize that Gen-X employees value sexual caution more than they do.

In spite of the growing trend toward sexual harassment policies and trainings, the number of complaints and legal claims from workers is growing. Part of the problem is a clash of generational cohort cultures. Managers from the Trailing-Edge Boomer Cohort may view offhand comments about having affairs as nothing out of line. They may, in fact, expect to have the occasional affair with a co-worker or employee. Even when they're sensitive and considerate in other areas, such as race or sexual orientation, some of them may not get the need for clear, sharp boundaries on sexual comments and conduct. They may think there's nothing wrong with tuning their PC screens to soft pornography sites while at work, for example.

Encourage your Trailing-Edgers to consider that what one person may view as innocuous another may view as highly offensive or troubling! The concept of a hostile environment needs to be emphasized for this group (as for all employees). Our advice is that, because of the wide variety of attitudes about all things sexual, employees in general (and perhaps those from this cohort in particular) need to receive even more training and warnings in the area of sexual harassment than they typically do. It only takes one Austin Powers in a workplace to create a lot of ill will and bad feelings. And while that sort of conduct may be viewed as humorous in a movie, it is likely to be viewed as highly offensive in the workplace.

FLASHPOINT: LEADING-EDGE BOOMERS' DESIRE FOR SELF-EXPRESSION AND TREATMENT OF WORK AS SELF-FULFILLMENT

Whether an employee or a manager, the Leading-Edge Boomer has a need to stamp each project with his or her personal touch. This can be a positive source of motivation, but it more often causes conflict over what is to be done, how to do it, and where to give the credit. This trait is a common source of conflict, resentment, and frustration for Leading-Edge Boomers' employees, who may feel they're not getting the individual recognition they deserve. Employees of Leading-Edgers frequently complain their boss is taking all the credit.

As the team concept has spread across the workplace, there has been a steady movement toward recognizing team accomplishments. As a result, individuals often feel that they're not being recognized for their individual contributions. Leading-Edge Boomers are especially likely to feel like their contributions aren't being recognized. To remedy this situation, make an effort to acknowledge each individual's input informally and often. Often, managers don't really know what each individual has contributed to a team effort. But employees do know, so all you have to do is ask them. In fact, making a habit of asking people to tell you what they personally did on a project is a good idea. Debriefing them gives them the chance to toot their own horn.

Also, make sure that employees have a chance to imprint their own personal touch and creativity on projects, when possible. Here's a simple example. In many organizations, there are standard formats for all internal reports, plans, and budgets. Every document that's generated tends to have a standard, dull design. What if you encouraged employees to do something creative with the cover of a report, for example? It's a simple opportunity for self-expression, but it's one that helps make it possible for individuals to feel that they can express themselves in their work.

FLASHPOINT: LEADING-EDGE BOOMERS' INDIVIDUALISM AND SKEPTICISM

> *When Leading-Edge Boomers gain senior management responsibility and use it to make radical changes without building sufficient support from older cohorts, serious conflicts arise with supervisors and the executive board. The radical in the corner office often gets turned out — one reason why executive turnover rates are dangerously high today.*

In the current business environment, most self-initiated changes are a good thing. If anything, organizations don't change fast enough, and fail to take the initiative as often as they should. Because Leading-Edge Boomers show their individualism and skepticism more readily than other cohorts, they are in the prime spot to interject new ideas and change. Their tendency to innovate should not be squelched. Instead, try to minimize the hurdles and bureaucracy (often imposed by older cohorts) that have to be navigated to champion a good new idea or make a sensible change. And make sure you ask your employees periodically to think of ways to make it easier to innovate, adapt, and pursue good new ideas. Why not put some Leading-Edgers in charge of taking suggestions?

FLASHPOINT: POSTWAR COHORT'S EMPHASIS ON STABILITY, FORMALITY, STRUCTURE, AND INSTITUTIONS

> *Postwar employees are slow to change and find it difficult to cooperate with younger, less respectful co-workers. At the executive level, this cohort frequently fails to recognize the need for change until it is too late. Postwar CEOs and board members have been known to block needed changes, insist on established processes to the detriment of innovative ideas, and ride their organizations into the ground. Younger cohorts have to learn how to talk to this cohort about change, and must learn how to overcome their instinctive resistance when the situation warrants.*

Change is probably faster outside your organization than within it, which means your organization, like many others, would profit by finding ways to up the rate of change. If executives from the Postwar or any other cohort are unintentionally shutting the change throttle, the reality is that *they are going to have to change.* When one cohort's instincts are hindering the progress of the company, the right strategic thing to do is to ask the out-of-step cohort to recognize this situation for what it is and do their best to be flexible and to adapt.

We encourage all arguments about how and whether to change — they may be painful, but they're likely to produce important strategic insights. So go ahead and have a lively argument about whether to change practices, plans, or other features of your business.

In most organizations, the individuals with the most independent and contrarian views are the least likely to be included in substantive discussions of strategy and plans. But they are the most likely to provide genuine insight and to inject new perspectives and ideas. For this reason, we recommend that all planning groups include some people who are viewed as difficult, disgruntled, or negative. Including potentially critical viewpoints in a dialogue can be a very positive thing indeed!

SOME GENERAL THOUGHTS ON MANAGING CONFLICT

Conflict can be beneficial or destructive, depending on which way it cuts. Managers need to be mindful of its power and manage it to bring out its positive aspects. Whenever you get a diverse group together, certain factors, including the following, tend to encourage conflict to arise:

- ✦ Different values
- ✦ Varied work habits and styles
- ✦ Different communication patterns
- ✦ Different cultural patterns regarding the expression of disagreement, anger, and other strong emotions
- ✦ Different world views
- ✦ Different points of reference

These are not minor things. They certainly have the potential to stimulate discussion and generate multiple viewpoints — essentials of open-minded, creative problem solving. But they also have the potential to break down communications and create enmity within work groups.

Managers need to be mindful of two imperatives as they lead increasingly diverse, multi-cohort work groups.

THE COMMUNICATION IMPERATIVE

Communication is hard work. Care, attention, and study are needed to make sure that it's effective within the workgroup and the organization as a whole. Increasingly, managers need to be champions of clear and rich communication in their organizations.

The more things you can do to encourage and improve communication, the better!

- ✦ Use facilitation skills (such as asking probing questions that dig beneath the surface) when running meetings.

- ✦ Use lots of open-ended questions when you're in one-on-ones with employees.

- ✦ Use e-mails, memos, and other standard interoffice communication media in two-directional or multi-directional ways by adding requests for comments and pass-along comments.

The goal is to get people talking more fully and in more detail about their work and the overall goals and direction of their workgroups.

Because of the importance of managing the communications environment, managers need to become experts in the facilitation and use of one-on-one and small-group interpersonal skills. There is a growing recognition of this fact, although practice still lags behind necessity. We take it as a good sign that some organizations are prescribing courses and workshops on interpersonal skills, facilitation, and communication for their up-and-coming leaders.

THE OVERLAP IMPERATIVE

Informal interaction with co-workers is growing less common, and it has been for a decade or more. People seem to have more work to do, and so they need to log more hours each day just to get through their pile. They don't have time to go out to lunch together or hang out at the proverbial water cooler very much any more. Also, the modern business has flattened so much that individual leaders have their hands full, and need both to supervise more people and to do more of their own hands-on work. They have less time to hang out and shoot the breeze. Much of their day is spent struggling to get through e-mails and reports and meetings and calls — all forms of communication to be sure, but none of them the rich, informal, personal kinds of communication that build rapport and strengthen personal ties. As a result, many managers never really get to know the people that work for them.

To counter this trend toward a lack of informal communication, we recommend managers plan and schedule something we call *overlap*. Overlap is simply time spent interacting in relatively personal and unstructured ways. Overlap encourages people to get to know each other better, to learn how to communicate with each other, to form friendships, and most importantly, to learn about each other and share some of the things that make them unique.

And, of course, overlap helps people better understand each other's generational cohort values . . . if only by osmosis.

If you haven't gone on a day trip or an informal lunch with a small group of your employees or co-workers, try it and see what happens. We bet that taking the time out of your schedule to hang out with the people you work with will produce some interpersonal breakthroughs and significant improvements in the strength and quality of the communication channels in the group.

You might think that your employees work in the same place every day, so of course they know each other. And, of course, *you* know *them*, too. But when we have the opportunity to explore this assumption at client companies or other organizations, we are often amazed to discover how little people really know about each other. For instance, employees may not be able to give any details about an associate's or direct report's family background, language skills or cultural heritage, or likes and dislikes.

We sometimes use simple surveys of communication style to help co-workers or team members discover who prefers steady pacing, who likes excitement, who is the planner, who is the creative one, and so forth — things that people need to know about each other to work well together, but things that people often don't know at all. Understanding the generational cohort values that emerge during the late adolescence and early adulthood coming-of-age years also helps a manager get the information he or she needs to know in order to train, motivate, and reward.

Even something as simple as a 10-minute break for coffee and snacks in the middle of a staff meeting can get some good overlap going, because everyone is together in the same place in a relaxed atmosphere that lets them interact. Sounds simple, and it is, but it can reap big rewards. Your people will be better able to truly work as a team and rise to challenges when they know each other. And you will have invested an ounce of prevention that could prevent many pounds of nasty clashes — those flashpoints that arise when people of different cohorts and backgrounds try to work together without understanding each other fully.

Conclusion

Managers constantly wrestle with how to provide employees with motivations and rewards that are reasonably standardized. At the same time, managers want to serve the individual interests of their employees. Resolving these impulses has always been a knotty problem, and generational cohort differences only make it harder to do so.

While working with different cohorts and encouraging all your employees to be as productive as possible is very difficult, we've found that communication and understanding on the part of managers goes a long way. You have to walk a fine line to achieve success, and understanding the different values that cohorts bring to their work environment is the first step. The next step is to establish a rapport with these different cohorts based on that understanding. When it comes to building effective cohort collaborations in the workplace, managers must be flexible, responsive, and sympathetic to the various values and affinities of each cohort. And most of all, they must learn to communicate in ways that bring people together, rather than drive them apart.

CHAPTER 11

RETHINKING EMPLOYEE MOTIVATION

A recent analysis done by the Gallup polling organization concludes that a whopping 55% of all employees lack enthusiasm for their jobs. And by Gallup's analysis, nearly 20% are so negative that companies would be better off letting them go, lest they poison the well even further.

News such as this potentially paints a discouraging view of employee motivation. Combine it with the rising tide of reports portraying younger workers as self-serving and lacking in loyalty, and you have a view of the modern workplace as some sort of revolving poker game, one in which each employee is out to maximize his winnings and has no sense of obligation to the others or to the sponsor of the game. And if employees don't like their hands, they just sit out for a while and watch the others work!

We really don't agree with such views. We see a lot of energy and drive in the average workplace. In general, we believe that employees are strongly self-motivated. They want to come to work and they want to do a decent job. When they report negative attitudes in surveys or when they do a consistently poor job, in our view that usually means there are problems in the way their work is designed or in the way they are supervised. Workers have plenty of raw energy and determination for employers to tap into — even if doing so isn't always easy.

This chapter focuses on ways of maximizing employee energy and enthusiasm, with special attention given to the role of generational cohorts.

CRAVE EXCITEMENT? TRY FISHING!

In Chapter 3, we described the high-energy, entertaining atmosphere of Pike Place Fish in Seattle. This fish market is an example of a workplace that appeals, in particular, to employees' sense of excitement and to their desire to express themselves as individuals through their work. Those two motivators — excitement and self-expression — are important to some employees. But not to all employees, by any means. So jobs at the fish market are a better fit for some people than others.

That people are particularly suited for certain types of jobs is an important insight, and we will explore it in this chapter. When you align employees' preferred motivators with their environment, you get exceptional levels of enthusiasm and high-quality performance.

As we discussed previously, the Gen X and N Gen Cohorts are a good fit for an exciting, adventurous workplace like Pike Place Fish. Not surprisingly, excitement is an important motivator for many members of these cohorts, and self-expression can also be important for them. By designing a workplace that offers plenty of opportunities for excitement and self-expression, the fish market does a good job of motivating and retaining members of these cohorts.

Appealing to specific work motives is a powerful management strategy. On the individual level, a manager and an employee can sit down and discuss what turns the employee on and then try to design a work experience that aligns the job with the employee's top work motives. In fact, Alex Hiam, one of the authors, has spent quite a lot of time teaching managers how to do precisely this, and we will share some of the specifics of the method in this chapter. In addition, managers can use their knowledge of cohorts to try to match groups of employees with motivating assignments and environments. There are multiple levels on which to pursue the goal of turned-on employees and high motivation.

Now That's Progress!

During the past 25 years, actual work time in the U.S. has increased by 160 hours a year — nearly a full work month! This despite computers, cell phones, and other high-tech gizmos that are designed to help us do more in less time. It's no wonder motivation has become such a hot management topic.

WHEN ONE SIZE DOESN'T FIT ALL

In our experience, some "motivators" can accidentally demotivate certain individuals or cohorts. Let's say, for example, that you want to motivate employees in your office to meet a challenging sales goal. Your way of doing this is to give a rousing speech filled with allegories about working together and teamwork, and to pass out ball caps and golf shirts emblazoned with the company logo. "There," you say to yourself, "that should get them going!"

Even if they are a bit discouraged by all the extra work, Postwars (and maybe even Leading-Edge Boomers, if the shirts and hats are the right status brand) will likely see these freebies as a nice gesture, and they will wear them with pride. As will N-Gens, who tend to respect authority and enjoy being identified with a group or team. In other words, for some employees this motivational tactic will work to some extent.

But when it comes to Trailing-Edge Boomers and Gen-Xers — the hardcore cynics in today's workplace — their reaction is likely to be, "Give me a break. You expect me to work 80 hours a week to meet this goal in exchange for a lousy shirt and hat! If I wear these at all, it'll be to clean out the garage or paint the house." For these employees, wearing the company logo might even be an embarrassment, a subtle admission that they have been duped into supporting the company line, which they all *know* is a lie anyway.

Effective motivation boils down to learning how to ask the right questions and finding out what motivates each employee on an individual level. For some, a company shirt and hat may be very motivating. But for others, a gift certificate for a massage, or even an on-site massage during a lunch hour, may mean more.

CUSTOMERS AREN'T ALWAYS RIGHT

Most companies these days struggle with how to motivate their employees. When pay raises, casual dress codes, and flex time don't keep the troops engaged, some companies have tried more radical approaches, including challenging such sacred maxims as "The customer is always right" and "Our shareholders come first." So companies such as Medtronic, which produces medical devices, have begun campaigns to elevate the status of their employees. If employees feel motivated by their jobs, they rationalize, the rest will follow. Among other things, Medtronic hosts holiday parties at which customers give tearful testimonials about how the company's pacemakers or other products saved their lives. Other companies pay big bucks to build employee confidence and loyalty by sending employees to seminars where they walk across a bed of hot coals.

But will this kind of approach work for every employee? Our answer is no. To maximize the performance of each individual, you need to try to maximize the fit between a person's job, on the one hand, and the person's basic work motives, on the other. For instance, a computer programmer who is highly motivated by a desire to achieve needs to be given personal opportunities to do challenging, important tasks, such as designing a top-level program for the company's accounting division. Giving such an individual other incentives — such as a public thank-you lunch or a bonus award — just won't do the trick.

WHY PEOPLE WORK

You and your employees may have many different work motives, or reasons for working. Work motives hold the key to boosting employee commitment and creating high performance — or, if a person's work motives aren't properly addressed, to addressing problems like turnover, bad attitude, and poor performance.

There are many possible reasons why people are motivated by their work, and people are usually motivated by more than one factor. For instance, most people would agree that they work for the financial rewards, at least to some degree. But people also place a high value on the intangible rewards of work, such as the friendships made, the pride of working with a good organization, and the sense of accomplishment that comes from doing something important and doing it well. Table 11.1 has a comprehensive list of work motives. You may want to go through and rate yourself for each one, with 1 meaning the factor doesn't motivate you and 5 meaning it's a strong motivator.

TABLE 11.1: WHAT IS YOUR UNIQUE INCENTIVE PROFILE?

Motivators	Rating	Definitions
Affiliation	1 2 3 4 5	Desire to feel part of the group with which you work. Pleasure in being associated with a great organization.
Self-expression	1 2 3 4 5	Urge to express yourself through your work. Desire to be creative.
Achievement	1 2 3 4 5	Drive to accomplish personal goals. Pursuit of excellence.
Security	1 2 3 4 5	Need for stability or reduction of uncertainty and stress.
Growth	1 2 3 4 5	Urge to develop your career to its fullest.
Excitement	1 2 3 4 5	Impulse to seek new experiences and enjoy life through your work.
Status	1 2 3 4 5	Motivation to increase your standing through your accomplishments.
Purpose	1 2 3 4 5	Need for meaning and direction. Desire for important work that really matters.
Competition	1 2 3 4 5	Competitive spirit. Desire to excel in relation to others.
Recognition	1 2 3 4 5	Need for positive feedback and support from the group. Desire to be appropriately recognized for your contributions.
Consideration	1 2 3 4 5	Preference for a friendly, supportive work environment where people take care of each other.
Control	1 2 3 4 5	Need for more control over your own working life. Desire for choice of working conditions or other options.
Rewards	1 2 3 4 5	Motivation to earn significant rewards or wealth from your work.
Responsibility	1 2 3 4 5	Motivation to play a responsible leadership role in the workplace or society as a whole.
Personal needs	1 2 3 4 5	Need to satisfy essential personal or family priorities.

Your top three or four motivators make up your current incentive profile (which may change, gradually, over time). Each of your employees has an incentive profile. When supervisors are aware of each individual's profile, they can better motivate and manage their people, and they can have more productive dialogues with them about what they need in order to perform at their peak.

How to Motivate Your Employees

Here is some good general advice on motivating employees:

- ✦ **Make your expectations clear:** Make sure employees understand your expectations upfront. This will alleviate frustration and make clear to employees what they need to do to succeed.

- ✦ **Reinforce both large and small improvements:** Don't save your praise for the completion of a big project. Give employees positive feedback along the way. Doing so will motivate them to do their best work.

- ✦ **Listen:** Take time to really hear what your employees are saying. Doing so will allow you to identify and address problems early on, while showing your employees you respect them.

- ✦ **Practice what you preach:** No one is going to be motivated by a dour, negative boss. Be upbeat and positive, but don't try to sugarcoat a bad situation.

- ✦ **Get out of the way:** Don't micromanage. Communicate what needs to be done, then step aside and trust your employees to do the job.

WHAT MOTIVATES EACH COHORT

Now we can look at how these work motives relate to the cohort model. Although each individual, naturally, has unique personal motivations for work, generalizing about the typical pattern for a cohort is possible. Cohort values and lifestyles are more consistent with specific motives than others. What this means is that certain work motives are more likely to be powerful motivators for each cohort than other motives. When we analyzed each of the cohorts for work motives, we found the patterns that are presented in Table 11.2.

TABLE 11.2: WHICH WORK MOTIVE IS IMPORTANT?

Work Motive	Ghost Cohorts	Postwars	Leading-Edge Boomers	Trailing-Edge Boomers	Gen-Xers	N-Gens
Affiliation	yes	yes				yes
Self-expression			yes	yes	yes	yes
Achievement	yes	yes				
Security	yes	yes		yes		
Growth			yes	yes		
Excitement		yes	yes	yes	yes	
Status	yes	yes			yes	yes
Purpose	yes	yes				yes
Competition			yes	yes		
Recognition	yes	yes	yes	yes	yes	yes
Consideration			yes	yes		yes
Control			yes	yes	yes	
Rewards	yes	yes	yes	yes	yes	yes
Responsibility	yes	yes				yes
Personal Needs			yes	yes	yes	yes

When you look at the pattern of motivators for any specific cohort, you get a good idea of what generally will appeal most powerfully to members of the cohort.

MOTIVATING EACH COHORT

Table 11.2 tells us which of the many possible work motives are likely to be dominant for each cohort, based on what we know about their profiles. We can go a step further and translate this information into some specific ideas about what is likely to motivate each cohort.

POSTWAR PERFORMANCE BOOSTERS

Here is a list of incentives that we recommend managers and employers use to motivate this cohort. Notice that many of these fit our traditional notions of what an incentive program ought to look like:

✦ Logo-identified or group-identified merchandise of all sorts, including clothing and personal-use items, such as mugs

✦ Public, visible roles and recognition

✦ Recognition of contributions to exceptional group achievements

✦ Symbolic rewards such as trophies or the use of the best parking space to recognize achievements

✦ Upscale, status-oriented rewards and gifts (watches, consumer electronics) or the use of a luxury automobile

✦ Trips to upscale resorts

✦ Participation in sporting events with a social dimension (such as a golf or tennis outing to a nice club)

These motivational methods and items are designed to appeal strongly to people who are motivated by affiliation with a company they can be proud of, by the achievement of goals for that company, and by the increased status that results from their achievements and the achievements of the company. The ideas we mention in the list are likely to work well for this cohort based on our overall profile of it, so they're what you might think of as safe bets when you're trying to generalize about how to motivate Postwars.

LEADING-EDGER PERFORMANCE BOOSTERS

This cohort emphasizes individualism and self-expression, but Leading-Edgers also have an interest in career growth and an orientation toward exciting, fulfilling work. Anything you can do that helps Leading-Edge Boomers feel that their lives are more meaningful because of their work will help keep them actively engaged in the workplace. Here are some ideas for incentives that fit their profile:

- ✦ Coupons or gift certificates that permit freedom of choice
- ✦ Roasting-style recognition of a person's unique personality and contributions
- ✦ Concierge services
- ✦ Recognition of exceptional individual achievements
- ✦ Recognition of contributions to exceptional group achievements
- ✦ Symbolic rewards (like trophies) to memorialize achievements
- ✦ Opportunities to attend career workshops or courses
- ✦ Time off or flexible schedules

In addition, consider Leading-Edgers' lifestage. They may be on the verge of or just entering the empty-nest stage, in which case fun things to do with their spouse (or rebound-relationship partner) are good motivators. A weekend for two at a spa would be great for this cohort.

Another way to motivate some Leading-Edge Boomers might be to let them take time off from work to volunteer a half-day each week or a full day each month with a nonprofit organization. Letting them do so would tap into the idealism of their youth, appeal to their need for self-expression, and build goodwill with community groups.

TRAILING-EDGER PERFORMANCE BOOSTERS

Although their motivators are similar to those of the Leading-Edge Boomers, Trailing-Edgers' main motivators are a little more oriented toward personal autonomy and the need for an emotionally supportive workplace. Being *nice* to Trailing-Edgers is a powerful way to keep them happily engaged with their work, and it's also a simple thing to do.

189

Here are some other examples of good motivators or incentives for Trailing-Edge Boomers:

✦ Frequent, small rewards to reassure employees that their work is still valued

✦ Contributions to savings or retirement funds

✦ Meals, massages, and sympathy

✦ Posting or sharing of individual work

✦ Appreciation and recognition from admired role models or mentors

✦ Participation in events that facilitate professional networking

✦ Rewards of time off

✦ Concierge services

Be *very* careful with pay levels and raises for this cohort. A cautionary tale illustrates the pitfalls in this area. "People aren't happy," an employee told *Federal Times* on the condition he not be identified. "They don't like coming to work here anymore."[1] That's an example of the kind of trouble Naval Sea Systems Command in Arlington, Virginia, ran into after a switch to a new compensation system that gives supervisors more flexibility to allocate pay raises based on merit. In theory, the new system is supposed to improve motivation and performance. But the problem is, employees don't think the new system is fair. They view the appraisal system driving salaries as highly subjective. Fairness is important to employees — and especially to those who are not very motivated by competition in the workplace. Trailing-Edge Boomers are at risk of being demotivated by competitive incentives such as the one introduced at Naval Sea Systems Command.

Many businesses have used such systems for years, and so their employees are more accustomed to the idea of performance reviews determining how much of a raise each employee gets. But in truth, many employees end up resenting such systems and feel that they're not sufficiently fair and accurate. So instead of motivating employees by rewarding exceptional performances, these systems can end up making employees feel upset or angry. Keep these systems fair in the eyes of employees, or you'll lose other cohorts besides the Trailing-Edgers. N-Gens are also especially sensitive to the fairness issue.

GEN-X PERFORMANCE BOOSTERS

Gen-X employees may respond well to incentives that seem similar to Boomer incentives, but we strongly recommend adapting them to the Gen-X culture and ethos. Get a Gen-Xer to redesign, or at least vet, your reward and incentive program before trying it, unless you are from this cohort yourself. Here are some general ideas for incentives that fit this cohort's profile well:

- ✦ Anything fun, such as travel, a night on the town, a change of location, or a temporary posting to a new area

- ✦ Tickets to entertainment events

- ✦ Things *they* think are fun — let them design the activity

- ✦ Travel options in which the employee chooses when and where to go and whom to go with

- ✦ Flexibility to select next assignment or co-workers

In addition, we also want to reiterate our concerns about turning Gen-Xers off accidentally by using any motivators or incentives that seem overly cheerleaderish and awaken their cynicism. Be careful of assumptions with this cohort.

If you're thinking, for example, of holding a weekend event at a local resort featuring a speech by the president of the company and another by a motivational speaker, followed by walking on hot coals and then dancing to big band music with your co-workers while wearing paper hats that say "Onward & Upward!" well, just run it by a few Gen-Xers first. If they roll their eyes, snicker, or say, "But I was planning to go skydiving with a couple of friends," then you know you may have a problem. You certainly don't want them to resent the time spent at a motivational event — it can become demotivating instead.

Careful What You Call Gen-Xers!

Name-calling is an obvious no-no. But to some employees, fancy designations like "associate," "partner," or "owner-operator" may be just as insulting as old-fashioned name-calling. The problem is that you can't change employees' roles just by changing what you call them. And in many cases, the new names reflect good intentions that have not been fully realized. According to *In Good Company*, a book from the director of the IBM Institute for Knowledge Management, employees will react negatively to being named to a new position unless they are also given significant new decision-making authority to go with the name.

This negative response is especially likely from Gen-X employees, so maybe you'd better avoid calling them anything other than what *they* want to be called. If you *do* want to increase their level of responsibility, great — but change their role first, then work with them to choose a name to fit the role. If you change the name without giving employees the new role, you will hurt morale instead of help it. Better yet, why not just change their role, and never mind about the name?

Source: Cohen, Don, and Laurence Prusak. In Good Company: How Social Capital Makes Organizations Work. *Harvard Business School Press, 2001.*

N-GEN PERFORMANCE BOOSTERS

In many ways, N-Gens' core values resemble those of members of the World War II Cohort — they tend to accept institutional objectives and viewpoints, and want to work and be recognized for helping achieve a greater good. They are team players, and like to be part of smaller teams within the larger organization. Older supervisors or managers from other cohorts may have the right general idea for motivating them, but miss by failing to match the motivator or incentive to their culture.

Here are some examples of incentives that fit this cohort's profile:

✦ Recognition through gifts of useful items for the work environment that employees can place and control the use of (such as a swing-arm lamp with dimmer or a CD player with headphones)

✦ Job rotations or short-term assignments that prevent boredom

✦ Entertainment (tickets or events, but make sure they are of *their* choice, not yours)

✦ Advancement to positions of greater responsibility

✦ Becoming members of a microteam that can bond to accomplish specific tasks and goals

We also recommend a simple but powerful motivator: Thank-you notes and frequent verbal recognition and encouragement. N Gens want to be noticed and appreciated and often feel like they're not getting enough attention. And if that's how they feel, then from a motivational perspective, they're right!

A recent survey conducted by Teenage Workforce Solutions for the National Grocers Association found that the number one consideration of working teenagers (N-Gens) is to be treated with respect (see the sidebar "What N-Gens Want in a Job"). This even beat out money, which came in fourth on the list, as a prime factor affecting whether N-Gens stayed in a job or went looking for greener pastures.

What N-Gens Want in a Job

✦ Respect: 92.9%

✦ Fair treatment: 92.3%

✦ Flexible schedule: 91.2%

✦ Money: 88.1%

✦ Fun: 87.2%

Source: National Grocers Association Press Release, "Survey Reveals What's Needed to Attract, and Keep, Today's Teenaged Worker," www.nationalgrocers.org, August 18, 2000.

Motivation with a Personal Touch

If you're looking for a good way to recognize and motivate your employees, the personal touch means a lot.

At Disneyland in Anaheim, California, one of the highest forms of recognition for cast members is to have their names painted on one of the Main Street USA windows for everyone to see. This kind of recognition is very public, and very personal, and it appeals to many Disney employees. Some who have received the award use words like "elated," "awed," and "dumbstruck" to describe their feelings about receiving such an honor.

Dallas-based Southwest Airlines also makes recognition very personal for its employees. After receiving the airline industry's Triple Crown award for best on-time performance, best baggage handling, and fewest customer complaints for the fifth consecutive year in 1997, Southwest's CEO dedicated a special plane to the workers and had the names of each of the company's 24,000 employees engraved into the plane's overhead bins.

But you don't have to go to such great lengths to recognize employees' contributions. Sometimes, a personal note or a sincere public or private thanks is enough to let employees know their contributions make a difference. Successful recognition and motivation is all about celebrating victories large and small, and connecting with people on a personal level.

Many managers find recognition difficult because it involves talking about their feelings, which makes them feel vulnerable. Also, many people are not confident in their skills to give a memorable thank-you speech or to write a meaningful note of recognition. But, as many experts point out, giving personal recognition is a learned skill, and practice makes perfect.

Source: Davidson, Linda. "The Power of Personal Recognition," Workforce, July 1999, vol. 78, p 44 (4).

CREATING FOUR WORK PATHS

As a manager, you make motivation decisions in a variety of contexts. Sometimes you're focused on one individual at one specific period of time. In such situations, we highly recommend going to a very fine level of analysis. Use the concept of the incentive profile to narrow down your focus on a few motivators that seem most likely to have a powerful effect. In doing so, your knowledge of cohorts should prove helpful.

However, you may also have to design basic long-term programs and policies. In this situation, you can't really customize. Certainly, it's not practical to have different plans and policies for every individual. It may not even be practical to do so for each cohort. That's why we recommend a high-level analysis for long-term decisions: A simple but powerful strategy for any employer today is to offer four main employment paths.

A four-path system helps improve the fit between the job and the various cohort values present in your workplace, and it accommodates individual differences. To simplify the task of aligning incentives to the specific work motives of individuals and cohorts, we have generalized work motives according to the same four-pronged strategy. Each of the four paths appeals to a different set of work motives.

STRUCTURED WORK PATH

The structured work path is most likely to appeal to Ghost and Postwar Cohorts. The key motivators include:

- ✦ **Affiliation:** Members of the Ghost and Postwar Cohorts like being a part of something larger than themselves. These employees wear the company logo with pride because it identifies them as being part of a group.

- ✦ **Security:** These employees like stability. Put them in jobs that don't involve a lot of change. While younger cohorts would be bored with the same old thing, older cohorts feel comfortable knowing what to expect each day.

- ✦ **Status:** Give these employees a sense that they are important and appreciated. Length-of-service awards are especially appealing to this group, as is anything that recognizes their accomplishments and helps to increase their standing in the group.

✦ **Recognition:** Make a point to acknowledge their achievement, even on small projects. And for larger accomplishments, don't miss an opportunity to thank them individually in a way that they will find meaningful.

✦ **Financial rewards:** Financial rewards are likely the way these cohorts are used to getting rewarded. But money alone isn't enough of a motivator for most people, so for maximum effect, couple it with something else, such as public recognition.

✦ **Responsibility:** Added responsibility often proves to be an excellent reward for members of the Ghost and Postwar Cohorts, but make sure this fits with individual needs. Some older workers do not want to be in charge and are happy simply completing the work that is assigned to them.

Traditional management styles and organizational structures tend to do a fairly good job of appealing to these motives.

INDIVIDUALIST WORK PATH

The individualist work path is most likely to appeal to Leading-Edge and Trailing-Edge Boomers, who tend to crave independence and self-expression. The key work motives for employees on this path are very different from those of individuals on the structured work path. Here is a summary:

✦ **Self-expression:** Self-expression is key, so offer Boomers plenty of opportunities to be themselves, do creative things, and leave their personal imprint. Let them coordinate and develop an internal website, or put them in charge of organizing a charity fundraising campaign.

✦ **Excitement:** Offer ways for these employees to enhance their personal experiences at work. Put them in charge of a departmental retreat, which might include anything from skydiving to bungee-jumping.

✦ **Growth:** Personal growth and development are important to Boomers, so make sure you give them opportunities for career advancement, or at least an opportunity for a lateral shift into a new area. They won't be content to plateau.

✦ **Consideration:** Leading-Edge Boomers, in particular, are looking for considerate, friendly, caring, humane treatment. They want their work to be more than just a job. Things like an extra day off for their birthday and flex time will show them that you care about them as a person, and that they are more than just a cog in a wheel.

✦ **Control:** Trailing-Edge Boomers, more than any other cohort, crave control. Let them decide where, when, and how they do their work by offering them opportunities to telecommute and work a flexible schedule.

✦ **Personal needs:** Flexibility and support for personal and family priorities is important to both Boomer cohorts, but for different reasons. Leading-Edge Boomers will appreciate eldercare referrals and time off to help aging parents. Trailing-Edge Boomers, meanwhile, will appreciate things like daycare referrals and flexibility to take their kids to the doctor or to attend a soccer match. Many companies have found that offering flex time and other family-friendly programs also helps reduce absenteeism.

EXCITEMENT WORK PATH

The excitement work path is most likely to appeal to Generation X, and the key to this work path is interesting experiences. Here is a summary of what this cohort expects from a job:

✦ **Excitement:** Opportunities to do new and different, amusing, exciting, even risky things at work (dressing up in costumes, for example, like at Pike Place Fish) are vital to the appeal of this path. To tap into this work motive, let employees dress as they please and offer an occasional offbeat outing during work hours (to go bowling or in-line skating, for example). The main thing is to keep employees on their toes, wondering what you will come up with next.

✦ **Status:** These employees don't want to toil away in oblivion. They want their accomplishments to help improve their status in the group. Take time to recognize their work publicly, and offer feedback on a regular basis.

✦ **Control:** Let employees decide when to work and where. Let them decorate their offices or cubicles any way they want. Giving younger employees some control over their work environment demonstrates that you trust them to get the job done.

✦ **Personal needs:** Give single employees without children the same opportunities to use flex time as other workers. They may use it to go to a movie in the middle of the afternoon, but if they come back recharged and work into the night, so much the better.

TEAM WORK PATH

This work path will appeal to the N Gen Cohort. In many ways, this cohort's core values are quite close to those of the World War II Cohort. Key motivators include:

✦ **Affiliation:** This cohort grew accustomed to working in study teams in high school and college, so they find a team-oriented approach highly congenial. Being a part of microteams of 4 or 5 people who meet and solve specifically-defined problems will have great appeal to N-Gens — you'll probably find they start meeting on their own time, after work for coffee or during informal pizza dinners, and get great satisfaction from bonding as a small team.

✦ **Purpose:** At this moment, N-Gens lack a well-defined global goal to give them meaning and direction. Nonetheless, they have a very real need for important work that really matters. Define a goal that gives them clear meaning and direction, and their team will attack it with zeal.

✦ **Recognition:** While all cohort groups like recognition, N-Gens crave recognition like no other. More than any other cohort since the World War II Cohort, they accept and internalize institutional (or corporate) missions and policies. Explicit recognition by an institution in the form of employee or team awards will spur them on to greater achievements.

✦ **Responsibility:** Because they believe in institutional goals, both corporate and societal, N-Gens willingly accept responsibility for doing their part. By and large, they don't feel qualified yet to be the overall leaders, but give them (or their team or microteam) a specific task and they will take it upon themselves to ensure its successful completion.

Conclusion

Motivation is one of the hottest topics in management these days. In fact, it has become a multi-billion-dollar business, and an entire industry has sprung up to meet the growing demand for motivational experts, some of whom command fees as high as $65,000 for a single session. But are any of these motivational efforts working? There is continued debate as to whether the industry really can boost performance through its many bells-and-whistles approaches.

The real question now is why these efforts aren't working better. Our answer is that there are no quick fixes. Simply throwing money at employees through cash awards or trinkets, or bringing in high-priced speakers, won't motivate employees long enough to make a difference. Sure, money can be a motivator, but to be effective it must be combined with other forms of recognition and serve as a symbol of something greater.

Plus, there's a common misperception that knowing how to motivate employees is an innate skill — either you have it or you don't. But nothing could be further from the truth. The ability to motivate is an *acquired* skill, and one that must be practiced day in and day out. In our opinion, it is one of the most valuable management skills you can learn. Here's why: If you don't learn to motivate people, your best people will quit and take a better job. Or even worse, they will give up and settle into mediocrity. You'll be left with poor performers and cynics, employees who don't leave because no one else wants them!

Back in 1924, researchers at the Harvard Graduate School of Business tried to find the optimum working conditions to maximize output at Western Electric's Hawthorne plant in Cicero, Illinois. They first added better lighting for an experimental group of employees, leaving another control group to work under the plant's normal conditions. Productivity increased for the test group. But it also increased for the control group, where nothing had changed. Baffled by these results, researchers measured other factors to explain the findings, but came away with nothing. When they returned working conditions back to the normal plant conditions for the test group, productivity continued to increase with each change. Still, researchers could find no explanation. When they finally asked the employees why their productivity had improved, the workers told them that participating in the study made them feel important and had improved their motivation.

The lesson here is that every employee has something he or she needs and wants in order to do a better job — and your role as a manager is to figure out what it is and then link it to performance in an appropriate way. It might be making the work important. It might be adding variety or excitement. It might be using one of the thousands of merchandise-, travel-, or event-oriented incentives. Whatever it is, if you can find it, you'll have more motivated employees. And understanding cohorts can help you find it.

Generational cohort management can also help you develop broad motivational programs by cohort, programs that can be further tailored to meet the very diverse needs of individuals in your organization.

ENDNOTES

1. Found on the *Federal Times* website, and used as a case example in Motivational Management trainings by the training firm of Alexander Hiam & Associates.

CHAPTER 12

THE NEW LEADERSHIP ESSENTIALS

B y now, you're probably thinking, "Wow. Managing sure can get complicated in a hurry when you mix a bunch of different cohorts together and call them a workforce!" The traditional leader typically does not respond well to the wrinkles and complexities that come with having many different workers, and as a result often has employees who seem strangely disconnected from their work and who are difficult to train and motivate.

Managers need to have a broad and flexible repertoire of leadership behaviors in order to handle all the demands of employee leadership in the workplace today. In this chapter, we provide a system that describes the ways in which managers can lead, and then we give you some cohort-related guidance for when to use which style.

Improving your leadership skills takes practice and a concerted effort. Following the advice we give you in this chapter is a lot like working out at the gym when you haven't exercised in years. It's painful at first, as you discover muscles you never knew you had. But after a while, you start feeling stronger and better about the exercises you're doing. Then, instead of using the same group of muscles all the time, you start trying different exercises and working different muscle groups to build overall fitness. The same goes with leadership — you need to try different approaches and use different skills in order to build your overall effectiveness.

TASK ORIENTATION AND PEOPLE ORIENTATION

When you think about leadership, you may think of a dynamic executive or supervisor who is good at inspiring his people. Someone like Jack Welch, the former head of General Electric. Or perhaps you think of a strong-willed leader like General George Patton, who people followed out of fear more than anything else. Or maybe you think of a warm and fuzzy Mr. Rogers–like leader, someone who gets the most from his people by treating them well and helping them develop to their full potential.

Each of these leader types might be effective in specific situations and ineffective in others. In recent decades, a gradual understanding has emerged that no one approach to leadership is inherently right. The right way to lead depends on the situation. And, naturally, one of the most important aspects of the situation is the people who are being led.

In this chapter, we explore the relationship between people's cohort values and their leadership needs. The first step in realizing that many different leadership styles are important came when researchers began to examine the difference between a highly task-oriented, structured management approach and a looser, more people-oriented approach. Task-oriented leaders seem naturally focused on the work itself. Their management style clearly directs people to do specific tasks in specific ways. They think a lot about the work itself, and not much about the people — except to check that the people seem to be doing the right jobs correctly. Are you a leader like this, with a task orientation? Many managers are.

At the other end of the spectrum are leaders who are very people oriented, and who think and talk a lot about what their people require to do a good job. This kind of leader is viewed as sensitive, helpful, and a good communicator. But this type of leader may also be perceived as disorganized, a poor planner, or lacking in technical skills, especially when a complex project needs to be done. Are you a leader with a strong people orientation? Many managers fall into this category, especially managers from the two Boomer Cohorts.

After many studies, researchers concluded that neither people- nor task-oriented management is completely effective. Managers need to flex back and forth, varying their management style to suit the situation. As theories of flexible management have developed, the old dichotomy of people orientation versus task orientation has been refined even further.

EIGHT LEADERSHIP STYLES DEFINED

In developing his leadership program, Alex Hiam, a member of our author team, has identified eight specific leadership styles, each of which has its place in modern management. The leadership styles are:

Reassure: The manager helps employees cope with the stresses and challenges of work life.

Challenge: The manager pushes employees by raising the level of challenge.

Empathize: The manager listens to employee's needs, understands how employees feel, and works with them to choose appealing goals.

Inform: The manager shows why a particular plan or direction makes sense and how it relates to employees' work.

Explain: The manager explains clearly *what* employees must do and *why* employees must do it, and makes sure they get informative feedback about *how well* they do it.

Direct: The manager oversees employees in whole units of work, telling them what to do and supervising and correcting the work as they do it.

Guide: The manager guides development by helping employees pursue stretch goals and try new things that improve their skills.

Delegate: The manager trusts employees to take on full responsibility for specific tasks.

Leaders need to be able to flex their style and manage using any of these approaches. For instance, if two organizations have to be integrated and there are many changes to handle in a hurry, leaders may need to provide plenty of reassurance and empathy to help overstressed workers through the transition. In a stable organization that has not changed significantly in several years but which now must respond to new strategic demands, the leader may need to provide a wake-up call using the challenge style. From tea and sympathy to wake up and smell the coffee, the leader's style has to change dramatically when the situation does.

Give Them Wings Before You Let Them Fly

Are you often disappointed when you assign employees a task and they do not do what you wanted? If so, maybe you are delegating too much too soon, pushing them from the nest before they are really ready to fly. Take time to make sure they fully understand what needs to be done and why before letting them go off on their own.

MIXING THE EIGHT STYLES: EXAMPLE ONE

Let's say that you recently hired Sally to fill an engineering position. Sally is right out of school, but she has several internships under her belt and seems confident and eager to learn. Since she's motivated to learn the job, you don't need to worry about her commitment, and that makes your life easier. You can use three main styles in managing Sally:

✦ **Direct:** In the early days, direct Sally so that she will have a chance to do the work properly under your supervision. Walk her through the process she is to follow and make sure that all of her questions are answered. This stage is almost like a dress rehearsal for the real thing.

✦ **Guide:** Later on, step back and let her take the lead. Offer support and advice as she gains competence through increasingly independent practice.

✦ **Delegate:** Finally, give Sally the chance to do the job completely on her own, without your looking over her shoulder. Just ask her to give you an occasional progress report so that you know she's still on the right track.

MIXING THE EIGHT STYLES: EXAMPLE TWO

Now, let's say you're managing Bob, who is a 10-year veteran of the company and who is a bit frustrated by his slow rate of advancement. While he is clearly capable of doing a good job, he often seems distracted by office politics and internal squabbles, and at times complains about tasks he is assigned to do.

Sometimes, employees like Bob are loath to do a task because they don't see why it needs to be done. As the manager, you may think that the rationale is none of their business! But people have a hard time working on projects or tasks if they think the tasks aren't important — or worse, if they think they're the wrong things to do.

When managing an employee like Bob, you must use your leadership skills to create a sense of purpose and to build commitment to a broader goal — and then to relate the specific work of the employee to that broader goal. In this type of situation, you can lean on three of the management styles:

✦ **Inform:** Share information in a logical way about the need for commitment to a broader goal or cause. Tell Bob, for example, "We need to meet our project startup goal, because if we don't, product supply will decrease, customer orders will fall behind, and that could hurt sales both short term and long term."

✦ **Empathize:** Sometimes commitment needs to be emotional, not just logical. That's where the empathize style can help. By listening to Bob and appreciating his feelings and perspective, you are better able to connect with him emotionally — and thereby, to connect him emotionally to the organization's purpose and plans.

✦ **Explain:** It's not enough to just use the inform and empathize styles to build a general commitment to an important goal or plan. You still must relate employees' specific actions and duties to the overall plan. How does Bob's work contribute to

205

the big-picture goal? This is where the explain style comes to the fore. It is perhaps the most important style available to managers because it is the critical link to getting employee buy-in.

In Bob's case, explain that unless project timelines are met, customer orders may drop, and the long-term success of the business could be at stake. This aspect of the explain style gives Bob a clear view of how his specific task contributes to the broader organizational goal. The explain style also helps employees evaluate how well they perform their tasks.

As a leader, you need to make sure that you provide plenty of clear feedback and that employees know they're doing a good job. We sometimes think of this as a view to task. When combined with a clear view to goal, it ensures higher than average performance because employees can always see a) why what they are doing is important and b) whether they are doing that important task well or not.

THE FAILURE OF LEADERSHIP TRADITIONS

As we noted earlier, Alex Hiam has done extensive studies of leadership styles to see how managers typically lead. Review the eight styles we defined earlier, and guess which one you think managers most often exhibit when dealing with their employees.

The answer is the delegation style. By far the most common leadership style is to delegate work to employees. Delegation means just telling employees to go do something, and then ignoring them (by and large) while they do it. In fact, delegation is often used by default, rather than design. That is, leaders abdicate leadership.

Delegation is appropriate when the manager knows that the employee:

✦ Has all the skills and knowledge needed to do an excellent job without help or correction.

✦ Has all the information and other resources that might be needed to do the job well.

✦ Wants to do the job well — is fully committed and motivated.

Who's Likely to Have Commitment Issues? Just About Everyone

Which employees most need to feel that their work is important and that they're contributing to the big picture? Which are most likely to lose motivation if they don't have this sense of purpose in their daily work?

If you thought of the Boomers, we agree with you. Leading-Edge Boomers' emphasis on self-expression and individualism predisposes them toward work with meaning or purpose. They don't want to be cogs in a wheel. They want to be doing something important, something that allows them to make a difference. A cause helps. A compelling goal is essential. Trailing-Edge Boomers have a similar urge toward individualism, although they want their job to be even more of a solo act. Add to this their natural tendency toward cynicism and distrust of institutions, and you have a group of workers who don't take any orders from management without questioning them. Trailing-Edgers want to know why they should have to do the task and whether it is really worthy of their unique, individual attention.

Leaders of Gen-X employees also find it necessary to create a sense of commitment. Managers of Xers can't assume that their employees are eager and willing to do the job and only need to be taught how. Xers won't climb the rigging unless they know why they need to — and unless they feel it's the right choice for them, personally, to do it.

Postwars are on their way out, and N-Gens are just getting started, so the two Boomer Cohorts and Generation X make up the bulk of today's workforce. That all three cohorts show tendencies to be somewhat disconnected from the work they do demonstrates just how important commitment building should be in your organization.

These are strict conditions. If they're not met, delegation fails. Because tasks have gotten more complex, and the speed at which tasks are completed has doubled or tripled, managers must not delegate until they are sure employees are ready and willing to do a particular job.

Failed delegation happens far too often. The employees don't know enough, or don't have enough resources (or the authority to get needed resources), or they don't really care enough to give it their best. The manager ends up catching employees after they've messed up, and is now irritated and disappointed. Things get negative in a hurry. The manager thinks the employee is stupid, lazy, or is goofing off. The employee thinks the manager is stupid, doesn't care, or is trying to sabotage the employee.

In good leadership, delegation is something the manager works carefully toward, building commitment and competence along the way. Trust should not be given prematurely, any more than it should be withheld once the employee is ready for it. Unfortunately, most managers do a lot more delegating than they really should, and they use the other styles of leadership that might prepare their people for the rigors of delegation less often than they should.

So why do managers delegate so much? Because 1) it's easy to just assign people tasks and then forget about them, and 2) delegation is the cornerstone of the Ghost Cohorts' leadership style. The military chain of command, which relies heavily on delegation, served older cohorts well during World War II and during the postwar era, but in today's work environment, this tradition fails the modern manager.

While we're on the subject, can you guess which leadership style managers are least likely to use? Not surprisingly, the answer is the empathize style. In fact, most employees say their managers do not lead in this style at all. Far from it — many seem more inconsiderate than considerate. They seem to actively avoid making any emotional connection with their people. Again, this is the ghost of older cohorts influencing our leadership styles in the workplace.

The World War II and Postwar Cohorts did not need or expect much empathy or sympathy in the workplace, especially from their bosses. They imprinted a top-down, impersonal leadership style that is still with us today. That is why leaders seem to do a lot of delegating and take very little or no interest in their employees' feelings and emotional needs. And that's why we now face the task of retraining managers so that they can begin to make effective use of the entire range of leader-ship styles.

These days, more and more personal issues are creeping into the workplace. Childcare, eldercare, substance abuse help, mental health counseling, and other personal issues have for the first time become concerns of employers. Companies have begun to realize that there's more to employees than their work life, and many are making an effort to offer expanded benefit programs that recognize the larger personal issues that may affect job performance. Times have changed, and with more and more dual-income families, there's no one at home to tie up the loose ends. While many old-style managers may not want to hear that the project didn't get done because the kids were sick or because Mom fell and broke her hip, the fact is that an empathetic leadership style is more likely to get results with an employee stressed-out by personal issues than a heavy-handed approach that tries to make the employee feel guilty.

FOUR PATHS TO LEADERSHIP

Hone your ability to use each leadership style, and then make a conscious choice of which to use in each situation. Period. It's a simple and powerful precept, and one that every manager already follows to some degree . . . and probably could follow to a far greater degree. However, the unique challenges of cohort management defy simple maxims. We were tempted to develop prescriptions for each cohort, but there are seven cohorts to consider and eight leadership styles. We're talking about a pretty big matrix here. And managers need to make constant, almost instinctive adjustments in their style to fit the constantly changing landscape of their workplaces. There must be a simpler way!

Indeed there is. The method that we recommend using to blend the eight leadership styles and the cohort approach revolves around those four different employee pathways from Chapter 11. In the remainder of this chapter, we offer some general advice about how to lead workers on each of these four pathways. For each of the four work paths, you need to have a separate management style.

STRUCTURED APPROACH

The structured work path is especially appropriate for older cohorts, including the Ghost Cohorts, whose values and traditions still shape our organizations, and the Postwars, who often sit at the very top of our leadership hierarchies. A structured approach emphasizes task-oriented, directive styles. It is not touchy-feely and does not disperse information to those who are being led. It assumes that if they're told what needs to be done, people will simply get to work and do it. The styles that work best for the structured approach are:

✦ Challenge (light a fire under them)

✦ Direct (tell them what to do, and oversee their work)

✦ Delegate (just tell them to do it)

Think about the great leaders of World War II. They used these three leadership styles pretty much to the exclusion of all others. The great general lays it on the line to the troops — we've got to take this beach or else. He tells them what to do, handing down detailed plans for the assault through his hierarchy. And then he sits back and waits for the reports, trusting his disciplined and competent organization to go and do the job. He delegates to his next in command, who delegates to his next in command, on down the line. Each time, the task is broken into smaller chunks to match the more limited responsibilities and authority of the next layer down.

That is the structured approach to management in a nutshell, and it does not take the full range of our eight leadership styles to execute it well. Generals Douglas MacArthur and George Patton never used the explain, empathize, or reassure styles, for example. They didn't need to. But for the younger cohorts, more and different leadership styles are essential. The limited and highly task-oriented style of the structured leader does not work very well for many of today's cohorts.

The brewery example from Chapter 1 clearly demonstrates the limits of this style. The older employees who stayed late to fix the broken equipment needed only a call to arms. Managers mentioned that there was an emergency, and that employees were needed who would stay late and help out, and this was enough to engage the older workers. They responded because of their strong sense of duty, responsibility, and the importance of conformity. Younger brewery workers, however, were obviously unmoved!

INDIVIDUALIST APPROACH

Members of the two Boomer Cohorts respond well to the individualist work path, as we explained earlier. This is because they are individualists who value self-expression — and, in the case of the Trailing-Edge Boomers, because they're cynical and don't necessarily believe the leader knows what he's doing. The cynicism of the Gen X Cohort makes Xers likewise doubtful of their leaders' abilities. Although we write more about them in the next section, some Gen-Xers respond well to the individualist approach.

The leadership styles that get the most from the two Boomer cohorts and are consistent with the individualist approach are:

- ✦ Inform (show employees how larger plans relate to their work)
- ✦ Empathize (listen to their feelings)
- ✦ Guide (encourage them to reach stretch goals)
- ✦ Delegate (just tell them to do it)

Of these four styles, Boomers are most likely to advocate for the inform and delegate styles. They often complain that they don't have enough information and that they need a more participatory environment in which they are privy to the details of the decision-making process. The inform style answers this complaint. They also tend to ask for more responsibility and to believe that they should be allowed to do projects without management interference. The delegate style would seem to meet this request, but it has a serious pitfall.

If a leader delegates prematurely, before using other styles to make sure the employee is fully committed and capable, then delegation will fail. The employee won't succeed, and both the employee and the manager will be irritated — often at each other!

Using the empathize style is essential because it bridges the gap between manager and employee and builds communication, understanding, and good rapport. It sets the stage for effective delegation later on by ensuring that both sides understand each other and know what is realistic and what is not.

Using the guide style, in which the leader provides plenty of richly informative feedback about performance and helps the employee develop a high level of competency, is also crucial. Leaders who allow Boomer employees to persuade them that they can be hands-off delegators fail to provide proper guidance, and their employees often fail as a result. The managers become frustrated with the employees, and the employees become frustrated with the managers. It may seem paradoxical for leaders to provide structured guidance to employees on the individualist work path, but think of it as training and developing your employees so that they have the competence to truly act as independently as their temperaments want them to.

A key lesson for modern managers is that independent-minded employees have to be prepared to succeed independently. If simply given enough rope, they will hang themselves, and tangle the leader hopelessly in their mess! Independence of spirit is a difficult thing for leaders to deal with, because it requires the leader to guide employees through enough experiences for them to acquire the real-world expertise needed to match their urge for independence.

On the other hand, the fact that many employees from the two Boomer Cohorts and the Gen X Cohort are eager for more independence means that they have a natural motivation to acquire more competence. This is a wonderful thing that aware leaders can use to full advantage, but only if they remember to provide coaching and guidance to build specific competencies.

Making Sure They're Really Ready

As the leader, you need to consider the practical issues and provide the structured experiences that are needed to ensure that your employees have all the knowledge and experience they need to succeed independently at each assignment you give them. Don't just take their word that they're ready!

EXCITEMENT APPROACH

The Gen-X employees in your workplace will generally respond better to the independence path than the structured path, as it introduces some leadership styles that fit them better. But they have some additional needs that, as we argued in earlier chapters, require the excitement work path. For these relatively young employees, work needs to be emotionally fulfilling and exciting. They want to feel like successful free agents, surfing their way through the workday. As the leader, you need to provide some good surf and then get the heck out of the way, dude. The core set of styles for managing on the excitement path is:

- ✦ Explain (tell employees why it's important)

- ✦ Guide (encourage them to reach stretch goals)

- ✦ Reassure (help them cope with stress of work)

The explain style is essential because these employees are liable to wander off and do something else that seems to be important or interesting if they don't understand the purpose of the tasks you've given them. As a manager, you need to provide plenty of leadership to give their specific assignments context, meaning, and purpose — and also to make sure they're aware of what to do and how to do it, and that they're currently doing it well.

In fact, managers' most common complaint about Gen-X employees is that they don't do what they're supposed to do. That's going to continue to happen unless the explain style is used often and fully to keep young employees oriented and focused on their work.

The guide style is also important. Like the explain style, it provides support and structure for these employees and is an important part of managing them. Gen-Xers often believe that they're ready for full delegation and want to be allowed to work independently. But they aren't ready. Not at all. So their managers try to direct them with close, heavy-handed supervision. But their free-agency urges are violated and they're bored. So they tug back by demanding freedom. When given it, however, they tend to do the job wrong or the wrong job. The only solution is to provide continuing guidance, walking alongside your employees on the excitement work path enough of the time that you can point out wrong turns and offer occasional tips and advice to keep them focused and learning. Their instinct for excitement will lead them right off the trail unless they have a good guide.

Don't direct your excitement path workers too strongly, or you'll find they rebel and run off into the woods. They don't want to walk in the back of the line. They want to be up front leading. Give them enough guidance that they can be up front without getting lost.

The final style for the excitement path is reassure. You might not think that free-agency advocates who ask you not to supervise their work need any reassurance, but they do. Don't let their occasional cynicism fool you — emotional support and a caring workplace family are important to them and help them feel comfortable and needed. You need to check in with them as a person, not as a boss, to let them know that they're appreciated and are doing well.

TEAM APPROACH

For the N Gen Cohort, what we call the team path works best. This cohort's values are in many ways similar to those of the World War II Cohort. Teamwork is big (quite a change from Gen-X free agency). N-Gens want to accomplish greater societal and corporate goals, and then they want to be recognized for their contributions. Accordingly, the management styles most appropriate to the team path are:

✦ Delegate (just tell them to do it)

✦ Challenge (light a fire under them)

✦ Inform (show employees how larger plans relate to their work)

You may be surprised to see delegate as one of the leadership styles to use for the team approach. Well, it's delegation with a twist. The delegation is not to an individual, but to a team specially assembled to accomplish the task at hand. The task must be explicitly defined — but once that has been done, the N-Gen team will work on and off the job to make sure that it gets done. They will accept the responsibility cheerfully and eagerly.

The Depression Era Cohort saved the country from starvation and financial ruin, and the World War II Cohort saved the world from evil. The N-Gen's ultimate challenge is yet to be defined, but they are willing to take on anything — the bigger the better! That's why the challenge style should also be thrown into the leadership mix when it comes to managing N-Gens.

The idealistic N-Gens want to work to accomplish some greater good. As a manager, you must inform them how a particular project fits into overall corporate objectives — why it's necessary and what the larger results will be that flow from a successful completion.

And with all applications of the team path, there must be explicit recognition at the successful completion of the project or the accomplishment of the goal. Recognize the team as well as the individuals on the team.

Are You Explaining Enough?

When you assign a junior member of your team to do a project, are you irritated when they ask questions about why it needs to be done? If so, you may need to plan a little more time next time to explain the big picture.

CONCLUSION

To sum up, the eight leadership styles cluster within the four management paths, and, as we have seen, align very closely with the different cohorts. The table below can help you decide which leadership style is most appropriate for a particular individual or group. If the individual or group is toward the leading edge of a cohort, consider whether one or more of the styles appropriate to the next older cohort might be best. Conversely, if the individual or group is tending towards the trailing edge of a cohort, give some thought to the styles that would normally apply to the next younger cohort.

And, of course, remember that people are individuals. They may have some characteristics of another cohort, no matter what cohort their age places them in. And even if most of their values are in line with one cohort, other values often get blurred for those whose coming-of-age years are close to those of another cohort.

TABLE 12.1: STYLES AND PATHS APPLIED TO COHORTS

Path	Structured	Individual	Excitement	Team
COHORT				
Postwar	Challenge			
	Direct			
	Delegate			
Boomer		Inform		
		Empathize		
		Guide		
		Delegate		
Gen X			Explain	
			Guide	
			Reassure	
N Gen				Delegate
				Challenge
				Inform

CHAPTER 13

CREATIVITY AND INNOVATION IN THE NEW WORKPLACE

We point out in Chapter 4 that the legacy of the Ghost Cohorts predisposes our organizations toward stability and away from informality, flexibility, and — of particular concern in this chapter — creativity and innovation. Some people like to joke that business creativity is a classic oxymoron — a combination of two fundamentally incompatible ideas. Although obviously an exaggeration, this joke taps into an essential truth.

Stability-seeking Depression-era employees and managers tended to see innovation as a necessary evil rather than as the main purpose of their work. If innovation was necessary to keep up or to face down a serious challenge, then, "By God, we'll do it." But in general, the hierarchical, ordered organizations they built were better at grinding a problem down than at redefining it and solving it.

However, creativity and innovation, even if they're rare, have always been an integral part of business. A healthy, growing economy is hard to imagine without them. The struggle today is to achieve a natural, consistent, and rapid rate of productive innovation and change in our businesses. Specifically, companies today have to be creative enough to *drive* change rather than to *chase* it — or even worse, run from it.

When we presented our four-path model in Chapter 11, we emphasized its importance in creating a safe haven and an appropriate development path for employees. The four-path approach emphasizes employees' needs. But we also observed that the four-path approach encourages diversity, and that there are business benefits to diversity of all kinds. As we look at the issue of innovation, we can add to our understanding of the organizational benefit of establishing four work paths: *When you create a multi-path culture, and permit and encourage employees to express themselves in different ways, you take a major step toward creating the innovative organization of tomorrow.*

To help you take workplace creativity even further, we provide some specifics in this chapter on how to manage for creativity and how to set up creative teams that are good at generating ideas and taking them all the way to fruition. These techniques can help you ramp up creative activity in your group or organization. The techniques we describe can be effective with any group, whether it includes multiple cohorts or not — but they work best when combined with an awareness of the different cohorts.

BALANCING INNOVATION AND PRODUCTION

These days, everyone knows that companies need to be able to change quickly. Each year, Fortune 500 companies control less of our economy as smaller, more nimble companies fast become the norm. Vast military might cannot prevent a terrorist attack, as we saw on September 11, 2001. And vast industrial might cannot prevent an entrepreneurial uprising. The certainty that past success means future profits has long since faded. We live in an age of creativity, an age in which organizations that *imagine* better often *do* better as a result.

From Loose to Tight to Loose Again

The four-path approach to management makes it easier to pursue what some experts have called a *loose-tight* organizational structure, in which your organization alternates between loose periods of creative opportunity-seeking and tight efforts to capitalize on new ideas with efficient processes that are based on them.

A key management challenge today is to somehow make it feasible for all employees to ask what-if and why-not questions. Engaging all employees in the creative quest is a radical thing to do. In fact, it is potentially very destructive. You risk losing efficiency, order, and discipline. Today's need for an upwelling of questioning and critical insight is at odds with the traditional well-ordered business hierarchy, in which members play their assigned roles. If you assign everyone the role of generating new ideas every day, you could get, potentially, total chaos.

A completely open and imaginative workforce probably sounds fun if you like excitement — as Gen-X employees often do. But it also sounds like a recipe for disaster. Work would be one continuous brainstorming session, a kind of creative party, with no time to settle down and do one thing long enough to produce anything positive from all the bright ideas. In fact, even when businesses exist in turbulent environments that reward creative risk-taking and opportunity-making, they have to strike a *balance* between invention and production.

We need the ability to recognize an opportunity to innovate and switch into creative mode rapidly and effectively. Then, we need to take what good ideas and inventions arise from that creativity and turn them into sound, efficient business processes and try to make money on them before they become obsolete.

COMBINING CREATIVITY AND WORK PATHS

As you might have figured out already, a production, or efficiency, focus is particularly suited to the Ghost and Postwar Cohorts, and others on the structured work path. It suits their preference for structure very well. And their tradition of management — while antithetical to some younger cohorts — needs to be kept alive in organizations for use in this phase of the innovation cycle. It also satisfies the organizational need for cyclical emphasis on stability in order to ramp up and cash in on good innovations.

But if you allow the structured work path to dominate, you will lack the ability to switch gears and behave creatively when you need to. And that is where the other three work paths come to the fore. The individualist path, which typically includes Leading-Edge and Trailing-Edge Baby Boomers, tends to attract creative types and it also encourages others to be creative (since everyone has latent creative capabilities). The excitement path, which typically includes the Gen X Cohort, is also innovation oriented, since it attracts and encourages people who embrace change and like adventure. And the team path can encourage creative solutions if the problem posed to the team is defined in the proper way.

While each of these work paths offers very distinct advantages and disadvantages, we recommend that you engage the various cohorts on these work paths in the pursuit of newer, more effective ideas. Let them be rabble-rousers, each in their own way, to counter the tendency of the stability-seekers to make your organization ever more efficient — and out of date. This is the real value of diversity in the workplace, and why managing by generational cohort and defining moments can be so powerful.

DEFINING THE FOUR ROLES IN THE CREATIVE PROCESS

In our consulting and training work, we often prescribe an activity Alex has developed called Creative Roles Analysis. It identifies the aspects of each individual's creative style and categorizes people according to the creative role they are most likely to play. These roles are:

- ✦ **Entrepreneur:** An entrepreneur is a compulsive asker of why and why-not questions. He follows a line of thought rigorously, often arriving at new insights as a result. He often visualizes new approaches and projects and is good at starting them, but he's not necessarily likely to follow each one through to the end before pursuing another, newer plan.

- ✦ **Artist:** The artist is highly imaginative and sees many alternatives. She crosses boundaries to make novel connections. Others may see her as offering visionary insights.

- ✦ **Inventor:** The inventor is capable of highly creative effort, but he prefers to have a clear focus or direction to guide the effort — he likes to focus the scope of inquiry on a well-defined goal. As a result, he's a great problem solver.

- ✦ **Engineer:** The engineer prefers to follow clearly defined steps. She's uncomfortable with protracted free association, and seeks order and structure. She's great at implementation as a result.

Whenever you undertake creative work, you can benefit from an awareness of which role is most important at each point in the process. By diagnosing the role requirements of the situation, you and your employees can either attempt to play the correct roles yourselves or you can cast a collaborator into the required role. And when you get stuck, you can check to see if you're thinking most productively for the role you're playing.

As you start using Creative Roles Analysis, we think you'll find that:

- ✦ When you know your own creative role, you are better able to broaden it on occasions when playing another role might be more helpful to you.

- ✦ When you know how your role compares to others' roles, you understand why you may not approach creative tasks as they do. You can then make an effort to accommodate other people's preferred roles, making collaboration easier.

- ✦ When you know what your most natural role is, you can decide where in the creative process you can be most effective. This knowledge permits you to divide up creative tasks with others in such a way that ensures that you take best advantage of your role preference.

Combining Employees from Different Cohorts to Create Innovation

Often, the most creative collaborations are between two or more people with differing creative temperaments. Many times, these people are from different cohort groups, as well. They work well together because, between them, they are better at playing the varied roles needed to see a creative effort through to completion.

Each of the four creative roles has an important part to play. In any creative endeavor, each of the roles comes into prominence at a specific time and gets in the way at other times. Table 13.1 shows a generic creative process.

TABLE 13.1: THE CREATIVE PROCESS

Phase	Creative Activity	Most Prominent Creative Role
1	**Initiate** Recognize a need or opportunity and ask questions that initiate the creative process.	**Entrepreneur** Inquisitive, curious, independent, enthusiastic, motivated, takes initiative, sees possibilities
2	**Imagine** Imagine many possibilities and expand the creative process.	**Artist** Imaginative, enthusiastic, original, intuitive, expressive
3	**Invent** Focus the creative process by seeing how to make the imagined possible and developing specific ideas.	**Inventor** Persistent, imaginative, determined, resourceful, focused
4	**Implement** Complete the process by pursuing successful adoption of the new idea or design.	**Engineer** Careful, disciplined, goal oriented, methodical, highly focused, consistent

To maximize creativity and innovation, the best thing to do in any project is to define specific roles according to the steps in Table 13.1.

When putting together a team that needs to be innovative, make sure you build your team out of at least four individuals, one for each of the four creative roles. You can add more people who have affinities for the different roles, or who provide needed expertise or authority or access, but make sure you cover the creative bases by building your project team around individuals who can take the lead at each phase in the project.

CONNECTING ROLES TO COHORTS

There are additional benefits when Creative Roles Analysis is combined with Generational Cohort Analysis. Different cohorts have different role tendencies. That is to say, while every cohort includes people who fit different creative roles, there are some overall patterns that allow us to generalize.

We can match specific cohorts to specific creative roles relatively well. And this means you can gain insight into the challenges of creative management by understanding which cohort groups are most likely to play which creative roles well.

Recruiting for Creativity

The hair salon chain SuperCuts decided to try and recruit particularly creative individuals to do hair styling in some of its Northern California stores. Salon employees who take a creative approach and enjoy doing something exciting for clients are especially good at satisfying clients — who themselves are often seeking excitement and individual expression in their hair styles.

But how to find and retain such employees? First, of course, they have to be managed in a looser way — they shouldn't be told exactly how to do their work, but should instead be allowed to take an experimental approach. And then the salons need to advertise that they're a safe haven for creative employees. SuperCuts chose to do this with appealing radio ads describing its need for creative employees. The ads ended with the tag line "That's not a job, that's artistic expression!"

ENTREPRENEURS

When we do management trainings, one of the things we always ask participants to do is to describe their ideal employee. When the list is compiled, it generally looks like a description of an entrepreneur.

Initiative, responsibility, innovativeness, resourcefulness, the ability to solve problems creatively and find opportunities — these are the qualities that entrepreneurs have, and increasingly they are the qualities that are most valued in employees, even by more established organizations. It seems like managers are always seeking people with entrepreneurial instincts, and always find them hard to identify or develop. But the classic description of the entrepreneur is not the only creative employee type, and most organizations have a wealth of creative resources, if they know where to look and how to nurture them.

The creative process begins with the entrepreneur because entrepreneurs have a practical perspective, but possess a creative instinct as well. They are good at seeing opportunities, at asking tough questions, and imagining new directions. They have great initiative.

Because the entrepreneurial role kicks off the creative process, it is a vital one. Without someone playing the role of entrepreneur, other creative capabilities and capacities lie dormant and never get engaged in a pragmatic quest for a new business idea.

Entrepreneurs are relatively rare in all cohorts. They are a precious resource (too bad traditional management styles tend to drive them away!). When we look at the qualities of the different cohorts, it is clear that Gen-Xers are more likely than other employees to step up to the entrepreneur role.

The Gen-X profile includes certain elements that are perfect for the entrepreneur role — in particular, a critical eye. If you think about it, the critical viewpoint is necessary as it opens the mind to the possibility of alternatives. You have to reject the status quo in order to imagine that there might be better ways! The Gen-X quality that is sometimes labeled as negative cynicism can be very positive and helpful if it's harnessed to the cause of innovation. The challenge is to engage Gen-Xers by giving them genuine opportunities to not only complain, but to engage in *constructive* criticism.

You want your Gen-Xers to not just say that things suck, but to suggest ways of making them better. You need to take their input seriously — even when their style is raw and you might be inclined to take offense. Focus on the substance, on the underlying insight, and challenge Gen-Xers with an invitation to point you and their working group or team in a new and better direction.

We recommend channeling members of this cohort into a constructively critical role by asking them to pose plenty of why, why-not, and what-if questions — and to share their answers with others. Those of this cohort who wish to are likely to play entrepreneur roles effectively, and are capable of bringing vision and imagination to the role.

ARTISTS

In most businesses, of course, you don't need large numbers of artists, in the traditional graphic arts meaning of the word. But as Creative Roles Analysis shows, your company does have a need for people who can bring the artist's imagination and insight to the task of innovation. Your artist might be someone who can articulate an exciting new concept for a distribution process — that is an art in the world of business creativity! Or perhaps it is someone who is willing to go off for a few days and come back with a new concept for how a software company could provide support to its product users over the web. Maybe your artist imagines a new color scheme for a point-of-purchase display and packaging, or thinks of new approaches to structuring supplier relationships. In one form or another, the artist's imagination is critical in opening up new possibilities and suggesting new paths for your business.

In one of the exercises we sometimes do for clients, we assemble a group of people and generate ideas for a possible solution to a problem — it could be any sort of problem. The idea is that if we come up with, say, 100 ideas instead of the 2 or 3 that seemed obvious to managers upfront, then out of those 100 ideas some really good alternatives might emerge. Sure, some hard work may be required to select and develop good, practical alternatives from the dozens of crazy ideas that come from an idea session. But without the open pursuit of fresh ideas, you don't have the building blocks to make good new alternatives. And your artists are most apt to be able to produce new ideas.

Both the Boomer Cohorts provide plenty of people who are good fits for the artist role. Creators by temperament, Boomers often enjoy the individualism of the artist role and can be trained fairly easily to express fresh and original ideas. And in a group of Boomer employees, there are often a number of amateur artists of one sort or another. So many

---

Ringing the Creativity Bell

Alexander Graham Bell was an artist, in the sense that we're using the term. His thinking style was highly imaginative and curious, but not very focused.

According to an *Encyclopaedia Britannica* entry, "Bell never lingered on one project. His research interests centered on basic principles rather than on refinements." And Bell's notebooks are full of "marginal memos and jottings, often totally unrelated to the subject at hand," an indication of a random style of thinking.

Bell's creative profile opened his mind to many possibilities and led him to generate important new ideas in a wide variety of areas. Few people realize that he founded *National Geographic* magazine and developed techniques for teaching the deaf, in addition to inventing the telephone!

Boomers understand this role already, and can help model it and show other employees how to bring out their artistic side.

When we do trainings or talks, we often ask our audience members to raise their hands if they know how to brainstorm. Everybody usually raises their hands. Then we ask for a show of hands from those who have used brainstorming in the past month to generate ideas for business.

Guess what? Usually all but one or two hands go down. This tells us that people know how to generate ideas — they're just not being asked to. And if your company doesn't take time to generate new ideas, you probably won't *have* many new ideas! It's that simple. So the key to stimulating your employees to take on the artist role is to make sure that generating ideas is on the agenda. Do some kind of idea-generating activity in every meeting and use e-mail to ask for ideas. Collect idea-generating techniques (there are hundreds) and circulate these among employees. One place to start is a little book called *A Technique for Producing Ideas* by James Webb Young, founder of the Young and Rubicam advertising agency. It's a short piece originally presented to a class at the University of Chicago business school in 1940, and while the tone may occasionally seem quaint today, the concepts are

But Bell's creative style had its down side. An artist can keep shifting focus from one imaginative thought to another and never take the time to develop a single invention fully. To overcome this potential limitation, Bell sought out people with the inverse of his creative style — engineers. Each of his many important inventions and projects was turned over to an engineer-style champion who could give it the diligent focus needed for implementation. These people would think about the project at hand, and not fill notebooks with stray ideas.

Bell had a marvelous instinct for assembling creative teams, whose members filled the range of roles needed to see his ambitious projects through. His mastery of Creative Roles Analysis (although he didn't use the term!) may well explain why he was able to be so successful as an inventor and entrepreneur.

fundamental to the creative process. It's one way to come up with fresh ideas, and without fresh ideas, innovation is impossible.

INVENTORS

The inventor's function in the innovation process is to *focus* wild new ideas, narrow the field down to one or a few strong candidates, then wrestle with them until they begin to look like actionable possibilities. Inventors have to take things from the world of imagination and abstraction into the world of reality.

If the new idea is for a product or other physical object, the inventor has to figure out how to actually make the thing — what materials to use and how to assemble them. The inventor takes care of all those practical concerns that the artist doesn't worry about when sketching a concept on the back of a napkin.

If the new idea is for a process — as is the case with many new ideas in the workplace these days — the inventor has to translate the concept into specific actions and steps. Again, the inventor has to bridge the gap from abstraction to reality. Invention is hard work. A process-improvement team can spend months and months achieving an improvement in a business process.

We must emphasize again that people who are naturally good at creative roles are relatively hard to find in most organizations. But when we look at cohorts, the one that pops out at us as having the most members who are suited for the inventor role is the N Gen Cohort.

N-Gens understand artistic thinking, since they grew up in households that were established by Boomer parents. In fact, many N-Gens are on the rebound from the free-form nature of these households, and are less artistic than their parents as a result. They like to see a bit more structure than their parents did. They feel a stronger need for collectivism, completion, and direction. But because of their upbringing, they still have one foot in the freewheeling world of the imagination.

We think that N-Gens are ideally positioned to translate ideas into the practical realm. Fire their imagination and give them the task of building something that might actually work, and they will take up the inventor's mantle. Participation in a project team that's charged with bringing a new idea to fruition is a great opportunity for invention-oriented N-Gens.

ENGINEERS

The engineer works closely with the inventor in a kind of hand-off from prototyping an idea to scaling it up for real implementation. The engineer's role in the creative process is to impose structure and scale up or otherwise implement the invention. In other words, the engineer takes the invention and creates a formal, bug-free business process or product. An engineer must have discipline and a sequential, structured style of thinking and working.

The engineer brings closure to the creative process. Highly creative people are not usually very good at flip-flopping to this completely opposite style of work, and so including some people who naturally play the role of engineers on any creative team that also needs to do implementation is a good idea.

Documentation is one aspect of the engineer's role — the development of systematic, established rules or procedures to make sure that practices get institutionalized. Engineers typically *love* red tape, so you want the other members of the team to stay involved, as a sort of counterweight, even after you turn an invention over to the engineer.

But you do want to let the engineer dominate the process when it moves into the implementation and execution stage.

Members of the Ghost and Postwar Cohorts are often well-suited to the engineer role. We also believe that some N-Gen employees — those who grew up in the more extreme, free-form Boomer households — are sufficiently eager to achieve rebound stability and order that they can assume this role and do it well. You may be able to charge a team that's heavy on N-Gens with both the invention and implementation stages.

EXPANDING CREATIVE CAPACITY

A creative endeavor often benefits from phase-by-phase shifts in the prominence of the entrepreneur, artist, inventor, and engineer roles. When people work on a creative endeavor, they can use their knowledge of creative roles to shift their approach, as needed, to move their work through all four phases of the process of creative development. That is to say, they can consciously vary the ways they approach their work in order to move it ahead.

For instance, if you're just beginning a solo project that you feel is difficult and will require creativity, you should try to play the entrepreneur role. Once you have defined the project clearly and well, and it has a fresh but practical focus and purpose, then you can switch roles and play the artist, then the inventor, and finally the engineer.

Because everyone tends to have a dominant creative role, it follows that everyone has a creative role that they are *not* as comfortable with. To expand our creative capacities, we need to increase our comfort with these non-dominant roles.

For instance, if you're a natural engineer, you can best expand your creative capacity by working on the style that is the least like the engineer. We call this opposite role an *inverse role*. In the case of an engineer, for example, the artist is the inverse. When engineers practice shifting from their naturally logical and organized style to the artist's naturally organic and intuitive style, they are able to benefit from a broader range of creative behavior. They can step out of their dominant role when necessary, benefit from the strengths of their inverse role, and then return to their dominant role with fresh ideas and insights.

The Ad Agency as Role Model

Ad agencies have to be both highly creative and highly efficient to succeed on a large scale. They have to be able to do highly creative work consistently.

Agencies often patch together informally organized groupings of employees for each project, with the groupings constantly rearranging themselves to reflect the latest projects. The creative people on these teams are selected and managed to maximize their ability to be creative.

Some of the creativity-enhancing management practices in ad agencies include:

✦ Low or no supervision of what people do on a daily basis and how they do it.

✦ High supervision of what people produce, with lots of selection and refinement of raw ideas and concepts.

✦ Emphasis on developing a wide range of creative approaches in very rudimentary or unfinished form as a spur to creativity from others.

✦ The ability to create the working style and environment each employee feels will maximize personal creativity.

✦ Free access to fellow employees to share ideas and stimulate creativity.

We've done some creativity training sessions in ad agencies, and we can report that the people who work in agencies are pretty much whom you might imagine: free thinkers, individualists, and some people who crave excitement, working intensely in informal, almost organic structures (if you can even call them structures). They look like you might expect, too: informal, with highly individualized approaches to office attire, and quirky, unique workspaces full of the things that inspire them and that remind them of past creative achievements.

In the same agencies, you also encounter people in suits with firm handshakes and clean desktops. These people are in charge of the structured, efficiency-oriented aspects of the business. Some of them are account managers who take care of finding clients and keeping them happy. They worry about deadlines and budgets. And then there are the media buyers, who spend their days seeking efficient ways to get those ads exposed in the media.

Defining the corporate culture of any successful large ad agency is difficult, because it really has multiple cultures. It has to be able to nurture creativity, but it also must be efficient, profitable, and good at delivery.

It is a constant struggle within advertising agencies to balance the needs of the creative and the business sides. The larger the agency becomes, the greater the tendency for the policies and procedures needed to manage the increased staff and workflow to impede the creative process. As Jay Chiat (founder of the Chiat\Day agency) once said, "I want to find out how big we can get before we get bad!"

To encourage creativity while letting his agency grow, Jay introduced a radical new concept in the mid-'90s: None of the staff would have offices. Rather, each employee would be issued a laptop on arrival at work, and they could go to any cubicle or meeting room to spend the rest of the day. Lockers were available for small personal items. The idea was to force staffers to interact with people from other groups and departments and force them into new workspaces to encourage fresh ways of thinking. The concept was a horrible failure and was soon abandoned, but it illustrates the lengths to which creative organizations are willing to go to enhance creativity.

USING YOUR INVERSE ROLE

To be a fully effective entrepreneur, inventor, artist, or engineer, you may need to use more than one style in the course of a creative project. Knowing what your natural style is helps you see what your creative strengths are — and also helps you to identify when and how to modify your style to incorporate other approaches. In particular, you can change your way of thinking by stepping into the inverse of the role that you typically play. In this section, we explain how to do precisely that. Follow these suggestions whenever you think you might be stuck or when you need some fresh insight into a project, problem, or opportunity!

IF YOUR DOMINANT ROLE IS **ENTREPRENEUR,** THEN YOUR INVERSE ROLE IS **INVENTOR**

To step out of your role, tell yourself that you do not have to do something that is completely new and different. Just making a modest improvement in an existing design can be sufficient! Also, encourage yourself not to worry about losing control. Let things come up and pursue them, regardless of whether you feel they fit into the current plan. To your inverse role, order and sequence are not important. New experiences and fresh ideas are.

Try to find some aspect of the problem or project to focus on just because it interests you, not because the particular aspect seems necessary, or even important, right now. Follow the smallest stream, not the largest river. Trust yourself to find a way to connect the stream to the river, even though the connection isn't on any map right now. Inventors can turn anything they find into a useful end result just by applying their natural ingenuity and insight.

Use incubation to improve your ideas. Take some time for an exercise break or a trip to a new place by yourself. See what your imagination comes up with while you're out of your normal realm.

YOUR BEST CREATIVITY TRICKS

An interesting exercise is to avoid writing anything down about your creative work for a whole week. Carry your ideas in your head and heart, repeating, refining, and strengthening them in your imagination to make sure that you don't forget them. At the end of the week, when you finally permit yourself to write them down, they will have been transformed into something new and wonderful.

In addition:

✦ Try working with your hands.

✦ Throw away your plans.

✦ Go for a long walk by yourself.

✦ "Shuffle the deck" and pick a new idea or approach at random, then see what you can do with it!

✦ Define the problem in as many different ways as you can, from the perspective of every constituency or every technical aspect that has relevance. Write down these definitions. New solutions will crop up; the best will apply to all or most of the problem definitions.

IF YOUR DOMINANT ROLE IS **ARTIST,** THEN YOUR INVERSE ROLE IS **ENGINEER**

To step out of your role, pick just one idea or project and dedicate yourself to it, to the exclusion of all other creative ideas. Talk to yourself about the advantages of persisting in one approach until you develop a high degree of comfort and perfection in it. Let go of your instinctive urge to constantly seek new experiences and perspectives, at least for a while. Find some simple, repetitive task, and try to embrace it and find the peacefulness of consistency.

Now apply this new style to the creative effort. Lay out a plan for yourself consisting of all the steps, in their necessary order, that are needed to finish the work. Examine the plan, making sure nothing is missing from it. Then make a promise to yourself that you will follow the plan, step by step, until it is done.

YOUR BEST CREATIVITY TRICKS

Reorganize your things (papers, for example) into lines or rows. Put the pile you need to work on in the front, the next one behind it, and so forth. Then work your way through the line, one item at a time. You'll find yourself completing more things more often, and your naturally imaginative temperament will ensure that your work still stays creative.

Also:

✦ Schedule yourself. It may be time to write (or draw?) a daily list and schedule.

✦ Clean up! When you bring more order to your workplace or living space, things will fall into place in your imagination as well.

IF YOUR DOMINANT ROLE IS **INVENTOR,** THEN YOUR INVERSE ROLE IS **ENTREPRENEUR**

To step out of your role, focus more on the long-term goal. Think about what you want to accomplish — what you want to complete — then ask yourself which of your ideas is most relevant to the end goal. Focus only on the goal-related work for now, setting aside other ideas and projects until you achieve the most pressing goal.

Also, try to impose more structure and order to your creative work. Sequential plans are helpful as you try to play your inverse role. Divide your creative work into three steps, give yourself a specific amount of time for each step, and track your progress on a calendar or in a journal.

YOUR BEST CREATIVITY TRICKS

Don't be afraid to change directions halfway there. You may discover another path and goal halfway through your plan that looks even more exciting. Great! You don't have to finish everything you start. You just have to finish *something* exciting and valuable — and make sure it really does get finished. So if you change your mind, make sure you write yourself a new plan.

Also:

✦ Get excited. Ask yourself which of your many ideas is most inspiring, then set yourself a goal and pursue it with enthusiasm.

✦ Write a plan. Try to stick to a logical sequence of steps to get from where you are now to where you want to be.

✦ Let your unconscious do the work for you. That is, immerse yourself in the various elements of the overall situation in the evening, just before going to bed. During the night, while you are asleep, your mind will be rearranging and recombining those elements into new and more creative patterns. Use the period when you are just waking to relate the new patterns to more conscious and specific goals and objectives. Often, that half-asleep/half-awake state will lead to breakthroughs of startling originality!

IF YOUR DOMINANT ROLE IS **ENGINEER,** THEN YOUR INVERSE ROLE IS **ARTIST**

To step out of your role, let go of your anxieties about finishing what you start and give yourself permission to take a playful, even irresponsible approach. Explore. Imagine. Collect ideas or things just because you like them, not because you know they are necessary to your project. Trust yourself to find some way to make them relevant later on.

The transition from engineer to artist is perhaps the hardest of all the role inversions. You may want to find some people whose temperaments are naturally artistic and spend a little time watching and imitating them. They have a secret life of the imagination that you never knew about. They are thinking or visualizing new things all the time. They are approaching their work and their lives through their senses and intuitions, not through logical thoughts. See if you can acquire the trick yourself and give it a chance. You are bound to find new and interesting approaches to your work.

YOUR BEST CREATIVITY TRICKS

Here are some ideas to help you shake up your normal way of thought and become more artistic:

✦ Use brainstorming and free association as much as possible. You need to break out of logical thought patterns to see new possibilities.

✦ Trust your senses. Think about how things smell, feel, or look, distracting your mind while it incubates the problem or project for a while.

✦ Ask lots of questions, especially "dumb" questions that get at things we treat as obvious, to find out if there is an insight you can glean or an assumption you've mistakenly been making.

✦ Try to redefine your problem or project. In fact, make a commitment to yourself that you will *not* do what is required of you, but will instead transform your task so that it can be done in a new and interesting way.

CONCLUSION

To sum up, achieving a consistently high level of creativity in an organization is one of the most difficult tasks facing a manager. Creativity, by definition, means new and it means change, and many employees find these concepts uncomfortable in the extreme.

That said, maintaining some level of creativity is essential for any organization that plans to grow and prosper. Without creativity, the organization may plow along for a time from sheer momentum, like a freighter that's lost its engines. Like a ship, the larger the organization, the longer it will maintain some maneuverability, even without power. Eventually, however, the momentum will be gone, and the ship will come to a stop, unable to control its course and buffeted by the winds and tides. Creativity is the engine that keeps the organizational ship moving ahead.

Creative Roles Analysis, combined with your new understanding of cohorts and how they interact, will ensure that your corporate creative engine keeps running with increasing effectiveness.

CHAPTER 14

PREPARING FOR A PROFITABLE FUTURE

This book has offered a number of insights that relate to age. Age does count, but it is *coming of age* that counts even more! We know that recent events are having a significant impact on society, particularly on young adults, and that we must be mindful of the implications for management. We have seen that five different generational cohorts currently dominate the labor force. Whether the terrorist attacks of September 11 will define a sixth cohort or whether the event will have a more subtle influence, shaping a value of security in the existing N Gen Cohort, is yet to be seen. We must be careful to wait and see what the fallout of this tragic event is before deciding that a new cohort has been formed.

We do know for certain that Postwars will be leaving the workplace over the next decade, taking with them their engineer approach and their build-it, fix-it, can-do mentality. In Chapter 13, we showed how creative implementation relies on people who can adopt the engineer mentality. The Postwars will be missed in the future, although the N-Gens, as they mature, may be able to play a similar role in the workplace.

We know for certain that over the next decade Leading-Edge Boomers will dominate the top levels in management. They will impose their values on the workplace even more than they already do. Because of this, the individualist work path will be refined and expanded, and will likely dominate organizations as, unconsciously or not, top leaders spread their way of thinking through the organization.

Eventually, we will see the oldest Boomers passing into retirement and part-time work. Even as Boomers start to fade from the workplace, we believe that they will have influence on succeeding managers. At the same time, we will witness the advent of another large wave of workers — the Boomers' N-Gen children, who will form the rank and file and who will bring another way of thinking into the work environment. Motivations and rewards will need to be adjusted to fit their needs and priorities as they unfold. While we have indicated the direction of these values in Chapter 9, they are still emerging and need to be monitored so that refinements and changes can be incorporated into managerial styles, practices, and policies.

In 2000, the Internet bubble burst, leaving many young people out of work. Because Gen-Xers staffed so many of these high-tech companies, their mentality of working 24-7 to quickly get to the pot of gold at the end of the rainbow seems to be fading. In the long run, that may be a good thing. The expectation of quick riches sapped energy away from developing a vision for the future, thus undermining the viability of many dot.coms. While the downturn in Silicon Valley and other high-tech hotspots, like Austin, Boston, and the Research Triangle in North Carolina, was a difficult time for many managers and employees, it did bring expectations back into line with those that held sway for most of the twentieth century.

AN EMERGING CYCLE?

Although it's too soon to be sure, we hypothesize that a cycle may be at work. A structured, engineering mindset (like that of the Ghost Cohorts and Postwars) makes way for a challenging, free-spirited mindset (think of the Boomer Cohorts) that in turn yields to a pragmatic, self-centered mindset (Gen-Xers). Then the more structured, team-oriented approach regains prominence (the N-Gens and those that follow). This cycle is consistent with the thesis advanced by Neil Howe and Bill Strauss in their series of books that started with *Generations.*[1] Howe and Strauss hypothesize that a predictable cycle of social change repeats itself every 80 years or so: A crisis period is followed by a high, which is then followed by an awakening, then an unraveling, leading to another crisis. These cycles, in turn, play a major role in forming the values that generational cohorts adopt as they come of age. Over the coming years, we'll see just how accurate this view is.

A BIG-PICTURE SOLUTION?

In this book, we have shared some of the insights and methods needed to bridge cohort-to-cohort gaps. When you consider cohort effects, you'll find you gain insight into many of the individuals who work with you, and perhaps insight into your own approach to work.

However, we must offer a word of caution. There are many occasions and situations in which dealing with a half-dozen or more unique categories of employees, and trying to bridge the gaps among all these individuals, is not going to be practical. For instance, suppose you're designing the curriculum for a leadership development program of the sort that most large companies now have. Although it would be nice to teach, say, six or seven different leadership methods, one for each cohort, you have to admit that today's training programs have difficulty teaching managers to use even one method well. A half-dozen methods are just going to muddy the waters. Management must be, above all, a pragmatic science if it is to do anyone any good in a real business!

Because we recognize the difficulties of separately addressing each cohort, we have developed a macro-analysis of generational cohort effects in the workplace. Although we wish that we could say our analysis has allowed us to fold all the cohorts together and create one silver bullet that can be used to solve every management problem, that's not the case. There will never be a silver bullet. But our analysis does lead us to a simple and powerful macro-view of what we think of as the generational cohort challenge in today's workplace. The four-path approach (introduced in Chapter 11) can be used now and in the future to help meet the needs of an ever-changing workforce.

Structured Work Path Principles

The structured path is indigenous to the traditional business organization, with its clearly defined roles, relatively slow career progressions, and relatively high sense of security for employees. The structured path reflects and speaks to the Ghost Cohorts' needs and traditions, and it also fits many Postwars. You might think that since the Postwars will be leaving the workplace in the coming years, the structured path is not very important anymore.

That's not the case. First, generalizations about cohorts never hold for *all* members of a cohort. Inherent aspects of personality and formative experiences that shape personality also drive a person's character. In other words, within any group of people of the same age, you will find some people who are atypical of their cohort. Some people's values are always going to be similar to those that characterize cohorts they don't belong to. Also, some of the tasks and roles in the workplace are best suited to and best performed by people who have a preference for tight structure. So it's important to have some of these people around! People who thrive on structure are very valuable, for example, in the implementation of plans and the transformation of innovations into well-oiled routines. They tend to create their own structure when it does not exist.

Even an organization that is dedicated to frequent change and the pursuit of competitive advantage through innovation periodically has the need to systematize new ideas and processes that have to be scaled up and replicated efficiently. In fact, an organization really needs more structure in order to accommodate more creativity. Chaos needs its balance. If you don't learn to create systems and impose rigor on processes very rapidly, you'll never learn to make products profitably or without errors.

Employees who are best suited to the structure path may not see eye to eye with the more flexible and creative folks on the other three paths, but they are the ones who can maintain some sense of order amid the chaos of the modern organization. So organizations certainly need to provide the structured path for those who find it appealing. How do you create a structured path? Here are some principles.

Provide Clearly Defined Roles and Duties

Formal, detailed job descriptions, work orders, action plans, and agendas are helpful. Every time things change, make sure that the formal mandate or instructions are updated to provide an appropriate structure for employees to work within.

MAKE SURE EMPLOYEES HAVE INFORMATIVE, SPECIFIC FEEDBACK ABOUT THEIR PERFORMANCE

People on the structured path need as extensive performance information as is humanly possible to provide. If they can become involved in generating and tracking performance data, all the better. An example of an information-rich feedback system for the structured path is a production process that's managed using statistical process control.

PROVIDE AS STABLE A VIEW OF THE FUTURE AS IS FEASIBLE

Within the limits of practicality, you need to let employees know what the future holds for them if they do their job well. You obviously cannot promise a steady, 20-year-long rise to the top. But you can give employees accurate information about where their job could go — even if the answer is nowhere. Some employees will be satisfied to stick with a decent job they can do well, and they will appreciate knowing that there is at least a little more permanence to their job than to those at other companies around them. So try to identify core work processes and the jobs central to them and steer people who value structure toward these core jobs. These jobs last a lot longer than many other jobs that are associated with special projects, new initiatives, and temporary teams — impermanent jobs that are ideal for workers on the excitement or team path, but that are not good for the structured path employee.

PROVIDE A CLEAR REPORTING STRUCTURE AND LINE OF AUTHORITY

The flexible, self-forming project teams that N-Gens like are a source of anxiety and frustration for those who prefer a high-structure work environment. So give employees the option of working in a more traditional hierarchy where they know who is in charge of what. Employees who like to be involved in a participative decision-making process can have a hard time accepting that others may prefer *not* to have to take on the responsibilities and ambiguity of such processes.

INDIVIDUALIST WORK PATH PRINCIPLES

The two Boomer Cohorts relish the term *participatory decision-making*. Having a voice is important to them — they feel good when they can express their individual viewpoints. Boomers have fought for more open lines of communication in the workplace and for a seat at the decision-making table.

They have also fought for opportunities to shape their own careers, rejecting the idea of a single, well-defined pathway and highly structured roles. They don't want to wear the uniform and think and act like others — even if it means accepting more risk and uncertainty in their working lives. The chance to be their own man or woman is important to them. They want to make a personal difference — which is very different from wanting to be part of the team. But they can make very able members of any team, as long as their involvement gives them opportunities to express themselves as individuals. Here are some principles and practices that help to keep individualist employees happy and motivated in their work.

ASK THEIR OPINION

Employees on the individualist path have a strong urge to express themselves. This needs to be acknowledged in decision-making whenever the decision affects them or their work. Where possible, engage these employees in decisions by encouraging them to voice individual opinions (as opposed to not asking their opinion or asking for a collective or group response). If you, as a manager, don't have time to listen to each of their voices individually, then ask someone else to facilitate a discussion in which they get the chance to speak their minds. Individualists feel that what is on their minds is unique and important, and this feeling should be respected as far as is feasible in the workplace.

ENCOURAGE THEM TO DESIGN THEIR OWN ROLES

Rather than giving each employee the same title and job description, for example, ask each of them to come up with a list of work goals and a plan for achieving them — and perhaps even suggest that they can design their own job title and business card, if appropriate. In the end, you may get the same work done by the same people, but by allowing them to participate in the details of setting goals and designing tasks, you give them the autonomy they need to become highly motivated and engaged with their work.

SEEK OPPORTUNITIES FOR PERSONAL CREATIVE EXPRESSION

The opportunity to come up with new or improved ideas, methods, processes, or products is a powerful motivator for employees on the individualist path. They will enjoy a chance to challenge themselves when doing so involves personal creativity. Make sure that you acknowledge individual contributions to larger projects too, so that the individual employees' contributions are visible to them and others in the group. Problem solving and innovations of all sorts are important opportunities for self-expression, so present them that way — employees on the individualist path are a great resource for solving problems or making needed changes. As long as they have some leeway to express themselves through their work, they will undertake major new challenges with a level of enthusiasm and energy that will surprise you.

ALLOW EMPLOYEES TO CUSTOMIZE THEIR ROLES

Employees on the individualist path may work far harder at a job that they feel they have invented for themselves than at the same job pushed upon them by their boss. And they are open-minded about career development options and don't mind nontraditional pathways, as long as they feel that what they are doing is appropriate for them and their special interests or talents.

EXCITEMENT WORK PATH PRINCIPLES

Gen-Xers, on the whole, are attuned to the excitement path. Xers are characterized by street smarts and a willingness to work very hard — but they are somewhat cynical and tend to act as free agents. They're in it for themselves, not for the greater good of the corporation. They're easily bored and need to be given plenty of excitement and variety in their tasks and assignments, otherwise they'll drift away. Think of them as if they are attending a talk, and you're doing the talking. How can you get them to sit in the front row and hang on your every word? What can you do to avoid having them slip to the back and nap, or worse, slide out the back door and disappear?

CHECK IN WITH THEM FREQUENTLY

A supervisor needs to ask employees on the excitement path at least once a week if they are bored or losing commitment. Let them know you want them to be actively interested and involved with their work. If they aren't involved, you need to know! Employees on the excitement path don't mind being brutally honest. They will tell you if they're getting bored, and will appreciate that you care enough to ask.

DO A MONTHLY WORK PLAN

A month is a long time if you're easily bored. Each employee should have a monthly meeting with a supervisor to go over assignments and set performance goals. Try to keep the employee moving through a series of assignments and special projects. Don't let the plan be "do your work well." Get specific each month about some new goals or directions to take the work.

CHALLENGE THEM

Don't feel bad about giving excitement-oriented employees tough challenges or difficult goals. They're happiest when they're working hard on exciting projects. If their work falls into a dull routine, they will look beyond their work for excitement and put their energy elsewhere.

How to challenge them? By implementing new ideas or programs, improving quality or speed of service, solving a problem, developing a new customer or market — any such challenge will do. And if you don't think they're ready to tackle a challenge, then consider giving them an assignment that will help prepare them for a larger challenge later on.

ASK THEM

Even if you do the three things above, you may still lose some excitement path employees to boredom. You don't really know what turns them on unless you ask them. Make a point of asking them for input about what they think would make their work more fun and interesting. This can be a part of those monthly planning meetings. Also, consider asking them to form a team or advisory committee that generates ideas for keeping the workplace exciting and interesting. They may come up with better ideas than you have. If they do, try to incorporate their ideas. If their ideas don't seem to fit into the current business model, then challenge the team to figure out how to make them work.

TEAM WORK PATH PRINCIPLES

As the value structure of the N Gen Cohort coalesces, they're starting to resemble the World War II Cohort in their core mindset. They tend to be team players, are more respectful of institutions and the Establishment than either the Boomers or the Xers, and are far more cause oriented and idealistic than the Xers. Play to these tendencies, and your N-Gens will respond.

ENCOURAGE TEAM FORMATION TO SOLVE PROBLEMS OR BRAINSTORM NEW IDEAS

N-Gens like teams — they even tend to *date* in teams, in the sense of going out in mixed-gender groups without two-by-two pairings. They don't crave personal expression like the Leading-Edge or Trailing-Edge Boomers, and they don't have the loner, free-agent style of the Xers. They want to strive and succeed as a team, and although a team structure imposed on them by superiors is better than no team at all, they prefer to form the teams themselves. Give them the opportunity.

GIVE THEM A GREATER PURPOSE TO PURSUE

Explain where their team task fits into the grand scheme, why it's important to the company, and, if at all possible, why it's important to society. They are young, but they really resent doing what they regard as menial or trivial tasks. Conversely, if they can be made to understand how the task is important, or why it's a vital link in the accomplishment of some greater good, they will respond with enthusiasm and energy that will amaze you.

GIVE THEM RESPONSIBILITY, *NOW*

N-Gens may be young in age, but their value structure is aligned with the people who won the war and built the bridges and highways and industries of postwar America — their grandparents. They *want* responsibility. Give it to them, and they will handle it.

Because they are young and relatively inexperienced, they may need guidance and constant feedback to keep them going in the right direction — but reinforce that the responsibility is ultimately theirs, and they will discharge it with honor.

RECOGNIZE AND REWARD THEM FOR SUCCESSFULLY COMPLETING TASKS

One important point of differentiation between N-Gens and members of the Depression and World War II Cohorts is that N-Gens came of age in a time of relative economic plenty. While the September 11 attacks and the recession that followed clearly will have a lasting impact, N-Gens have not experienced the degree of tough times that the World War II and Depression Cohorts did. So while N-Gens are team players, they are not into self-sacrifice. They want to be recognized and rewarded! They will find toiling away in relative obscurity, even if they're working for a good cause, very unfulfilling.

OPTING IN OR OUT OF WORK PATHS

The thing about a multi-path approach to employee management is that you really need to allow employees to choose their own path. You don't want to force anyone, or you defeat the purpose of improving the match between individual employee wants and the employer and workplace. So how can you make sure that each of the work paths is an *option,* not a requirement?

First, make sure employees know they have the option of being in or out. If a Gen-X employee consistently says she does not want her job to be more exciting and that she wants stability instead, don't keep bugging her. Don't direct challenges her way unnecessarily. Don't change her work plan monthly — maybe a six-month planning horizon, or an even longer one, would be better for her. The point is that our cohort profiles give us only a general idea of how people behave and what they want from their work. So always check in with individual employees. Then let them guide the final conclusion about which path fits them best.

PARTING THOUGHTS

In this book, we have introduced the concept of generational cohorts, groups of people with common core values that were formed by their shared coming-of-age experiences. We have offered you ideas about how to improve the way you manage these different cohorts. In particular, we continue to stress that one management style will not be very effective in a workplace that includes at least five generational cohorts — and that four work paths need to be deployed.

Our approach is so very new that many of these ideas are just that — ideas. We know that generational cohort *marketing* works, and that these ideas as applied to managing in the workplace are theoretically sound. But each industry, each company, each workforce has its own unique and individual elements, and thus we leave the operational interpretation and execution of the four work paths to you. We are sure that managing by generational cohorts will open up new ideas for you as a manager. And we hope you will find these ideas of use in increasing the productivity, creativity, and satisfaction of your workforce.

ENDNOTES

1. Strauss, William and Neil Howe. *Generations: The History of America's Future, 1584 to 2069.* New York: Broadway Books, 1992.

EPILOGUE

In our previous book, *Defining Markets, Defining Moments,* we concluded with a discussion of a recurring pattern of events as postulated by authors William Strauss and Neil Howe in their widely acclaimed book *The Fourth Turning: An American Prophecy.* Strauss and Howe offer an intriguing theory based on predictable cycles of societal change. By tracing Anglo-American history back to the War of the Roses in the mid-fifteenth century, they make a remarkably compelling case for their argument that in a span of around 80 years, there are four recurring patterns, which they call *turnings.* Those turnings are:

✦ Crisis

✦ High

✦ Awakening

✦ Unraveling

These are recurring periods; every 80 years or so, the cycle repeats itself. A crisis period is followed by a high, followed by an awakening, followed by an unraveling, leading to another crisis. In the most recent cycle, the crisis was the Great Depression and World War II. This was followed by the high of the postwar period. The awakening was the turmoil and social unrest of the '60s and '70s. And the unraveling is happening now. We are due to begin the next crisis cycle in about 5 to 8 years.

Strauss and Howe also postulate that a predictable personality type forms during each turning, based on which turning was happening in people's coming-of-age years. Although they derived their cyclical patterns from historical research, and we discerned our cohorts from market research and empirical marketplace data, the two match up quite closely. The key difference is that over the period from the 1920s to the present, we postulate that seven distinct *cohorts* exist, with their formative coming-of-age periods from 5 to 18 years in length, based on critical defining moments of the times. Strauss and Howe, on the other hand, see five *generational* cycles during that period, each of which is (or will be) about 20 years in length. However, there is no fundamental conflict between our cohorts and their generations. Rather, they are complementary, and we accept the recurrent cycles that Strauss and Howe put forth: Cohorts are smaller, shorter waves with peaks and troughs overlaying the longer, recurring 20-year-long generational swells.

Strauss and Howe characterize the generational types as:

+ **Artists:** Born during crises, overprotected as children, came of age during highs. Artists are structured, process-oriented, indecisive as leaders, and pluralistic. In our cohort terms, this is the Postwar Cohort.

+ **Prophets:** Born during highs, indulged as children, came of age during awakenings. Prophets are moralistic, individualistic, energetic, and highly self-aware. These, we call the two Boomer Cohorts.

+ **Nomads:** Born during awakenings, underprotected as children, came of age during unravelings. Nomads are pragmatic, free agents, pessimistic. These, we call the Gen-Xers (with overlaps at either end with the youngest of the Trailing-Edge Boomers and the oldest of the N-Gens).

+ **Heroes:** Born during unravelings, attended to as children, came of age during late unravelings and early crises. Heroes are relatively selfless, competent builders, outer-directed, team players. These are the N-Gens.

These groupings, not coincidentally, correspond to our four-path management approach. The structured work path, designed for the Postwar Cohort, will in theory work for the children of the oldest N-Gens, who should start entering the workplace in about 20 years.

As we enter the first years of the 21st century, each of the generational cohorts is progressing through the workplace, achieving seniority over time. The structured work path, which has dominated (particularly in mature industries) due to the preponderance of Postwars at the top, will give way to the individualist work path as the Leading-Edge and Trailing-Edge Boomers replace Postwars. This transition, which has already started, should in theory be replaced in 10 to 15 years by one that installs the excitement work path as the work path of choice. However, as Gen-Xers age, their orientation toward stimulation and away from routine may be replaced by their other dominant characteristic, a whatever-it-takes pragmatism. Particularly if, as Strauss and Howe predict, America enters the next crisis, which calls for a more structured management style, the excitement work path may quickly give way to the team work path.

While thinking about the management style most appropriate 10 years in the future may seem like a purely academic exercise, this book has focused on generational cohort theory and how it can help you better understand, manage, and motivate your employees *today*. Each cohort can be optimally led with a management path that taps into its core value structures. And as the different cohorts age and move up in the organization, management strategies and tactics can be refashioned to reflect their different value systems. In devising future management plans, the key thing to remember is this: In a world of ever more rapid change, cohort values are the one constant.

We believe this generational cohort approach will result in an improved management style that will take you to new heights of employee understanding and managerial effectiveness. We wish you great success.

APPENDIX

THE BACKGROUND OF GENERATIONAL COHORT THEORY

Although the application of cohort theory in a management context as outlined in this book is new, the foundations of the cohort concept as a recognized academic construct date to the late 1920s. In 1928, the German philosopher and sociologist Karl Mannheim raised the notion of groups of people bound together by historical events in his analysis titled "The Problem of Generations," which was contained in a larger work titled *Essays on the Sociology of Knowledge.*[1]

Mannheim and almost all later writers used the cohort hypothesis to examine political attitudes and behavior. Mannheim postulated that "late adolescence and early adulthood are the formative years during which a distinct personal outlook on politics emerges" (*ibid*). He specifies age 17, "sometimes a little earlier, and sometimes a little later," as the beginning point of this attitudinal development, and suggests that by age 25 the process is over. He differentiates clearly between the concept of a cohort, which is socially determined, and a generation, which is a biological construct (a grouping of offspring from parents). Mannheim suggests that cohorts are only formed when political and historical events occur and make an important impact or impression on a society. In a time of great social stability, or, for example, in peasant societies with little mass communications, cohort formation will not occur. After all, values can't be influenced by events that don't happen or that people don't know about.

Mannheim's thesis was adopted and expanded by Norman B. Ryder in a paper titled "The Cohort as a Concept in the Study of Social Change," read at the annual meeting of the American Sociological Association in 1959.[2] Ryder was a demographer, not a sociologist, and he introduced the notion of *demographic metabolism,* wherein a society persists beyond the lives of any individual member, "continually receiving raw material by fertility and discharging depleted resources by mortality." Ryder defined a cohort as "the aggregate of individuals (within some population definition) who experienced the same event within the same time interval."

Ryder goes on to say, "The cohort record is not merely a summation of a set of individual histories. Each cohort has a distinctive composition and character reflecting the circumstances of its unique origination and history." And for Ryder, the events that shape each cohort's uniqueness are those that happen when the cohort members are becoming socialized— becoming adult members of society. Exactly when that socialization occurs in terms of an individual's lifestage is open to interpretation, and probably isn't critical. What *is* critical is that the key period is young adulthood, the so-called formative years: "Cohorts may be defined in terms of the year in which they completed their schooling, the year they married, or the year in which they entered the work force full-time." These are all young-adult lifestage events.

Numerous papers followed Ryder's, but almost all continued to be in the area of sociopolitical analysis. Neal Cutler's "Political Socialization Research as Generational Analysis: The Cohort Approach vs. the Lineage Approach" again drew the distinction between cohort and generation.[3] Ryder had earlier called for empirical research to validate the coming-of-age hypothesis, and in 1985 the challenge was accepted by the Institute of Social Research at the University of Michigan at Ann Arbor. Under the direction of Drs. Howard Schuman and Jacqueline Scott, the institute did a study that was reported in *American Sociological Review* under the title "Generations and Collective Memories."[4] The abstract states:

A national sample of adult Americans was asked to report 'the national or world events or changes over the past 50 years' that seemed to them especially important, and then to explain the reasons for their choices. The resulting data were used both quantitatively and qualitatively to explore hypotheses relating to generational effects, life course, and collective memory. Broadly speaking, different cohorts recall different events or changes, and these memories come especially from adolescence and early adulthood. The reasons for mentioning various events and changes also differ across cohorts in ways that indicate that generational effects are the result of the intersection of personal and national history.

For the last sentence, we would say "the intersection of cohort and lifestage."

Schuman and Scott found that 33 historical events over the past 30 years were frequently recalled as especially important by respondents. The most important (as ranked by the number of first mentions) were:

- ✦ World War II
- ✦ Vietnam War
- ✦ Space Exploration
- ✦ Kennedy Assassination
- ✦ Civil Rights Movement
- ✦ Threat of Nuclear War
- ✦ Advances in Communications
- ✦ The Depression
- ✦ Computers
- ✦ International Terrorism

✦   General Moral Decline

✦   Women's Rights Movement

When the ascription of the significance of these events is plotted against the age of the individual when the event happened, it is evident that people regard as most important those events that happened when they were 17 to 23 years old: "In sum, age is clearly the most general predictor of memories for events and changes over the past 50 years, and the graphing of age relations provides strong evidence that in all or almost all such cases, age represents cohort effects, which in turn have their origins in adolescence and early adulthood."

This then is the theoretical underpinning of cohort analysis. While there have been a number of books that speak to managing on the basis of generations, our application of the more detailed and refined segmentation by cohort values is, to our knowledge, a first.

ENDNOTES

1. Mannheim, Karl. "Das Problem der Generationen," reprinted in *Essays on the Sociology of Knowledge.* London: Routledge, 1928.

2. Ryder, Norman B. "The Cohort as a Concept in the Study of Social Change," reprinted in the *American Sociological Review,* Vol. 30, (1965), 843–861.

3. Cutler, Neal. "Political Socialization Research as Generational Analysis: The Cohort Approach vs. the Lineage Approach," *Handbook of Political Socialization: Theory and Research,* edited by Stanley Allen Renton. New York: Free Press, 1977.

4. Schuman, Howard and Jacqueline Scott. " Generations and Collective Memories," *American Sociological Review* Vol. 54 (1989): 359–81.

INDEX